Data Analytics Applications in Latin America and Emerging Economies

Data Analytics Applications

Series Editor: Jay Liebowitz

PUBLISHED

Actionable Intelligence for Healthcare
by Jay Liebowitz, Amanda Dawson
ISBN: 978-1-4987-6665-4

Data Analytics Applications in Latin America and Emerging Economies
by Eduardo Rodriguez
ISBN: 978-1-4987-6276-2

**Sport Business Analytics: Using Data to Increase Revenue and
Improve Operational Efficiency**
by C. Keith Harrison, Scott Bukstein
ISBN: 978-1-4987-6126-0

FORTHCOMING

**Big Data and Analytics Applications in Government:
Current Practices and Future Opportunities**
by Gregory Richards
ISBN: 978-1-4987-6434-6

Big Data Analytics in Cybersecurity and IT Management
by Onur Savas, Julia Deng
ISBN: 978-1-4987-7212-9

Data Analytics Applications in Law
by Edward J. Walters
ISBN: 978-1-4987-6665-4

Data Analytics for Marketing and CRM
by Jie Cheng
ISBN: 978-1-4987-6424-7

Data Analytics in Institutional Trading
by Henri Waelbroeck
ISBN: 978-1-4987-7138-2

Data Analytics Applications in Latin America and Emerging Economies

Edited by
Eduardo Rodriguez PhD

CRC Press
Taylor & Francis Group
Boca Raton London New York

CRC Press is an imprint of the
Taylor & Francis Group, an **Informa** business

AN AUERBACH BOOK

CRC Press
Taylor & Francis Group
6000 Broken Sound Parkway NW, Suite 300
Boca Raton, FL 33487-2742

First issued in paperback 2022

ISBN 13: 978-1-03-247674-2 (pbk)
ISBN 13: 978-1-4987-6276-2 (hbk)

DOI: 10.4324/9781315164113

Visit the Taylor & Francis Web site at
http://www.taylorandfrancis.com

and the CRC Press Web site at
http://www.crcpress.com

Contents

About the Editor vii
Contributors...ix
Introduction xi

SECTION I   EVOLUTION AND ADOPTION OF THE
ANALYTICS PROCESS

1   Evolution of Analytics Concept..3
    EDUARDO RODRIGUEZ

2   The Analytics Knowledge Management Process 21
    EDUARDO RODRIGUEZ

SECTION II   ANALYTICS KNOWLEDGE APPLICATIONS IN
LATIN AMERICA AND EMERGING ECONOMIES

3   Analytics Knowledge Application to Healthcare 53
    ESTEBAN FLORES AND ISABEL RODRÍGUEZ

4   Diffusion of Adoptions on Dynamic Social Networks: A Case
    Study of a Real-World Community of Consumers 73
    MAURICIO HERRERA, GUILLERMO ARMELINI, AND ERICA SALVAJ

5   Prescriptive Analytics in Manufacturing: An Order Acceptance
    Illustration 91
    FEDERICO TRIGOS AND EDUARDO M. LÓPEZ

6   A Stochastic Hierarchical Approach for a Production Planning
    System under Uncertain Demands.....................................103
    VIRNA ORTIZ-ARAYA AND VÍCTOR M. ALBORNOZ

7   Big Data and Analytics for Consumer Price Index Estimation..........131
    PATRICIO COFRE AND GERZO GALLARDO

8 Prediction and Explanation in Credit Scoring Problems:
   A Comparison between Artificial Neural Networks
   and the Logit Model 141
   EDGARDO R. BRAVO, ALVARO G. TALAVERA, AND
   MICHELLE RODRIGUEZ SERRA

9 A Multi-Case Approach for Informational Port Decision Making 159
   ANA XIMENA HALABI-ECHEVERRY, MARIO ERNESTO
   MARTÍNEZ-AVELLA, DEBORAH RICHARDS, AND
   JAIRO RAFAEL MONTOYA-TORRES

10 Data Analytics to Characterize University-Based Companies
    for Decision Making in Business Development Programs 187
    LEÓN DARÍO PARRA BERNAL AND
    MILENKA LINNETH ARGOTE CUSI

11 Statistical Software Reliability Models 207
    FRANCISCO IVÁN ZULUAGA DÍAZ AND
    JOSÉ DANIEL GALLEGO POSADA

12 What Latin America Says about Entrepreneurship? An Approach
    Based on Data Analytics Applications and Social Media Contents ... 229
    LAURA ROJAS DE FRANCISCO, IZAIAS MARTINS, EDUARDO
    GÓMEZ-ARAUJO, AND LAURA FERNANDA MORALES DE LA VEGA

13 Healthcare Topics with Data Science: Exploratory Research
    with Social Network Analysis 253
    CINTHYA LEONOR VERGARA SILVA

Index 265

About the Editor

Dr. Eduardo Rodriguez is the Sentry Endowed Chair in Business Analytics, University of Wisconsin-Stevens Point, analytics adjunct professor at Telfer School of Management at Ottawa University, corporate faculty of the MSc in analytics at Harrisburg University of Science and Technology, Pennsylvania, visiting scholar, Chongqing University, China, strategic risk instructor, SAS (suite of analytics software) Institute, senior associate-faculty of the Center for Dynamic Leadership Models in Global Business at The Leadership Alliance Inc., Toronto, Canada, and principal at IQAnalytics Inc., Research Centre and Consulting Firm in Ottawa, Canada. Eduardo has extensive experience in analytics, knowledge and risk management mainly in the insurance and banking industry.

He has been knowledge management advisor and quantitative analyst at EDC (Export Development Canada) in Ottawa, regional director of PRMIA (Professional Risk Managers International Association) in Ottawa, vice-president, Marketing and Planning for Insurance Companies and Banks in Colombia, director of Strategic Intelligence UNAD (Universidad pública abierta y a distancia) Colombia, professor at Andes University and CESA (Colegio de Estudios Superiores de Administración) in Colombia, author of five books in analytics, reviewer of several journals and with publications in peer-reviewed journals and conferences. Currently, he is the chair of the permanent Think-Tank in Analytics in Ottawa, chair of the International Conference in Analytics ICAS, member of academic committees for conferences in knowledge management and international lecturer in the analytics field.

Eduardo earned a PhD from Aston Business School, Aston University in the United Kingdom, an MSc in mathematics, Concordia University, Montreal, Canada, Certification of the Advanced Management Program, McGill University, Canada, and an MBA and bachelor in mathematics from Los Andes University Colombia. His main research interest is in the field of analytics and knowledge management applied to enterprise risk management.

Contributors

Víctor M. Albornoz
Departamento de Industrias
Universidad Técnica Federico Santa
    María
Santiago, Chile

Guillermo Armelini
ESE Business School
University of Los Andes
Santiago, Chile

León Darío Parra Bernal
Institute for Sustainable
    Entrepreneurship
EAN University
Bogotá, Colombia

Edgardo R. Bravo
Department of Engineering
Universidad del Pacífico
Lima, Peru

Patricio Cofre
Metric Arts
Santiago, Chile

Milenka Linneth Argote Cusi
Business Intelligence and Demography
    (BI&DE)
Bogotá, Colombia

Laura Rojas de Francisco
School of Management
Universidad EAFIT
Medellín, Colombia

Laura Fernanda Morales de la Vega
School of Humanities and
    Education
Tecnológico de Monterrey
Mexico City, Mexico

Francisco Iván Zuluaga Díaz
Department of Mathematical Sciences
EAFIT University
Medellin, Colombia

Esteban Flores
ARE Consultores
Mexico City, Mexico

Gerzo Gallardo
Metric Arts
Panamá City, Panamá

Eduardo Gómez-Araujo
School of Management
Universidad Del Norte
Barranquilla, Colombia

Ana Ximena Halabi-Echeverry
International School of Economics and
    Administrative Sciences
University of La Sabana
Bogotá, Colombia

Mauricio Herrera
Faculty of Engineering
University del Desarrollo
Santiago, Chile

Eduardo M. López
Tecnológico de Monterrey
EGADE Business School
Monterrey, Mexico

Mario Ernesto Martínez-Avella
International School of Economics and
    Administrative Sciences
University of La Sabana
Bogotá, Colombia

Izaias Martins
School of Management
Universidad EAFIT
Medellín, Colombia

Jairo Rafael Montoya-Torres
School of Management
Universidad de los Andes
Bogotá, Colombia

Virna Ortiz-Araya
Departamento de Gestión
    Empresarial
Universidad del Bío-Bío
Chillán, Chile

José Daniel Gallego Posada
Department of Mathematical
    Sciences
EAFIT University
Medellin, Colombia

Deborah Richards
Computing Department
Macquarie University
Sydney, Australia

Eduardo Rodriguez
Sentry Endowed Chair of Business
    Analytics
University of Wisconsin–Stevens Point
Stevens Point, Wisconsin

Isabel Rodríguez
ARE Consultores
Mexico City, Mexico

Erica Salvaj
School of Business and Economics
Universidad del Desarrollo
Santiago, Chile

and

School of Business
Universidad Torcuato Di Tella
Buenos Aires, Argentina

Michelle Rodriguez Serra
Department of Engineering
Universidad del Pacífico
Lima, Peru

Cinthya Leonor Vergara Silva
Data Science Group Instituto
    Sistemas
Complejos de Ingeniería (ISCI)
University of Chile
Santiago, Chile

Alvaro G. Talavera
Department of Engineering
Universidad del Pacífico
Lima, Peru

Federico Trigos
Tecnológico de Monterrey
EGADE Business School
Monterrey, Mexico

Introduction

There are several books on developing, in an independent way, the technical aspects of analytics and its use in problem-solving and decision-making processes. This book concentrates on understanding the analytics knowledge management process and its applications to various socioeconomic sectors in a comprehensive manner. The analytics knowledge applications are presented using cases from Latin America and Emerging Economies where a solution has been achieved.

The Latin American and Emerging Economy examples are especially interesting to study because they can incorporate the whole analytics process. They are also good reference examples for applying the analytics process for SME organizations in some developed economies. Furthermore, the selected cases are a means to identify multiple tacit factors to deal with during the analytics knowledge management process implementation. These factors which include data cleaning, data gathering, and interpretation of results are not always easily identified by the analytics practitioners. This is driven by the fact that analytics process descriptions come mostly from developed economies with very solid and mature organizations that have already overcome several barriers in implementing analytics.

This book introduces the steps to perform analytics work in organizations starting from problem definition and data gathering to solution implementation and its evaluation. This book is organized into two sections: Section I includes Chapters 1 and 2. Chapter 1 is about the evolution of the analytics concept and the factors that are converging for the adoption of the analytics knowledge and process. This chapter presents the alignment of analytics concepts, their evolution, and the relationship to strategy formulation and management control systems. In Chapter 2 the focus is on the analytics knowledge adoption and the presentation is based on the review of the Analytics Knowledge Management Process. The presentation of the Analytics Knowledge Management Process is developed with a review of the analytics knowledge management subprocesses: analytics knowledge creation, analytics knowledge storage and access, analytics knowledge transfer, and analytics knowledge application.

Section II is related to the applications of analytics knowledge to real-world cases. There are 11 cases included with a wide spectrum of topics and explaining the theoretical treatment that some of the applications require. These cases cover several socioeconomic problems faced by Latin American and emerging economies. The selected cases pay special attention to the description of how to combine analytics methods and techniques, data integration, and appropriate analytics knowledge.

This book crucially facilitates the understanding of analytics methods and techniques of almost every person in an organization. Given that the number of techniques and methods available to analytics practitioners is very large, this book concentrates on explaining the strengths and weaknesses of methods and techniques commonly described by authors. This approach is in search of supporting business managers and professionals who seek to design and control the application of their analytics arsenal.

This book is written for leaders in areas such as marketing, planning, risk management, production and operations; students of MBA and MSc in management-related areas; industrial engineering, applied economics, executive education programs, and for educators, researchers, students, and practitioners in management and information technology and related fields.

This book has a concentration on analytics knowledge management subprocesses, review of problems in multiple sectors in Latin America and Emerging Economies, review of several analytic techniques to solve problems, and the use of the most updated methods associated with the problems. The cases to illustrate the analytics process in action comprise in Chapter 3 the application of analytics in healthcare services in Mexico; Chapter 4 presents the application of social networks in the process of product adoption in Chile; Chapter 5 introduces the order acceptance illustration for prescriptive analytics with a case in Mexico; Chapter 6 includes the uncertainty aspects of analytics reviewing a case from Chile for improving production planning; Chapter 7 shows how scrapped data can be applied in the creation of macroeconomic indicators in Latin America; Chapter 8 offers a comparison of credit risk classification methods using Peruvian bank data; Chapter 9 shows an analytics application for the understanding of ports management based on information systems development using Colombia's data; Chapter 10 introduces the use of analytics knowledge application in education comparing the entrepreneur education in Colombia and Peru; Chapter 11 brings to the analysis the ICT problems where analytics knowledge can be used illustrating the definition of software reliability in a Colombian university decision; Chapter 12 shows the use of text analytics for the understanding of the concept entrepreneurship in Latin-American economies; and finally in Chapter 13 an application of social media analysis is presented to review what people are saying in Chile regarding the healthcare services.

EVOLUTION AND ADOPTION OF THE ANALYTICS PROCESS

Chapter 1

Evolution of Analytics Concept

Eduardo Rodriguez

Contents

Summary 3
The Planning Process Experience and the Analytics Process 4
Adoption of Management Ideas from Mathematics and Science..........................9
Computational Capacity and Use of Data 11
People's Skillset and Its Development 12
Common Principles of Management Theories..13
To Develop a More Intelligent Organization 15
References..18

Summary

This chapter is a reflection on the evolution of the concept of analytics. Analytics as a concept has been for many years in management practice under different labels. Analytics has been part of the management thinking evolution that introduces a scientific approach to make decisions, solve problems, and create knowledge. The use of the analytics process is based on an aggregation of concepts that looks for converting data into actions. The purpose of this chapter is to describe how through time we have been looking for a better use of data resources combining rationality, intuition, and the knowing methods that physical sciences use.

The Planning Process Experience and the Analytics Process

In this chapter, there is a mention of the historical events with the purpose of understanding the influence of concepts in the current level that analytics has and its future. However, the aim of this chapter is not to enumerate the historical events in the life of analytics but to review the factors that influence the analytics wave in business. There are several factors in the management practice that converge positively in order to consolidate analytics in the current and future business environment such as bigger computational capacity, access to data and technology at affordable cost, use of statistics and applied mathematics in more areas of organizations, and the development of social sciences.

This chapter presents how the concepts have been used in an isolated way for years and how the use of several management concepts across disciplines has been very slow in their adoption in organizations. The main point is to observe that decision-making and problem-solving processes are a combination of formal and reason-based approaches with intuition in organizations. This chapter prepares for an understanding of Chapter 2 regarding the analytics knowledge management process. The analytics knowledge management process includes the adoption of the analytics process that is considered in this book as a technology (How) in organizational settings.

To start there is an example in management processes evolution that can guide us to an understanding of the analytics process adoption. This means we need to learn from the experience of creating a planning process and planning departments in organizations. The analytics process is under the same stage of evolution as strategy design and strategic planning were many years ago. Strategic and operational planning processes are a crucial part of the current organizations' life. Management meetings are held every year to discuss objectives and to develop strategies to achieve the defined objectives. Plans are part of the definition of corporate performance evaluation metrics. In general, the whole organization will continue monitoring the development of plans, strategies, implementations, results, etc., over periods of time. In general, it is possible to say that currently a planning process is completely embedded in organizations. Plans are part of the strategy design as the means to achieve organization's goals/objectives. Plans are setting the goals that are used as the corporate performance evaluation framework. Planning is a process that is fed by data and the good data use and the knowledge created from the data will be the source of appropriate organizational plans.

However, the planning process is under permanent review, the same as the ways to design and to implement strategies. Strategies design and strategic planning are topics that occupy permanent management's work. The planning process is looking for reducing uncertainty through the knowledge created from the data and the adjustment to the conditions of the markets. The differentiation between strategic planning from creating and designing strategy is very important for the whole organization in order to learn how to use new tools like analytics in the planning process. Regarding this differentiation Martin (2014) wrote "True strategy is about placing bets and making hard choices. The objective is not to eliminate risk but to increase the odds of success." It could be possible to say that the adoption of the planning process in organizations is generalized but it is in a permanent improvement and evolution according to the access and use of tools and resources available such as the analytics process and its arsenal of methods and tools.

The review of the strategic planning includes the precision in the concepts used, the process of planning itself, and the ways to implement it. For example, Mintzberg (1994) who has been one of the main contributors to the understanding of strategic planning process has included precision in the concepts that show in his own work on strategic planning the mistakes in the use and definition of the concepts within the strategic planning process. Sometimes planning is a limited process in organizations, which focuses on the creation of documents that will be reviewed periodically and not really a way to conduct the organization to achieve the goals. There are several traps in strategic planning. One of them is to believe that a plan is the solution for everything or the answer to any market change. This experience from the planning process evolution is potentially similar to what we can expect of the analytics process: a great acceptance, possibly a fashion and huge expectations, but we need to understand that the analytics process will be a process that requires a permanent learning process inside the organization.

Moreover, many questions have emerged in the strategic and operational planning processes implementation: Not only questions about the best way to define objectives/goals but also about the structure of the process to permeate plans inside the organization. The development and introduction of a plan require a consistent and aligned set of business processes, people, and technologies to improve performance and sustainability of the organizations. Organizations are trying to monitor the organization's adaptation to the business environment in order to keep a competitive position.

Nowadays, organizations have planning processes in most of the cases and some organizations have planning departments and some departments have planning areas or teams. Organizations perform the planning process with more formalism than others using several techniques. These techniques include quantitative and qualitative tools. However, not all organizations in the same market use the same techniques even though planning is a core process to discover how to proceed and to act in the present and future market conditions. Analytics is part of both planning and strategy design and analytics tools are potentially the same in organizations and their planning processes but the way to leverage strategic steps using analytics tools is what will show the difference at the time of competing in a market.

The experience with the planning process development and its adoption is similar to what the analytics process needs to go through. The analytics process implementation needs to learn from the planning process adoption and its experience in organizations. The analytics process has not only a role in supporting the planning process, but also to support strategy design and implementation through tactical actions. It is in the strategy creation where analytics starts providing more sense for organizations in using the systematic approach for solving problems and making decisions. Analytics will contribute to discovering better insights to adapt the organizations to current and future business environment situations. Products and markets development, which are core tasks in a value chain in organizations, might be the ones that can lead the search of a higher benefit of the analytics process. Differentiation based on analytics can be a permanent process to improve in order to add value to organizations.

Moreover, on the one hand, the analytics process needs to learn how the planning process operates and where analytics can be useful. The analytics process is going from strategy design to implementation (operationalize the strategy) including a permanent strategy feedback review. The feedback is the way to learn based on data and analytics is about learning from data for predicting, describing, controlling, and optimizing organizational processes. If there is no review or follow-up of the results in each period possibly there is no understanding where the organizations are located in the space of the competitive strategy dimensions that Porter introduced (Porter 2008). Even more, the analytics process is required for defining objectives and these objectives probably might not be simple numbers/figures but intervals of values around targets and metrics of variation of the expected results. For example, strategic plans are formulated for certain periods of years and the goals of everyone in organizations are per year most of the time leading to a short view and commitment of employees for maintaining the organization's competitive advantages.

On the other hand, the analytics process needs to learn from the planning process that organizations are systems with memory and the accumulated data will be the vehicle to learn from experience and how to apply the analytics process in a proper manner. The memory based on data requires methods to show options to discover opportunities and control possible risks. Risks are not necessarily only related to negative events or bad results but also associated with the lack of understanding of good results. In the end, what is keeping the organization up is how to proceed for a better understanding of the problems and how to tackle them.

Analytics contributes to the creation of knowledge management systems that put the created knowledge from data in people's hands to use it and act as enhancing business processes. Analytics helps organizations to keep track of the company in the market and to provide confidence intervals where the goals can fall. To achieve that level people in organizations are trying to understand how goals are converted into numbers that represent variations of expected results. Variation of results represents risk of the organizations that need be identified, assessed, and controlled. The same as in the planning process the analytics process is moving from the stage of thinking in having a wonderful analytics process to the stage of having a valuable analytics process to develop in organizations. The journey from the idea of having analytics to value generation has its ups and downs. Several projects with Big Data are not going well (Tyagi and Demirkan 2016) because of a lack of understanding of organization's objectives, management issues, etc. This means the analytics process adoption requires maturity levels not only on data management but also in the management and understanding of the analytics process.

In general, analytics is evolving from being isolated and problem-specific tasks to a discipline fully integrated into the strategy creation and strategy implementation support. This can be possible if people, technology, processes are aligned to strategy and the learning of working interdisciplinary within and across the organizations grows in order to contribute to the strategy design and its implementation in a better way. The value of analytics is not only in the methods or capabilities but also it is in the development of a solid culture to solve problems and make decisions using what organizations have in term of minds, data, and tools (models, applications, and so on).

Analytics needs for its adoption and value creation to develop an analytics knowledge management process that will be the vehicle to conduct the analytics to work. The evolution of analytics is associated with several efforts that start with the appropriate definition of problems and the learning of techniques and methods to use for solving those problems. In particular analytics adoption requires to learn from the experience and to take advantage of opportunities such as

■ Better access and use of tools and means to perform the analytics work. In an organization the process of using the analytics tools has been very slow as this note from Bursk and Chapman (1963) illustrates because it looks like today's conversation. However, they are talking about how in 1950 the approach for solving problems in management was influenced by scientific approaches. They pointed out, referring to management practice, that organizations are using methods that "… drawing in depth both on mathematics and on social sciences, and by utilizing intensively the high-speed electronic computer, researchers are beginning to give to the decision-making process a scientific base akin to the established methods which have long provided the bases for research in physics, biology, and chemistry."

■ Acceptance of the work was based on reason and intuition to solve problems and make decisions. Buchanan and O'Connell (2006) pointed out: "Of course the gut/brain dichotomy is largely false. Few decision makers ignore good information when they can get it. And most accept that there will be times they can't get it and so will have to rely on instinct." And they continue saying that Peter Senge in *The Fifth Discipline* (1990) suggests that it is better to use reason and intuition together. The following two stories illustrate the use of mix of reason and intuition in developing analytics capacity and show the use of the most important ingredient in analytics: people's thinking and its structure to connect data, knowledge, and intuition.

Around 1943 Abraham Wald, a very important mathematician who lived between 1902 and 1950, explained what a correct way of thinking is, showing the process of gathering data for making decisions. Wald's team was interested in understanding what type of protection (armor) the airplanes should have during the attacks on air. People in his team started getting data from the airplanes that came back to the base and observed where the bullet impacts of the enemy were. Wald observed that the sample was not the correct one for solving the problem. Wald expressed: "What you should really do is add armor around the motors! What you are forgetting is that the aircraft that are most damaged don't return. You don't see them. Hits by German shells are presumably distributed somewhat randomly. The number of damaged motors you are seeing is far less than randomness would produce, and that indicates that it is the motors that are the weak point" (Wallis 1980).

Another example to illustrate analytics thinking is related to the way to infer or predict results through reason. Sometimes it is not required to have sophisticated methods but a good approach for understanding the problem and the logic for using the data available. Ruggles and Brodie (1947) presented a great example of analytics reasoning for estimating during the World War II the production of tires, German tanks, and other enemy equipment. The method used was based on estimations using the serial numbers of the products. The analytics methodology was better than using the traditional intelligence methods of reporting or "more abstract methods of intelligence such as reconciling widely divergent prisoner of war reports, basing production estimates on pre-war capabilities or projecting production trends based on estimates of the degree of utilization of resources in the enemy country" (Ruggles and Brodie 1947).

We have seen that analytics adoption can take a similar path as the planning process took and we have observed the need of introducing an analytics knowledge management process in organizations. In the following paragraphs there is a description of the analytics knowledge evolution and its adoption based on the convergence of the following factors: first, the adoption of ideas from mathematics and science in management. Second, improvement in computational capacity and use of data. Third, the development of people's skillsets and finally as a fourth factor the use of a common set of principles that several theories in management have. We use as a principle that the purpose of the analytics process and the analytics knowledge management process is to create more intelligent organizations. More intelligent organizations need to connect concepts, capabilities, mindsets, and behaviors the same as analytics implementation needs a review of several management theories. This review shows that the management has tried to approach methods of knowing used in physical sciences and there is a search of a scientific method that supports evidence development for the problem-solving and decision-making processes. Possibly the methods used in natural sciences can help to reduce bias or lack of objectivity, because of limited knowledge or reduced view of problems to solve in the management practice.

In the next section, we start observing how ideas from mathematics and science have been adopted in the improvement of management practice in particular preparing the land for the analytics process adoption.

Adoption of Management Ideas from Mathematics and Science

There are many concepts of natural sciences and mathematics adopted in management and presented through several management theories. Ideas about the scientific method from Descartes to our days have been developed based on the use of a systematic approach to solve problems and obtaining evidence to test hypotheses and consolidate theories. The concept of a scientific method in organizational studies has moved far away from the times of observing the results on organization's processes assuming employees as resources (Taylor's approach) that can be organized as raw material and machines. These days there is a better view about industries and organizations regarding human resources and scientific methods. This view is concentrated on improving the capacity to know systematically, learn from experience, measuring for understanding the business processes, and to act in organizations. Organizations are trying to reduce the lack of understanding of the value of analytics knowledge observing that the economy these days is based on knowledge development. The analytics process is suiting in this organization's view because analytics is based on a scientific approach for solving problems and a means to create knowledge and develop actions for improving business processes.

Another point to keep in mind is that management used methods considering the tasks, variables, factors, etc., as facts or better to say following a deterministic world. The search of better knowing methods involved, for many years, only a deterministic approach for problem solutions (formulas, scenarios, what-if analysis ...) but better understanding of the reality has shown the need to include uncertainty and to incorporate randomness in problem analyses. There are new and very important analytics knowledge process tools, techniques, and methods combining deterministic and stochastic approaches to solve problems. The understanding of randomness started with figures such as Pascal, Bernoulli, Gauss, and many others arriving to the formalization of probability theory under Kolmogorov and the development of analysis and measure theory. The formalization is led by the need of axiomatization of mathematics according to Hilbert's contribution to mathematics construction. At the same time, applied mathematics development incorporated risk concepts and differentiate risk from uncertainty. New applied mathematics theories to management were created by scientists such as von Neumann and Morgenstern introduced game theory and operations research started with scholars like Dantzig, Raiffa, Ackoff, and many others.

The mathematical apparatus of analytics was developed many years ago with the development of applied mathematics, computation, and information systems. However, the adoption of analytics in business has been affected because of the adoption of applied mathematics and use of computational resources. It has had barriers in the appropriate use of data, understanding of the fundamentals of analytics and mainly in people preparedness. Moreover, the adoption of applied mathematics in management could be similar to what has been the changes in applied mathematics and to what Paul Cootner pointed out in 1964 (Cootner 1964) in the preface of Mandelbrot's book (Mandelbrot et al. 1997): "Mandelbrot, like Prime Minister Churchill before him, promises us not utopia but blood, sweat, toil and tears. If he is right, almost all of our statistical tools are obsolete … Surely, before consigning centuries of work to the ash pile, we should like to have some assurance that all our work is truly useless." It implies the need of reviewing new ways to understand problems in the risk analytics world and in general in the analytics approach for problem solving.

Analytics has been part of the life of people in business and in various related disciplines. The concepts that are coming from mathematics in many cases are not immediately applicable to the real-world problems but possibly these concepts and results can be applied in the long run. The applications can be in business or in different sciences and engineering. Some of the applications of mathematics have grown and consolidated very well for more than two centuries, but they have been isolated areas and developed in specific industries like actuarial science in the insurance industry. Actuaries were the analytics people in organizations for many years (insurance companies) but only few years ago we can find actuaries working in several areas in insurance companies, including marketing, or in other economic sectors. These days to use probability theory and to talk about Bernoulli experiments is more common in business (finance, marketing) as it used to be some years ago. However, the concepts are coming from Bernoulli, Bayes, Legendre and others from the eighteenth century. The same happens with the slow adoption of concepts of prescriptive analytics because, for example, Lagrange multipliers are also from the end of the eighteenth century or linear equation solutions and Markov Chains model are from the beginning and end of the nineteenth century, respectively.

The adoption of mathematical models in management has taken a long time as we discussed in the previous paragraphs. The following example of the Brownian motion model adoption in management confirms this slow adoption process of analytics in management. The Brownian motion is the description of the particles movement that was used in biology at the beginning of the nineteenth century. The mathematical model was presented by the French mathematician Bachelier (1879–1946) who was associated with the speculation concepts in finance. Brownian motion model was used later in physics by Einstein at the beginning of the twentieth century; in management it was used in the development of mathematical finance. However, the model was used at the end of the twentieth century with the option pricing model of Black and Scholes. In light of the growing interest of connecting problems and applied mathematics tools the search of new knowledge from data sets motivated the development of data mining tools. The data mining methods include statistical-based tools such as regression models and machine/algorithm-based solutions such as artificial neural networks, support vector machines, and many more. Baesens et al. (2009) indicate that "Data mining involves extracting interesting patterns from data and can be found at the heart of operational research

(OR), as its aim is to create and enhance decision support systems. Even in the early days, some data mining approaches relied on traditional OR methods such as linear programming and forecasting ...."

Finally, many techniques that we currently use in analytics work have been developed for more than 50 years. We learnt that solutions to business problems based on analytics are from the good understanding, alignment, and organization of people, techniques, data, and problems. The OR beginning is around the time of the creation of Radar. "Operations research (OR) had its origins in the late 1930s when a group of British Royal Air Force officers and civilian scientists were asked to determine how the recently developed radar technology could be used for controlled interception of enemy aircraft" (Assad and Gass 2011).

Computational Capacity and Use of Data

The computational capacity or the use of computer-based technology has influenced the adoption of the analytics process in business. Information systems were developed with and without computers. They have used computational process in batch and real time. These days with Big Data and parallel computing we are working in batches as we used to in the 1970s. The computational capacity has been improved over time because of the development of computer languages and the approach to create analytics-oriented languages including the use of mathematical/statistical tools and syntax, which helps in the creation of applications improving efficiency in the coding process.

Computational effort is related to the development of using data and to the organization of steps required to obtain/access appropriate data and its process. Data are converted to fuel the analytics process that needs to organize through standards, data repositories' creation adapted to structured and nonstructured data. From these data structures traditional activities, related to marketing, credit, and other management areas, started using data that leads to study problems in more dimensions and obtaining better prediction capabilities.

There has been a review of algorithms to improve the time of answer. The computational capacity has been improved not only because of new logical components but also because machines and networks are working at a higher speed and with better performance. The access to tools for computational purpose through open-source applications such as R, Python, Hadoop and family, Spark, etc., contributes to create solutions and to provide access to organizations with less resources but it requires to have people with analytics knowledge. Additionally, the computational capacity has contributed to the development and use of solutions such as customer relationship management (CRM), supplier relationship management (SRM) Supply Chain Management applications, social media, etc. Data are converted into an asset in organizations requiring governance to expand the data use among more people in organizations.

Computational capacity allows to apply several analytical techniques to small or regular data sets the same way as Big Data. Techniques are available for all sizes of organizations and computational capacity is accessible in most of the cases; however, the appropriate use of techniques and computational capacity is a matter of having trained analytics users. Users who will develop clear problem definitions, test or review model assumptions, model conditions, and deal with issues of using a high volume of data. Issues such as the level of garbage that data can have and the possible creation of bias in answers to problems. This means that having access to data or computational capacity is not enough for developing in an appropriate way the analytics process. A factor that has a remarkable influence in the adoption of analytics process is people's skillset, which will be discussed in the following section.

People's Skillset and Its Development

Analytics knowledge management process has as the main component the human capacity to learn and to use knowledge. Any analytics knowledge management system will incorporate people and technology working together. In organizations there are technical people who have been prepared for many years and are growing in their capabilities, the issue is that in most of the cases the number of technical people is not enough to influence and to develop solutions to the immense variety of problems in organizations. There is an issue to solve in the number of technical people in analytics but is at management level where the analytics process understanding can have more barriers to overcome. There is a need of building a bridge between technical people and management in order to develop a common language around obtaining meaning from data, to find better solutions, and to make better decisions. Management schools need to do more efforts in improving their education about analytics and its integration into other common fields such as marketing, finance, operations, and human resources.

People's preparation for developing the analytics process in organizations requires improvement of analytics skillsets, minds, and behaviors. People's skillsets are the means to create and apply analytics knowledge developed through data management and modeling processes. People in organizations need to connect the dots of management theories in order to understand what to use in the analytics process according to specific problems, such as quality, productivity, performance evaluation, strategy development, and many others. People deal with the limitation of using techniques across disciplines and knowledge domain contexts. People in analytics need to understand the knowledge domain contexts in order to create value with the analytics process.

In the journey of developing people for analytics process adoption it is required the acceptance of the use of reason and intuition in the decision-making and problem-solving processes. The views from Simon (1969) indicating that the decisions are not totally rational or the introduction of prospective theory by Kahneman and Tversky (1979) are examples of the conceptualization around the need of using rationality and intuition for understanding complex problems and their solutions. Moreover, people in organizations need to understand that improvement of manufacturing, business processes, and the use of methods to define problems require the connection of solutions with methods to measure. People are the creators of these connections and creators of the measurement systems that will help to achieve a better strategic intelligence development.

Common Principles of Management Theories

In this section, we review some of the management theories that have several concepts and principles in common that are part of the analytics knowledge management process. One of the most popular and current theories in management is lean thinking. Womack and Jones in 1996 introduced the idea of defining values based on the customer's experience regarding products, time, price, and organizations' capabilities. The concept of waste was included as crucial in the analysis of business processes. Waste defined as resources that are not required to perform tasks and business processes.

However, these principles, on the one hand, are part of the analytics process which comprises operations research and information systems concepts, techniques, and problem resolution methods. The concept of having customers in the center of the business analysis has been part of the management practice/education for years, particularly in the marketing or TQM perspectives. Furthermore, to develop the best process for organizations (efficiency and optimization) has been part of the manifesto of operations research from the insertion in military and business worlds. The purpose of eliminating waste when products and services are developed and transformed in offer to customers is immersed in the principle of the best solution search for processes improvement.

On the other hand, the analysis of steps looking for clarification of the value of activities and the connection with business goals have been the fundamentals of analysis and design of information systems. Methods for developing the analytics process and information systems have evolved to a closer interaction between users and developers/analysts as it is in the agile approach. Nothing is more in a search of perfection than the creation of mathematical models and information systems. The analytics process brings together the principles of creating value-added and customer/user satisfaction under the premise of using appropriate customer knowledge. This customer knowledge is focused on what customers/users want and what is required for having access to satisfy their needs. The enhancements in the levels of accuracy and performance are strong filters created in the analytics process for accepting new solutions in the analytics knowledge management process in order to add value to organizations. In general, we could say that analytics has been part of the organizations' management but has been used under other labels.

As it is shown in the previous paragraphs it is possible to observe in other management theories how the analytics knowledge has been part of management development. The confusion of names, labels, and presentation of ideas could create the low understanding of topics that organizations have been talking about for years. For example, in the Goldratt's theory of constraints (Goldratt and Cox 2004) the review of problems and solution starts with an understanding of the possibility of best solutions under specific settings and under resource specifications. What Hammer and Champy (2006) proposed about the reengineering process is aligned with the way as applied mathematical models created knowledge. A point in common with reengineering is that in the analytics process the creation of the solutions is based on the expected results and not concentrated on performing isolated tasks. These tasks are using models/techniques that will turn data into actions and will review the use of the resources in the best possible way according to the business and industry development.

Deming (2000) in the definition of TQM locates the customer in the center of the organization's actions and focuses its ideas on the direction of collaborative work, continuous improvement, and a systematic plan development with permanent feedback. The analytics process is in essence a permanent improvement process that requires the work of diverse groups of people and ways to think and tackle problems. Analytics deals with strategic and tactic problems that have to be solved by multidisciplinary teams in a collaborative way. Furthermore, and the basis of this book, the analytics knowledge management development starts using Nonaka's work (Nonaka and Takeuchi 1995), who introduces the knowledge creation dynamic through the learning and use of the knowledge to develop external outcomes that are solutions and actions to improve business processes. The process of knowledge management emerges from creation and accumulation of knowledge to the capacity to share/transfer and develop solutions to organizations' problems.

Another common aspect of several management theories is the use of a scientific method in management. The scientific approach of defining a problem and defining a process to solve the problem using evidence to test hypotheses is closer to the management practice as it used to be. Lean Analysis, Six Sigma, and Service Science are based on measurement systems creation, validation of ideas and concepts, review of the results, and generation of control means to maintain the business processes in good performance. Besides, the concept of uncertainty and risk through time is incorporated into the measurement systems. Organization's performance evaluation starts with the development of deterministic methods and evolves to stochastic-based ones. The support of the measurement and control systems for performance evaluation of business processes is based on the analytics knowledge management process using theories and fundamentals from mathematics, statistics, and computer science.

In summary, the analytics process and analytics knowledge management process have been present in management in implicit and explicit ways through the management theories. What has not been easy for people in business is to identify communalities of the theories and concepts in order to avoid jumping from one theory to another reducing the positive effects of continuity, consistency, and permanent review of business processes based on known principles. Additionally, people have been behind the use of methods of experimentation, use of mathematical thinking, and modeling processes for turning data into insights and actions. Connecting dots among management theories and conceptualization can be a very strong way to develop analytics in organizations because there are improvements in education and the contact with data and technology is more common. One can start by defining objectives based on data analytics, creating information systems that help to measure what the organization wants to achieve and to take care of. Methods and techniques can be used because of better data flowing through the organization producing a dynamic of models and information systems enhancements or as Saxena and Srinivasan (2013) expressed: "In our view, analytics is the rational way to get from ideas to execution." This means that analytics might be a strong part of the management development but a clearer understanding is required as we develop the analytics process for improving performance of organizations.

To Develop a More Intelligent Organization

This is the last point to review in the factors influencing analytics adoption. The concept of an intelligent organization is associated with the capacity of organization's adaptation to the conditions of the markets and the possibility of solving more problems, and making better decisions under constraints such as time, uncertainty, and resources access. The assumption in this book is that the better the intelligence development the better the adaptation and, on the contrary, better adaptation means more intelligent organization. There are several aspects to reflect about the way to develop intelligent organizations based on the analytics knowledge management process, some of them are the following.

First, to transform an organization into a more intelligent organization is related to the capacity to use in a proper way information and knowledge, in particular the use of analytics knowledge. Regarding this view Bazerman and Chugh (2006) pointed out "Bounded awareness can occur at various points in the decision-making process. First, executives may fail to see or seek out the key information needed to make a sound decision. Second, they may fail to use the information that they do see because they are not aware of its relevance. Finally, executives may fail to share information with others, thereby bounding the organization's awareness."

Second, it is important to use knowledge resources that are available; in particular the formal knowledge that is already created and provides insights for managing organizations. The organization needs to learn and to use what has been learnt. In this regard Cascio (2007) asked: "Why Don't Practitioners Know about Research That Academics Think Is Very Important?" Reflecting on this question possibly in the analytics process application there is a need to understand the new results about techniques, tools, sources of knowledge, and data management across the organization.

Third, a more intelligent organization needs the development of means to define where the organization has to go, this means to know if the objectives and goals are appropriate, feasible, and required. In organizations people can fall in the trap (Hammond et al. 2006) of the bias of using evidence to confirm what the current point of view is, to validate former decisions, or to follow what the instinct is telling us. These traps avoid the penetration of the information/knowledge in organization's process contradicting what we need to perceive or receive from the analytics work. To be aware of traps in the management decision-making process there are some controls to follow, but the most important is the follow up to the results of predictions, forecasts, development of time series of performance, risk key indicators, etc.

Fourth, intelligence is associated with the process of converting data into knowledge which can add value in the organizations. Davenport et al. (2001) commented: "The problem is that most companies are not succeeding in turning data into knowledge and then results. Even those that do are doing so only temporarily or in a limited area." However, the steps to convert data into a valuable knowledge for organizations need some capabilities for the data to knowledge transformation as Barton and Court (2012) pointed out: "In our work with dozens of companies in six data rich industries, we have found that fully exploiting data and analytics requires three mutually supportive capabilities ... First, companies must be able to identify, combine, and manage multiple sources of data. Second, they need the capability to build advanced analytics models for predicting and optimizing outcomes. Third, and most critical, management must possess the muscle to transform the organization so that the data and models actually yield better decisions."

Fifth, to become an intelligent organization requires to follow the steps of adoption of technology in organizations (In Chapter 2, the adoption of the analytics process as technology will be presented). The adoption of analytics starts with an understanding of the concepts associated with the analytics process itself and connecting these concepts with enhancements of organization's intelligence actions. This means, for example, that the concept of business analytics might be used to describe the development of intelligence with a double approach of business value achievement and implementation of the analytics process. Sheikh (2013) summarized the concept of analytics saying: "... two different perspectives to lay out the characteristics of analytics: one is related to how business value is achieved and the other regards how it is implemented." Sheikh (2013) continues saying that the business view is about the use of products, technology, or services to contribute to the analytics solution creation.

In summary, in this chapter we have reviewed a group of factors that are affecting positively the development of analytics knowledge. These factors led to find a better understanding of what the analytics process adoption means. In general, the analytics concept continues its evolution based on the improvement of the following:

1. Data organization, cleaning, and preparedness to be studied.
2. Development of people's skills from various disciplines to deal with models and with data itself.
3. Testing capacity to review the assumptions, stress testing of models, review of interpretations, and development of the systematic way to manage feedback.
4. Governance of the analytics process is developed in the way that can be creative using learning from experience for building new solutions. The Agile Manifesto used in information systems can be a way to develop. Permanent feedback and interaction with users are crucial.
5. The dynamic between learning and teaching analytics. The valuable process of analytics for organizations is that the speed of new models/tools/faces of problems requires a better interaction among stakeholders and understanding of opportunities and limitations to create solutions. It is crucial to open the black box of tools and models in analytics and to identify how people can grow in understanding and development of new models and solutions.
6. The process to embed analytics in the knowledge domain. Interpretation and meaning are the factors to create impact of the analytics work. These factors are only possible to obtain if the context is clear for the outcome interpretation. From this point it is important to understand that the expert knowledge will have the value of creating new analytics knowledge and at the same time to find the away to a proper use of techniques. For example, the implementation of better management control systems based on analytics capabilities is required and mainly with reporting systems based on XML documents (XBLR business reporting standard).
7. A process for selecting the best models including the criteria for using them: interpretability, simplicity, possibility to develop/build on it, automation, accuracy, etc.
8. A blend of reason and intuition and hard and soft techniques in problem solutions. Possibly in the development of analytics knowledge there is room for creating a concept of soft analytics as it was introduced in the soft OR concept as Heyer (2004) said: "It was in their ability to address these increasingly complex problems that soft OR methods gained credence. As opposed to the traditional or hard methods, soft OR employs predominantly qualitative, rational, interpretative and structured techniques to interpret, define, and explore various perspectives of the problems under scrutiny."

Chapter 2 introduces the concepts that can be followed for understanding analytics adoption. This chapter presents the main aspects that we have learnt from general technology adoption. The main point presented in this chapter is the description of the analytics knowledge management process and within it the understanding of the analytics process as a technology that for its adoption follows the general technology adoption experience.

References

Assad, A. A. and Gass, S. I. (Eds.), 2011, *Profiles in Operations Research: Pioneers and Innovators*, Springer, New York.

Baesens, B., Mues, C., Martens, D., and Vanthienen, J., 2009, 50 years of data mining and OR: Upcoming trends and challenge, *The Journal of the Operational Research Society*, 60(1), 16–23.

Barton, D. and Court, D., 2012, Making advanced analytics work for you: A practical guide to capitalizing on big data, *Harvard Business Review*, 90(10), 78–83.

Bazerman, M. H. and Chugh, D., 2006, Decisions without blinders, *Harvard Business Review*, 84(1), 88–97.

Buchanan, L. and O'Connell, A., 2006, A brief history of decision making, *Harvard Business Review*, 84(1), 32–41.

Bursk, E. and Chapman, J. (Eds.), 1963, *New Decision-Making Tools for Managers*, The New American Library, New York.

Cascio, W. F., 2007, Evidence-based management and the marketplace for ideas, *Academy of Management Journal*, 50(5), 1009–1012.

Cootner, P. H. (Ed.), 1964, *The Random Character of Stock Market Prices*, The MIT Press, Cambridge.

Davenport, T. H., Harris, J. G., De Long, D. W., and Jacobson A. L., 2001, Data to knowledge to results: Building an analytic capability, *California Management Review*, 43(2), 117–138.

Deming, W. E., 2000, *Out of the Crisis*, MIT Press, Boston.

Goldratt, E. and Cox, J., 2004, *The Goal: A Process of Ongoing Improvement*, Routledge, New York.

Hammer, M. and Champy, J., 2006, *Reengineering the Corporation: A Manifesto for Business Revolution*, Rev Upd edition, HarperBusiness, New York.

Hammond, J. S., Keeney, R. L., and Raiffa, H., 2006, The hidden traps in decision making, *Harvard Business Review*, 76(5), 118–126.

Heyer, R., 2004, *Understanding Soft Operations Research: The Methods, Their Application and Its Future in the Defence Setting*, DSTO Information Sciences Laboratory, Edinburgh, Australia.

Kahneman, D. and Tversky, A., 1979, Prospect theory: An analysis of decision under risk, *Econometrica*, 47(2), 263–292.

Mandelbrot, B. B., Gomory, R. E., Cootner, P. H., Fama, E. F., Morris, W. S., and Taylor, H. M., 1997, *Fractals and Scaling in Finance: Discontinuity, Concentration, Risk*, Springer, New York.

Martin, R. L., 2014, The big lie of strategic planning, *Harvard Business Review*, 92(1), 78–84.

Mintzberg, H., 1994, *The Fall and Rise of Strategic Planning*, Prentice-Hall, New York.

Nonaka, I. and Takeuchi, H., 1995, *The Knowledge-Creating Company: How Japanese Companies Creates the Dynamics of Innovation*, Oxford University Press, New York.

Porter, M. E., 2008, The five competitive forces that shape strategy, *Special Issue on HBS Centennial. Harvard Business Review*, 86(1), 78–93.

Ruggles, R. and Brodie, H., 1947, An empirical approach to economic intelligence in World War II, *Journal of the American Statistical Association*, 42(237), 72–91.

Saxena, R. and Srinivasan, A., 2013, *Business Analytics, International Series in Operations Research & Management Science*, Springer, New York.

Senge, P., 1990, *The Fifth Discipline: The Art and Practice of the Learning Organization*, Currency Doubleday.

Sheikh, N., 2013, *Implementing Analytics: A Blueprint for Design, Development, and Adoption*, Morgan Kaufmann, Waltham, MA.

Simon, H., 1969, *The Sciences of the Artificial*, The MIT Press, Cambridge.

Tyagi, P. and Demirkan, H., 2016, Biggest big data challenges, *Analytics Magazine*, November/December, 56–63.

Wallis, W. A., 1980, The statistical research group, 1942–1945, *Journal of the American Statistical Association*, 75, 320–330.

Chapter 2

The Analytics Knowledge Management Process

Eduardo Rodriguez

Contents

Summary 22
Introduction...22
Learning about Analytics Knowledge Adoption...23
    The Analytics Process as Technology 24
    Learning about Technology Use 25
Adopting the Analytics Process 28
    The Principles to Adopt the Analytics Process 28
Developing an Analytics Knowledge Management Process 29
    Analytics Knowledge Creation 30
    Analytics Knowledge Storage and Retrieving...31
    Analytics Knowledge Transfer 32
    Analytics Knowledge Application...35
Reflections on the Analytics Process Adoption..35
    Understanding the Problem: Going to the Customers.................................36
    Learning from People's Experience: Minds and Behaviors Influence...............38
    Developing and Transferring New Analytics Knowledge and Capabilities
    for Operations 40
    Revisiting all Stakeholder's Needs: Looking for Niches................................ 42
    Building on Measurement Results and Benefits..43
    Developing Governance to Keep Alive the Innovation Process,
    Collaborating for Better... 44
References 47

Summary

Currently, there are not only new digital technologies to support organizations but also to a volume of data that grows as a potential valuable asset in organizations. However, there are limitations in organizational capabilities to obtain knowledge from data, use the knowledge to solve problems, and support the development of answers for complex problems and decisions. This is possibly because of a lack of understanding of the required capabilities, reduced development of capabilities, limited human expertise and understanding of analytical tools, low use of the technological tools, and poor communication capabilities in the organizations. In many cases, the inappropriate use of new technology and analytics knowledge in organizations reduce the search for solutions to support multidisciplinary and interdepartmental work for problem solving.

This chapter is uniquely designed to provide an integral view of the use of analytics knowledge and technology as a symbiotic process to solve problems. This chapter complements the previous one and moves beyond the understanding of some factors for developing the analytics knowledge and concentrates on the analytics process adoption. The chapter also presents the analytics knowledge management process and some examples to illustrate it. Technology is referred to, in the chapter, as an analytics process and a review of technology adoption is studied with the purpose of learning from it to implement the analytics process.

Introduction

The aim of this chapter is to review the ways to develop competencies in order to adopt analytics knowledge and its process in organizations. There are two main streams to analyze the general problem of competencies improvement associated with the capacity to adopt analytics knowledge and its process. On the one hand, organizations need to develop the learning process to use in the best way (efficiently and effectively) new analytics knowledge. On the other hand, organizations need to gain competencies to contribute to developing analytics knowledge.

This chapter is based on the problem, in organizations and not in individuals, of how organizations can develop an analytics knowledge management process to improve the adoption of analytics knowledge and process. This means there is an interest in what an organization is, how the organizations learn and improve analytics capacity, and how they develop a knowledge management process to support analytics adoption. In the process of analytics knowledge application, it is possible to contribute to creating new technologies as well but this is out of the scope of this chapter. The application examples in the chapters of this book are based on the search of solutions to specific problems. They are part of the illustration of the analytics knowledge application as a subprocess of the analytics knowledge management process.

In particular, this chapter covers the following topics:

■ Bases of the concepts in the analytics knowledge management process and analytics knowledge management systems design.

■ Design of a basic plan to improve people's competencies in analytics, understanding and use of analytics capacity based on the knowledge management processes.

■ Connection of technology use with analytics and other capabilities that organizations are demanding. Learn the meaning and application of various technological and analytical tools for improving the decision-making process in each organization.

■ Introduction of approaches to reduce the misuse of intangible capital in organizations. Understand the potential use of different technological and analytical tools for multiple kinds of problems. Gain knowledge to improve the processes related to the way to do more with what is available in the organization (Scope Economies).

■ Guidelines for the process of improvement capabilities of different stakeholders for managing and participating in discussions related to the use of technology and analytics in decisions and problem resolution. This is to develop competencies to participate in the interdisciplinary and interorganizational problem-solving processes where technology plays a crucial role for strategic definitions.

Therefore, the following sections present the foundations to understand the company as a learning system, a knowledge management framework, and the concepts associated with analytics knowledge and the analytics process adoption.

Learning about Analytics Knowledge Adoption

The purpose of adopting the analytics process starts on the one hand, with an understanding of WHAT we need to know about analytics and on the other hand, with the answer to HOW organizations are learning about analytics and its process. To answer these questions a first step is to define the analytics process as a set of six main activities, as follows (Rodriguez 2017):

1. Problem definition, delimitation, definition of scope through the needs of the business.
2. Data management as the source to create analytics knowledge.
3. Model management as the knowledge creation process.
4. Development of understanding and meaning as the analytics knowledge that can be valuable for the organization.

5. Analytics knowledge sharing and transfer as the organization's capability to exchange analytics knowledge.
6. Analytics knowledge application as a way to develop a permanent improvement of business processes.

The analytics process includes the What and How of analytics; however, the adoption of the analytics process requires the design and implementation of the analytics knowledge management process. The reason is that the analytics process adoption is not only a problem of adoption of techniques or IT technology, but also a problem of human interaction, user experience, and development of solutions through analytic knowledge sharing, and appropriate use of analytics knowledge in the knowledge domain. In summary, the analytics process adoption is a problem of creating meaning. The concept of adoption is not how much a company invests in analytics tools, but how the analytics process is really embedded in the organizations and how users are finding that the analytics process is providing value to what they need to do at work. The analytics knowledge management process is developed through four subprocesses: analytics knowledge creation, analytics knowledge store and access, analytics knowledge transfer, and analytics knowledge application. In this book, the analytics process represents the technology to transform data into knowledge and actions and the concept of adoption of technology not only refers to the adoption of software/tools, but also to the human interaction with the analytics techniques and tools. The following concepts: technology, techniques, models, and methods are crucial for providing meaning to the transformation of data in an organization's asset and as a generator of organization's value.

The Analytics Process as Technology

The concepts of technology, techniques, models, and methods are at the core of understanding of the analytics knowledge management process. The first is to understand what we mean by technology in this chapter. Cardwell (1994) provides us the guide to review the concept of technology: "At the heart of technology lies the ability to recognize a human need, or desire (actual or potential), and then to devise a means—an invention or a new design—to satisfy it economically." In this manner, we are going to use the concept of technology as equivalent to the analytics process as a whole and we will review the technology adoption experience to guide the analytics process adoption. The analytics process requires techniques, models, and methods to create analytics knowledge and actions, data, soft approaches to solve problems, and computation capacity to achieve the goals performing specific tasks. The analytics process is systematically organized in order to provide solutions and to perform activities supported by analytics knowledge data/text mining, optimization, simulation, etc. They are considered as part of technology, and deal with a group of techniques associated with different problems or knowledge development sources.

A technique (Regression Analysis) is used as the way (HOW) or as the process that people use to perform analytics actions, develop models, and tools in order to obtain the results of the analytics process. These models are the abstraction of the reality (the regression model that is built with estimated parameters) and can be qualitative, quantitative, graphical, etc. The models and software are converted into tools for understanding data and create meaning. The difference with methods is just in the scope of the steps and at the level where they are used in a work or research setting. The methods in the regression setting, used as the technique example, can be associated with dealing with variable interactions, backward, stepwise, forward analyses for variables selection, outlier identification, and assumption validation.

We explore the models of technology adoption to understand how the analytics process can be adopted. Dealing with technology requires not only an understanding of different types of technology but also the proximity of technology to humans. To provide value and to discover how to do things based on the use and advances of science in organizations require technologies, techniques, and methods. People's capacity to use technology, technique, and methods is the bridge among data, business process, and analytics knowledge to contribute to the problem-solving and decision-making processes. Moreover, technologies are developed from many different sources and knowledge fields. There are technologies associated with medical and biological studies, and the use of technologies in economic problem resolutions. Nevertheless, technologies are for answering human needs; in particular, analytics technologies require to be very close to the day-to-day life of people in organizations.

Technology is growing through two different ways. On the one hand, technologies can be developed by evolution of the technology itself in each area like an ongoing technology process. This refers to enhancements and improvements to technology that already exists. On the other hand, technology can be related to the revolution of solutions, creating disruptive technologies, and in which technology cannot meet the need of users–customers, but they are the new ways to do things (Baltzan et al. 2012).

People's needs are evolving and technology is providing solutions to many of these needs. However, not all knowledge fields are at the same level of advance. Analytics technologies have advanced at a high speed in the last decades. Users have advanced as well but in some cases the gap between knowing how to use a technology and how to contribute effectively to solutions of problems is growing. This gap is generated by various factors, in particular people in organizations are not improving their competencies for a more effective and efficient use of technologies, and creation of techniques or methods to solve more complex problems or support more effectively the decision-making process.

Learning about Technology Use

In many cases, technology access is possible and users' preparation is limited to take advantages of the technology. The best example is with the use of spreadsheets.

The original VisiCalc (created by Dan Bricklin and Bob Frankston at the end of 1970s) had most of the functionality that most people use on a day-to-day basis in the current work environment. However, currently there are applications that are thousand times more powerful than VisiCalc, but people's capacity to use new capabilities is very limited. The spreadsheet can be used to solve multiple problems, but the solutions have not been approached by the user because of limited skills to use the tool. This limited use of technological resources can be converted into risks, operational and strategic risks, for organizations because of non-appropriate use or because the technology is not used to leverage competitive advantages for organizations and create changes in costs structure or priorities definitions. Another good example of not using technologies in an appropriate way appears in universities as indicated by Agbatogun (2013) that the faculty members can access technological solutions to improve their classes, but the level of use of these technological solutions is reduced. The reasons for the low use are related to the academic status, academic qualification, gender, motivation, and discouragement affect the use of digital technologies.

These above examples indicate that the analytics process adoption is affected in the same way as other technologies by the user's preparedness for using technology, acceptance of the new methods to support business processes, and the ways to measure the value of technology. Dai et al. (2012) have explained how some technologies were evolving in digital television terrestrial broadcasting (DTTB) systems, including digital video broadcasting-terrestrial second generation (DVB-T2) to solve more problems of information increment supporting Internet and broadcasting. The DVB-T2 technology is an example of emerging technology that requires adoption based on the review of many other similar technologies to solve similar problems. In the analytics process, a complex step is the selection of the tools/models to use in the solution of some problems. There are many algorithms and statistical techniques to solve some specific problems. The analytics process adoption faces the issue of selection of techniques/methods and tools. In organizations the changes in technology use are evolving according to the data growth, data access, and the problem-solving process; however, the measure of technology adoption is highly based on the expected return of investment, the capacity of disruption, or opportunity.

Technology adoption requires the review of the adoption measurement parameters and methods that involve user experience indicators and improvement in the value added to multiple business processes. For example, Tanriverdi and Ruefli (2004) examined what has been the adoption of the technologies in organizations and the investment/return analysis. They said "In particular, we examine the notion that managerial interventions in the form of IT investments and activities can affect the risk/return profile of a firm. Such interventions would have the objective for a given level of return of reducing the chance of loss or the magnitude of loss-or both." This means that the value of technology can be in the risk control purpose of the organization because as they continue explaining "Risk, as chance and magnitude of loss, captures an aspect of performance that is not captured by return or by cost." No adoption of technology because of limited return can affect risk control or attention.

As a complement to what Tanriverdi and Ruefli (2004) expressed about the technology adoption metrics, Scheer (2013) pointed out that technologies are bringing new risk to organizations as well, which needs to be taken into consideration in any technology adoption process: "Emerging technologies are underway in a wide array of industrial applications and need fields. When innovating on technologies, one main objective is to improve the management of safety related to their emerging risks." In the terms of Bryenjolfsson and Hitt (1996), IT brings benefits in productivity and consumer surplus, but not in profitability or said in a different way technology might not produce a payoff (Kohli and Devaraj 2003). Organizations and technology adoption are affected by no motivation to use new technology or by possible wrong use, of the acquired/developed technology. The analytics process can be one of these technologies with limited use which do not meet the expectations. The analytics process creates a lot of expectations on one's capacity to solve problems. These expectations need to be managed among stakeholders and to ensure that people understand the limitations of the analytics process. This reflection on the measurement of technology adoption applied to the analytics process adoption opens the question about organizations' preparedness for the analytics process adoption.

Moreover, technology, in particular the analytics process, is not having the same effects in all organizations or in all areas of the business. For example, Zhu et al. (2004) have indicated that technology readiness is a factor that positively contributes to the e-business value and the size of the organization is negatively related to the e-business value. In addition, e-business is associated with the internal resources and that for launching an e-business the financial resources and government regulations "are more important in developing countries, while technological capabilities are much more important in developed countries." This point in the context of the analytics process can be associated with a better use in some areas of the organizations. In the e-business atmosphere some strong actors of the market are using what is available for web and text analytics in studying the content, use, structure, sentiment, traffic, access to data, and many more.

In analytics the computational tools are not the only objective. They are part of the means to develop analytics knowledge. Technological tools are a complement to human actions involved in managing business processes which need people's competencies in order to use technology properly. On the basis of this point, people can have access to technology but the correct use of technology will depend on how the organization prepares people to adopt the emerging technologies. Davenport and Prusak (1998) expressed that for knowledge in general, we need to understand the interaction of internal users', who are exchanging analytics knowledge and require the means for access, transfer, and apply that analytics knowledge. An organization, as a knowing system (Stehr 2002), maintains the dynamic of analytics knowledge exchange and it is part of the knowledge that flows into organizations through trained people, who use technology in order to create economic growth and competitive sustainable advantages.

Another aspect to learn from technology use is that one thing is to use the emerging analytics technology and another is to contribute to the development of technology itself. In analytics, it is common in order to use analytics techniques and tools and at the same time in order to contribute to the development of them. The number of algorithms to solve analytics problems grows very fast. However, new changes in the business environment and new options (models, algorithms, computational solutions, etc.) to solve a problem affect people's adoption of the new technology. Often people are overwhelmed with the number of emerging methods that they cannot assimilate. Universities and many organizations can contribute to new technology adoption, but universities cannot do everything. The fast paced technological evolution requires a fluid assimilation and understanding among organization's stakeholders. Professional associations, internal learning and development areas and, in general, all departments in organizations are required to keep people up to date for the proper use of technology. This means that people who are prepared to use analytics knowledge and maintain a learning process might generate change and better return of investment in improving organization's capabilities.

Adopting the Analytics Process

In this section, there are two subsections to understand the adoption of analytics. First, we present some principles that frame a technology adoption model for the analytics process and second, the review of the knowledge management processes and the basics of a knowledge management system to support an analytics adoption model.

The Principles to Adopt the Analytics Process

The previous sections explained that technology adoption requires to be connected to the organization development, innovation, and improving people's competencies. To maintain technology in permanent evolution an innovation business environment might be an enabler. In this way, the first proposed principle is that the analytics process adoption requires to count with a permanent innovation business environment inside the organization. Innovation is at any level within business processes, new products, new markets, or new ways to perform actions. In general, innovation is a two-way process within any organization: from senior management to technical areas and vice versa. Senior management should make a review of the problems considered important to study and to support not only the appropriate definition of the problem, but also the way to find a solution and its implementation through the organization's staff and technology involved in the search of these solutions. From the technical areas to management direction in innovation, there is a flow of proposals to improve business processes and to introduce new products, services, markets, etc., which will be part of the innovation process. Moreover, the stages of innovation should not only review the relationships of market–customer–company and industry but also the vision of the business, policies, responses to the market, and the development of those responses based on the employees' analytics knowledge.

Innovation is directly related to factors that motivate changes in an organization. These changes can be related to product or market development, which are strategic decisions associated with analytics work according to the PwC's Global Data and Analytics Survey (2016). The creation of new products is not the end of the innovation process, because it is essential to understand how new ideas are adopted, how they are introduced to the organization, and how they are aligned with new additional/complementary technologies as the analytics process will be.

The second principle affecting the analytics process adoption is related to dealing with operational risk. The most common definition of operational risk, first published by the Basel Committee, includes the loss, direct or indirect, that is a result of failure in internal processes, people's actions, and systems performance. Many of the risks in the operational risk categories can be related to the use of technology, techniques, and methods and the analytics process is part of the risk control strategies design. This is the case as the analytics process is used for detecting internal and external fraud, employee's malpractice, safety issues in the workplace, potential damage to physical assets, possible disruption of business and systems failures, and low quality of execution, delivery, and processes management.

The third principle is associated with strategic risk. The analytics process is involved in the identification of business objectives, analysis of the variation of the objectives and goals, strategy design, management control systems, and governance models, among others. The adoption of the analytics process starts with the definition of business objectives. Strategies to achieve the goals/objectives and governance models require the development of new capabilities: design of new tools, coordination, integration and aggregation of multiple information systems, and analytics techniques.

These capabilities' improvement are based on the analytics knowledge management process and its subprocesses: analytics knowledge creation, analytics knowledge storage, analytics knowledge access, analytics knowledge transfer, and analytics knowledge application. In the next section, these processes are introduced.

Developing an Analytics Knowledge Management Process

This section proposes the development of an analytics knowledge management process to deal with analytics knowledge and process. In this section, it is adopted the technocratic approach as Earl (2001) described in his article about the strategies for knowledge management practice. The reason is to focus on processes, analytics knowledge flow, and understanding. The practice in any possible analytics knowledge management strategy will include subprocesses that are described as follows.

Analytics Knowledge Creation

Analytics knowledge is divided into two categories: explicit and tacit. Explicit is codified analytics knowledge and can be presented by documents, code, and design of tools/means to perform analytics work. Tacit is the knowledge in the people's mind. The concept of creating analytics knowledge is observed in at least three ways: first is in the use of analytics to create knowledge; a second is to create analytics knowledge for the development of new technologies, and the third is the knowledge creation about the use/adoption of analytics in the organization. The SECI (socialization, externalization, combination, internalization) model (Nonaka and Takeuchi 1995) adapted to analytics knowledge represents analytics knowledge creation as a dynamic around development and use of analytics as follows: first, a *combination* process that is a conversion of explicit knowledge in analytics to explicit knowledge in analytics. This process represents the systematization of analytics knowledge that includes codification or documentation. The analytics knowledge could be transferred to people to grant access and use analytics during analytics process steps such as prototyping solutions and after solutions implementation.

The second process in knowledge creation is *internalization*, which means to pass from explicit analytics knowledge to its tacit analytics knowledge. This is the way to learn to work on the solution of the problem that deals with analytics through action. This is the learning process that is required to apply analytics knowledge in a further step of a problem or in different problems. The third process is *externalization* wherein the tacit analytics knowledge is converted into explicit analytics knowledge. This is presented through different means, methodologies, models, metaphors, and concepts related to analytics that people have access to. The process requires ways to transfer and to share analytics knowledge. And a fourth process is *socialization* where tacit analytics is converted into tacit analytics knowledge as well. This means the conversion of experience and practice with analytics in new experience and practice with analytics keeping the human interactions.

Alavi and Leidner (2001) state that organizational knowledge creation involves developing new content and replacing the content already in place. Analytics knowledge creation is related to the organization's social and collaboration capacity to grow analytics knowledge as Nonaka (1994) indicates. The *ba* or spaces for knowledge creation are different according to the SECI model (Nonaka and Takeuchi 1995); however, it is possible to say that the analytics knowledge creation is a permanent and dynamic flow as Alavi and Leidner (2001) explained: "The four knowledge creation modes are not pure, but highly interdependent and intertwined." Furthermore, analytics knowledge creation involves the new content creation, replacements of content, and the tacit component creation involves analytics knowledge movement at individual, group, and organizational levels. A good example of moving in the analytics knowledge creation process is the cloud computing capabilities for the analytics process. Once the cloud computing was introduced as storage, it was transformed into a service that includes capacity for processing data, a central repository of software, access to use of the software itself, and means to collaborate and develop projects that integrate many different resources.

People in organizations and organizations themselves started looking at cloud computing as a new resource and a way to manage some administrative issues in management information systems. The services were defined and developed and people started identifying and using those services identifying: Infrastructure as a Service (IAAS), Platform as a Service (PASS), and Software as a Service (SAAS) that are included in the cloud computing conceptualization.

Cloud computing can be associated with the study of mutual value creation (cocreation) between service systems or organizations. Cocreation and cloud computing are concepts to leverage the analytics knowledge. Cloud computing is a means of collaborative use of system tools, process capabilities, and knowledge in the organization. There are many different potential applications with inherent risks as well that will need to develop ways of using the SECI model in order to prepare organizations to deal with the new future of this technology.

Another example is when organizations realized that they have many information systems and one problem to solve that is related to performance evaluation of the organization. In these cases, there is a need not only to work with financial information but also business and competitive intelligence data from marketing, human resources, and operations. Organizations started adopting technology-related enterprise resource planning (ERP), customer relationship management (CRM), supply chain management (SCM), etc., in order to integrate processes and to develop more analytics capabilities to use shared data and technology of the organization.

Analytics Knowledge Storage and Retrieving

Analytics knowledge storage and retrieval refer to the need of managing–organizing the analytics experiences included in organizational memories; the reason is that analytics knowledge is created and at the same time forgotten, but new users of analytics need to learn from experiences in order to avoid a longer and sometimes tortuous learning curve. There are different forms of keeping organizational memories such as through databases, data lakes, information systems, documentation, document management systems, models workflows, Predictive Model Markup Language models (PMMLs), networks of experts, and so on. Moreover, there is a difference between individual and organizational memories applicable to analytics process adoption. At the individual level, the memories are personal experiences, emails, notes, and mainly individual observations where experts can be involved, while at the organizational level memories refer to the organizational activities that can be in documents, documentation formats, or sections in information systems for business processes, databases, data lakes, systems to support decisions, etc.

The systematic way to develop a process for maintaining the memories of the individuals and organizations provides the support for new users and at the same time the way to update the current means of analytics knowledge storage when changes are performed.

Analytics Knowledge Transfer

Analytics knowledge transfer is a process where communication capacity within and outside the organizations is crucial. There are barriers for good communication and for improving a communication flow (Argyris 1994). These barriers refer to dealing with defensive positions that reduce the capacity to learn and to discover the real problem, superficiality in the problem definition and solutions, and to have a kind of blind that reduces the awareness of what the attitude in front of the problem and what the potential solutions is.

This kind of barriers creates various limitations in a learning process, adoption of changes, fear, and at the end a half-truth related to the problem to solve, lack of capacity to dig deeper into the issues, and the potentiality to find solutions. Regarding these points, in the current environment organizations need more people motivated to think and formulate valuable inputs in the improvement process and in consequence better analytics knowledge transfer. Analytics introduction requires people inside the organizations who act as leaders of change and adoption through the generation of means for better understanding of the analytics process.

Rodriguez and Edwards (2012) have indicated that communication of analytics work, in particular in risk analytics, has to be improved in terms of flow and integration of policies in order to improve the understanding of board of directors and executives. Human communication is crucial in the analytics knowledge transfer and there is a need of searching for effective methods to communicate analytics work. In the case of communication of the analytics process among technical areas, executives, and the board of directors to improve the decision-making process Samoff and Stromquist (2001) pointed out: "Decision-makers have very short attention spans and they are unwilling or unlikely to read more than a few sentences on a topic. If so, for knowledge to be useful it must be presented succinctly." This is complemented by Uzzi and Lancaster (2001) who indicated, "learning, like knowledge transfer, is a function of the type of relationship that links actors."

In organizations, the risk analytics understanding by the board of directors and executive committee is positively correlated. But the board understanding is not associated with the effectiveness of means used to communicate the risk policy and results. This can be interpreted as a need to work more on the content of the messages and development of the communication actors' preparedness for understanding the analytics messages than the communication means themselves.

However, even though Dickinson (2001) introduced knowledge as a factor to reduce risk in organizations, there is not any clear identification of the means to improve knowledge transfer to control risk. In particular, to transfer that knowledge that is in documents or codified results, or to share the knowledge that is in the minds of the employees. The interest in understanding a means to develop communication is part of the purpose of what Eppler (2008) expressed saying that communication can be improved using tools such as "knowledge visualisation suites, dialogue techniques, knowledge elicitation methods."

Not only that good communication means are required, but also there is a need to develop teamwork and the influence of communication within it. Organizations need people working together under different leaders, areas, and teams as interconnected cells of the analytics process. It was expressed by Argyris (1994) that leaders and subordinates demand better communication in order to think of the organization as a whole and not just in their specific role. Furthermore, as mentioned by Peterson (2006), risk culture is related to developing the environment of working together inside the organization for solving enterprise risk issues.

This example of risk knowledge transfer leads to an analysis of what analytics knowledge transfer needs in organizations.

■ *Exploiting opportunities for transferring emerging analytics knowledge*: Two ways to analyze a situation of analytics knowledge transfer can be based on other technologies or human-related actions. Alavi and Leidner (2001) expressed that knowledge transfer has formal and informal, personal and impersonal methods; each one with different technological solutions. They pointed out: "... between individuals, from individuals to explicit sources, from individuals to groups, between groups, across groups and the group to the organization." On the one hand, technologies that act as means to transfer analytics knowledge can be the web-based technologies: intranets, cloud services, etc. On the other hand, human interaction plays a crucial part in analytics knowledge transfer. The transfer process can use presentations, storytelling, network connectivity, and short summaries of the specifications of new analytics techniques and mainly the correct use and potentiality problem resolution using analytic techniques. Analytics communication needs documents with content and structure based on questions to answer, problems to solve, and a message development associated with engagement and participation in the implementation and sustainability of the analytics process use.

  Opportunities for better analytics knowledge transfer can be considered in at least three areas: explanation of the new analytics knowledge applications to more problems, application to multiple disciplines, and the way to complement technologies and process improvement initiatives in organizations.

■ *Build strengths for transferring analytics knowledge*: To develop strengths in transferring analytics knowledge requires several actions and capabilities.

These capabilities are related to people and technology as well. For example, people's capacity to present the analytics process and problem resolutions in a simple way use models that are accurate and that people can understand in the way that they operate, support everything with visual methods when this can be possible, improve the capacity to talk in public, and to express the ideas in a presentation with order and effectiveness, introducing some level of passion in order to communicate the interest and the potential value offered with the ideas and concepts. It is extremely important to express the analytics ideas in the business language; this is to give context to the analytics process.

People can have the capacity to represent many ideas in a graphic form (analytics visualization) in order to summarize and to describe relationships and components of concepts and results related to a technology or a system. However, people's efforts need to be systematic and with the structure in information and knowledge systems that provide a means to sustain and spread these efforts.

■ *Manage the weaknesses for transferring analytics knowledge*: The weaknesses can emerge from the identification of the gaps to fill, limitations, development of stakeholders to adopt the analytics work, and organizational dynamic to deal with. There are examples of weaknesses in analytics knowledge transfer that affect the analytics process adoption. An interesting case is the adoption of CRM technologies based on social networks as it was in British Telecommunications plc in the UK implementation (Orlikowski and Thompson 2010). In this organization, CRM was supposed to support customer service but because of lack of training and limitations in preparedness of internal users the good technology support was negative to maintain the high reputation of BT in its customer service.

■ *Deal with threats for transferring analytics knowledge*: There are multiple types of threats related to credibility in the implementation of analytics processes such as trust, issues of security, management of concepts, terminology, misuse, and adaptation to the contexts of analytics models and concepts. Possibly, the most important threat is to consider that the analytics process can be introduced and the systems implemented and forgetting that a good implementation requires a process of aligning people, technology, means for performance evaluation, incentives, and controls to work using the analytics process.

The misuse of technology (analytics process), accuracy, and security in the new digital technologies implementations is converted into a headache in organizations. Many of the issues of stealing information and reduced capacity to control instruction can be a big time consumption. In Baltzan et al. (2012), there is a presentation including several measures that organizations have to take in order to maintain healthy systems, policies of using the web, management of data, testing of solutions/models, and the estimation of downtime costs in processing data.

Analytics Knowledge Application

Alavi and Leidner (2001) indicate that knowledge application is associated with competitive advantage development and for that there are three mechanisms to create capabilities: directives, organizational routines, and self-contained task teams. Analytics knowledge application might be summarized as the creation of actions in organizations, the support to develop sustainable competitive advantages, and the improvement of the innovation process. Fostering and acting in innovation processes and the creation of competitive advantages are part of the value of the analytics process. The competitive advantages are possible if the analytics process is generating differentiation in the core activities of the value chain of the organization. A purpose is that analytics be a means to reduce the fast copy of advantages in organizations by competitors. The second part of this book is dedicated to analytics knowledge application. There are applications in several sectors, different types of problems, and several models to use.

In the next section after reviewing the analytics knowledge management subprocesses, we use examples of new technologies introduction to illustrate how based on the clarity of the expected benefits organizations are adopting and promoting their technology solutions.

Reflections on the Analytics Process Adoption

This section is about the technology adoption drivers and it is illustrated using various types of examples in organizations. The reflections about the implementations of technology are the fundamentals for understanding aspects that the analytics process requires for its adoption. The focus of the presentation of these drivers of technology adoption is based on the benefit that these organizations achieved when they adopted new technologies. From these examples, it is possible to identify lessons to learn and use for the implementation of the analytics process in organizations.

Adoption of technology is not just to use Internet or specific technologies in very particular solutions; adoption is the way to embed technology in the business processes and in the development of distribution channels, products and services, people, and operations. For example, creation of content using digital technologies (Jin and Li 2012) is a subject that includes decisions related to new technology investments, strategic changes, operational changes, etc. This means adoption of new technologies is not straightforward; it is defined by impact (value added to the organization), and the management of stakeholders' expectations. This means in the decision of adopting new technology it is important to have a clear understanding of strategic and tactic decisions made and to make.

Some of the drivers for general technology adoption are, on the one hand, reduction of costs, efficiency improvement as Mukora et al. (2009) pointed out "Future sources of energy are less economically competitive than conventional technologies, but have potential to reduce costs through innovation and learning. Tools for modelling technological change are therefore important for assessing the potential of early-stage technologies." On the other hand, the drivers are related to the capacity to lead innovation and development of competitive sustainable advantages in the organization.

Thus, the adoption of technology touches several aspects of an organization which are growing in complexity. In the rest of the chapter, we are going to show six approaches that can help to manage the complexity in the adoption of new technologies and that are applicable to the analytics process adoption in organizations:

■ Understanding the problem: going to the customers
■ Learning from people's experience: minds and behaviors influence
■ Developing and transferring new analytics knowledge and capabilities for operations
■ Revisiting all stakeholders' needs: looking for niches
■ Building on measurement results and benefits
■ Developing governance to keep alive the innovation process, collaborating for better

Understanding the Problem: Going to the Customers

Define the problem, what is the organization trying to solve? This is the beginning of the technology adoption. This means the analytics knowledge management process starts with a problem identification and a definition of the problem scope and blocks to solve the problem. The problem definition is the crucial step to identify and to show if the new technology has meaning and potential value inside the organization. A good problem definition can be associated with the answers to the following:

■ What is the root cause of the problem to solve?
■ What is a good description of what is happening?
■ How big (size or magnitude) is the problem?
■ What are the metrics used to describe the problem?
■ How do I know there is a problem?
■ What are the indicators?
■ Where is the problem occurring?
■ What is the process name and what is the location/team where the problem is happening?
■ Who is involved in this process?
■ Who are the key stakeholders?
■ When did the problem become an issue?
■ Since when has the problem been felt (even if not initially noticed)?
■ How is this affecting the users?

- Clear roles and responsibilities
- Clear ownership and accountabilities for reference documents and contacts
- Authorization process for new document, contacts, and subsequent updates
- A review process of the actions, updates including review frequency
- A communication standard, for example, naming convention and document properties required under the new technology

Furthermore, the problem has to be clearly identified through a feedback process to enable continuous improvement and as Damodaran (2001) stated: "Documented reports of underperformance of ICT systems over several decades reveal that a major factor contributing to the disappointing outcome is the inadequate understanding of the user requirements and thus failure to design new technologies to meet those requirements. To address this problem it is important early in the innovation cycle to identify and predict human needs and wants."

A good problem definition is connected with the measure of the impact of technology adoption potentially using a balanced scorecard that connects the expected results and risk. Fitzgerald et al. (2013) have suggested that the evaluation of impact can be affected because of

- Definition of the inappropriate Key Performance Indicators
- Changing the culture
- Lack of management skills
- Limitations of IT systems
- Data integrity concerns
- Not enough data
- Too much data

These aspects do not include the lack of review of the variation of the results that is an observed need of the current systems of performance evaluation. Variation control is what could be the priority in an organization given the continuous changes and the existence of capacity to improve permanently the business processes through technology use. For example, investment in technology-based services can go in the direction of having better relationships with customers and maintain a more stable relationship with them. Starbucks started including Wi-Fi access in their locations without a clear value return but they reviewed the concept of the Wi-Fi service in order to connect Starbucks with the customers. The strategy produced very good results in the organization's performance (Fitzgerald et al. 2013). In the same way as Starbucks, organizations are in the process of finding ways to adopt new technologies. They are creating business cases, fostering digital transformation working more in a cross-wide manner among areas that adopt or have new practices with new technologies.

However, the Starbucks example is not the rule; there are examples of a no good technology adoption. In some cases the problem is not well defined and the adoption of technology is delayed because of

■ Lack of urgency and the vision in terms of where to go and reduced identification and share of the benefits of the new technology introduction. To this is added the need of picking a direction. These things can be a more complex barrier when internal politics is involved and not clear incentives are designed.

■ People's knowledge and current capabilities status quo. There are issues regarding the attitudes of older workers, legacy technology, and innovation fatigue.

■ The need of making a case for digital transformation that people understand and buy.

Fitzgerald et al. (2013) additionally indicate that the use of the Digital Technologies Maturity Index is a way to connect the vision and the adoption of new technologies in organizations. Not all organizations are in the same level of using technology, the same as digital technologies organizations in the analytics process are in transformation from gut and intuition-based decision-making process into a culture of using data evidence in problem-solving and decision-making processes (The Economist IU 2014). On the basis of this index it is possible to classify organizations based on a combination of factors affecting the investment in digital technology for supporting the organization's operation and the way the organizations are developing management and human capital within the organization. The analytics process is based on digital technologies and the analytics process contributes to the digital technologies development as well. The important aspect to consider is that a clear definition of a problem to solve will open the window to validate the value of the new technology.

Learning from People's Experience: Minds and Behaviors Influence

A review of the Nasbitt et al.'s (1999) work indicates that technology cannot exist without a context. The context is tied to people's experience in the business processes, and people's contact with technology in everywhere and in their daily life. The experience of the members of an organization is converted to develop human skills. Human preparedness for technology adoption is crucial. In particular, in the analytics process adoption humans and solutions based on computational capacity need to create a permanent symbiosis. No absolute automation will be possible and not all solutions can be reached to meet accuracy and simplicity goals.

Carroll and Broadhead (2001) presented examples in which the adoption of some digital technologies was not producing the results as expected. Technology by itself cannot modify some minds and behaviors in the employees. For instance, using emails cannot be inversely correlated to the use of papers. In many cases users, companies, and suppliers recognize the increment of paper after introducing emails. Additionally, in e-business there are myths regarding implementation costs, customer's behavior, and speed of development that in some projects were not meeting expectations. Human preparedness for technology adoption is crucial.

Likewise, Diaz (2010) provides an example in the education setting showing how many of the steps in the process of adoption of a new technology are related to the lessons learned reviews. Diaz mentioned "… in Online Learning many faculty members correctly assert that while today's students enter institutions having had some exposure to Web 2.0 tools such as Facebook, they lack an awareness of how those tools can be used for learning." Additionally, students can reach a good level of comfort using the learning technology and are open to deal with troubleshooting even though through trial and error to deal with a new tool. The other group of users, professors, in many cases takes a long learning curve to adopt new technologies in classes.

There are additional points to learn from the experience of the BT Group with the introduction of a social CRM (Orlikowski and Thompson 2010) as mentioned before. The search for the benefits is in many different aspects of the organization but possibly the main one is related to improvement of customer experience, new service, and products development with a highly friendly customer touch. The purpose of BT social CRM was to find a means for people expressing their concerns and claims and to answer the customer's queries creating ways to operationalize the answers—answers that required follow up and to move from different levels of resolution and possibly escalate to several areas in the organization. The experience put in evidence that for the organization to support a social CRM had challenges in

- Training and change mindsets and skills of employees. They were required to adapt to a high volume of contacts/inquires where it was difficult to postpone answers.
- Speed and visibility. Everyone can see what is happening, how the answers are provided, many things can arrive in minutes.
- Difficult to plan the process to provide an answer. Many things were arriving in different ways, various issues to solve, and the work flow cannot be organized.
- Capabilities development inside the organization. Find the way to grow the system and to plan additional levels of use and development.

Not all CRM implementations are as complex as it was at BT but it depends on the expectations, people's use of the technology, and the type of problems to solve. Even though the CRM implementation at Ross Video (CNRC 2016) was not as difficult as in BT, possibly the problem and scope was smaller and easier to assimilate in the organization. At Ross Video the CRM software was enabling salespeople to make better decisions more quickly, dramatically improving their ability to satisfy customers and close deals. The introduction of the new system helped in

- Reengineering each process within its sales chain.
- Reducing the duration of its weekly sales conferences by 50%.
- Improving regional sales managers' effectiveness by 10% thanks to live, accurate access to all data for all customers 24/7.
- Improving sales coordinators' effectiveness in processing and fulfilling orders by 50%.

Developing and Transferring New Analytics Knowledge and Capabilities for Operations

The analytics process is part of the improvement of efficiency and efficacy in operations. In particular, analytics knowledge transfer is a priority for adopting the analytics process in operations. Once analytics knowledge is created, people need to understand what the analytics process implementation can do and what cannot be done for the organization's areas and their business processes. As we mentioned before, there are several vehicles of transferring analytics knowledge: from the use of intranets, extranets, or in general portals to support conferencing, chats, storytelling, and coordination of social activities—social networking inside the organizations. These means of analytics knowledge transfer require strategies for transferring analytics knowledge and to convert it into actions/operations, two of them are given below.

First, finding meaning and common language among stakeholders: The basic strategies are supported by the data gathering process and the way that people/users start talking the same language related to the new technology. Some points to consider are the ones given below:

- Understanding the technical terms
- Clarifying knowledge requirements
- Identifying related problems to solve
- Identifying opportunities to improve
- Understanding the demography of the new technology adopters
- In the same way as in the analysis and design of information systems, a crucial part in the analytics process adoption is to gather correct data about the needs and requirements of the system

And as a second strategy to keep in mind we have the development of means to spread out the analytics knowledge and understanding problems and solutions. This can bet through

- Creating web pages in an intranet to connect the potential users, experts, and general stakeholders

- Gathering information from different teams and stakeholders
- Initiating an educational program about the concepts used
- Introducing people from different groups in a benchmarking process
- Developing a pilot on a tool already used (it can be new too): prototyping
- Positioning influence for using the new technology in several cases
- Providing examples or cases of solutions to some problems/issues similar to the new technology to be introduced
- Describing the technology currently used and potentially useful solutions

The analytics process adoption can be an experience in New World Technologies introducing ERP (CNRC 2016). The main aspect to understand in this example is that the introduction of ERP helped the organization to make better decisions based on a more efficient and effective access to information. The experience with ERP modified the way to do business, bringing the following benefits:

- Improvement in productivity.
- Improvement and reduction in data entry. Duplication was reduced.
- Better service to customers. Faster answer to customers with response time to next day of the inquiry.
- Production time was reduced. Not only leads were supported in a faster way but also production costs were reduced.
- Provide the opportunity to change the business model manufacturing parts in Canada instead of offshore.

The adoption of new technology requires a good fit to the operation and the use and understanding of the new knowledge. This is the case of Imprimerie Maxime Inc. (CNRC 2016) in search of better capabilities for printing. This is a clear adoption of technology because of the owners' understanding of the business requirements and a good fit of what in the technology market was available. The adoption of the technology was faster because of the specific solution created for the printing industry. This integral solution comprised the quotation process, production planning and control, and accounting in the printing industry. The benefits were directly related to the increment in sales, better margin, better productivity, and a faster answer to customers' inquiries. The new technological option gave the opportunity to plan new employees hiring in order to support positive business perspectives.

Moreover, to change the business operation adopting new technology implies the permeation of new knowledge into the organization. In the case of Telco, which is a telecommunication company, the study by Khanagha et al. (2013), regarding the adoption of cloud computing, shows that the adoption was faster because of presenting, providing examples, and discovering potential issues such as embedding the new technology into traditional areas of business and because of the potential effects of the business models. In the experimentation program, the company engaged people to this new technology project in order to create the positive environment of dealing with the new technology. This experimentation gave the opportunity of transferring technical knowledge and understanding issues to solve problems, such as having a common language for working. Once this experimentation program grew the decision to make was if they need to grow the program or to shrink it. The decision was to shrink it as a program and to start pushing the business units toward the adoption of the technology and finally to embed the new technology in the organization, disappearing the program as a program because the new technology should be part of the whole organization's life.

This case indicates the value of having a gradual process to introduce a new technology, as it is the analytics process, keeping the assets in the current operation as a complement of the new technology introduction and mobilizing the new knowledge across the organization.

Revisiting all Stakeholder's Needs: Looking for Niches

The concept of permanent feedback in the analytics process implementation is associated with the permanent review of user's needs. Revisiting stakeholder's needs, with the new technology in mind, helps to identify the pain points that would be reduced with the new technology use. Thus, to assess stakeholders' new technology knowledge, needs, and possible solutions is a practice that helps the implementation of new technologies as it is in the case of the analytics process. A practical way to revisit stakeholders' needs is using an experimentation process for discovering use and misuse of the new technology. This experimentation can be through the development of a test using updated prototypes to put close to the users the new technology and the potential solutions to their problems.

Delacruz (2009) commented about the permanent review of the technology adoption among stakeholders "Little did I realize then how time consuming and all-encompassing learning, studying, and adapting technology to teaching would become." This is in the setting where technology is used for teaching and for improving the learning–teaching processes, where the teachers are not prepared for technology adoption and the adoption takes time. This means revisiting the stakeholder's needs in a systematic way will help to

- Obtain a clear voice of the internal customer—this is a tool you can use to gather feedback on the pain points experienced by the new technology audience.
- Benchmark other groups in the organization—what have other teams done with respect to their responsibilities and the technologies in use, what applies to the task owners, and where the new technology can leverage work performance.

A permanent review of stakeholder's needs is a means to find applications to new technology and opportunities to integrate areas in organizations. The example of United Services Automobile Association (USAA) (Ross and Beath 2010) as a financial service organization that totally focus on market and on technology aspects illustrates the involvement of stakeholders and the permanent review of their needs. USAA services are in the field of financial services with a total operation based on the web, telephone, fax, ATMs, and mobile channels. The basic strategy in this organization was to act as a direct marketing company that is in the search of being an integrated enterprise. This purpose is highly demanding from innovation in processes and technology. These two areas of innovation and use of technology for business improvements required to create a well-planned structure to prioritize processes.

The structure to prioritize process was based on a project governance schema that was looking for projects where alignment and integration were the core of the new project's definition. This is alignment to the strategy and creation of value through integration. Stakeholders in this case grew from one area to involve all areas in the organization because of looking for having a holistic view of the projects implementation. The USAA identified four steps to develop any project which are applicable to the analytics process as technology: align, integrate, design, and build the solutions to the business. Additionally, the cost efficiency and time to deliver were the key points of control of the plan including a satisfied IT group. In innovation processes, people were involved, they were asked for ideas/answers to keep the project sponsors motivated. Furthermore, everyone was conscious of being part of a permanent learning process with a constant identification of barriers to overcome.

Building on Measurement Results and Benefits

The adoption of technologies could contribute to the goal of more intelligent organizations. The analytics process is part of the process of achieving smarter organization's outcomes. The identification of improvement is based on the measurement process of selected performance variables. The measurement process will create metrics to identify the variation that represent the achievement or not of the expected results. The metrics to choose should relate back to the problem statement, goals, and objectives and are the key factors determining the success of the new technology implementation. The metrics are also a way to know where the implementation and its sustainability may have fallen slightly off track. The "control" phase and the metrics that come along with it will allow making any adjustments to the framework to ensure it continues to answer the needs of the users.

As it is so important to measure the "right" things, project leaders should develop these metrics on partnership with subject matter experts and leadership. The measurement process is a path to connect the dots in the analytics process use for strategic and tactic purposes. Charam (2007) pointed out "In my observation, people who create organic growth that is profitable and sustainable connect the dots sooner and are on the offensive." In the U.S. Securities and Exchange Commission (Wixon and Ross 2012), new technology adoption led to work more efficiently and smarter with a better evidence-based decision-making process. The project focused on what is important to answer for the organization, using data and analytic tools, looking for actions to perform. A way that the organization proceed to be smarter is based on reviewing the experience with customers' claims and complaints, creating a web-based submission process, creation of a market intelligence office to triage what was coming from the web submission, reviewing and documenting the processes, learning and putting in practice solutions and answers. They created an examination process for organizations in terms of compliance as well.

All of these above points supported the development of shared data, creation of automated processes with central data repository and workflow clarification, creation of an organizational structure to develop and support collaboration, transparency and integration of the changes and new actions. For all of these steps, they value the expertise development and leverage the individual skills. The motto of U.S. Securities and Exchange Commission was working smarter and with focus. For achieving their goals in the project implementation they mixed digital technologies with activities on people and on the solution of the customer's issues, providing the use of technology and analytic tools and processes, fostering people to discover and use, based on their responsibilities, in many other problems and solutions.

Another example associated with measurement needs and the influence in technology adoption is Delta-Q (CNRC 2016). The firm implemented a Design for Failure Mode Effect Analysis (DFMEA), a method used by engineers to document and explore ways in which a product design might fail in real-world use. The final expected outcome of using this technology was to develop a product with a much lower failure rate than would be possible without DFMEA. It may be several years before a measurable change in the failure rate will be apparent. However, it is already evident that productivity has increased. It is a direct benefit to Delta-Q to have more people with a higher level of design knowledge, and may lead to more innovation, problem solving, and productivity growth.

Finally, it is important to mention that the measurement of the level of maturity for adopting technologies can help to expect different outcomes in implementation. In the analytics process, people will start working with not complex problems and basic tools to move to higher levels in sophistication that demand more data and resources. For example, Mougayar (1998) presented the concept of Cybermaturity, The author indicated that executive education and awareness topics around cyber solutions were the key in the development of the services based on the web. These points included things such as understanding of buyer/seller models, drivers, transactions, relationships to the strategic planning process, etc. This is an opportunity to measure the level of the learning process and the understanding that the business can have of using new technologies.

Developing Governance to Keep Alive the Innovation Process, Collaborating for Better

Technology adoption needs governance. Sponsors and users need to be motivated and oriented to keep the technology creating value in a permanent way.

In particular, the analytics process would provide more solutions to problems but the development of analytics capacity needs permanent improvement. The following points can contribute to better governance of technology adoption:

■ Accountability (clear ownership, clear process, clear roles, and responsibilities) and ownership of the steps in the analytics process
■ Consistent creation, update, and review of analytics process (formal documented process and timelines)
■ Fostering collaboration (built-in validation process, cross-team participation, broader engagement, alignment)
■ Sustaining integrity of the analytics process (acceptance and adherence to the governance process)
■ Developing a consultation group/experts identification
■ Revision schedule of actions, solutions, implementation, and feedback at different levels in the analytics process
■ Discussion times in meetings and review of planning steps for improving technology adoption

Governance for technology adoption is associated with continuity. Continuity requires a consistent governance process but that deals with the changes that are emerging. For example, the analytics process use data in different formats and the problems to solve will be not only about data but also how things are connected, how artificial intelligence provides support to organizations, and how humans will interact and manage the new technology. Negroponte (1995) pointed out "One way to look at the future of being digital is to ask if the quality of one medium can be transposed to another." This is one of the reflections related to the digital introduction of almost everything where a human is involved. The point is that not everything is possible to manage in the same way and under the same standard when new technologies are in place. Governance will help for the adaptation of process and people to maintain the adoption of new technology.

Governance is a step to maintain business processes alive and the innovation process will affect governance at the same time. The adoption of the analytics process is related to innovation development in organizations. Supervalu (Quaadgras et al. 2012) illustrates the adoption of technology and its relationship with governance and innovation. In Supervalu, the main purpose was the search of integrating processes and creating a culture of sharing that includes, at the same time, a creation process of shared tools. Employees learnt how to use the technological means in order to develop ideas and to find solutions to problems in multiple areas. Moreover, the company modified an organization's governance and provided more empowerment to the regional managers in order to achieve the vision of being very close to the neighbors where the stores were located. To get there Supervalu created a clear profile of the kind of regional directors they wanted to have and the willingness to use the shared tools and consolidate a sharing culture.

Now, management control systems at a micro level are represented by the implementation of technology and means to consolidate strategic and tactic steps in organizations. For example, Dutton et al. (2006) pointed out "The Internet exemplifies an emergent social technology that has co-evolved through the contributions of many individuals, groups and institutions ..." Furthermore, it is possible to say that organizations require governance in the analytics process adoption through

- Fostering understanding and conviction
- Formal mechanisms of participation mixed with informal ones
- Talent and skills development of solving new problems
- Role identification and adjustment to new environment

The effect of governance needs to be related to the achievement of goals pointing to real value added because of technology adoption. In their book, Weill and Broadbent (1998) give a clear presentation of the purpose of investing in new technologies which can be adhered to in the analytics process. This purpose is related to increase value addition in the organization with the premise that investment in technology is similar to investment in other assets. Thus, we need a governance process that will lead the organization to clarify the expected value from technology adoption through the improvement of operational infrastructure, risk management, and people capabilities. Another aspect of governance in technology is the governance of data as a priority for implementing the analytics process. As we mentioned, the volume of data grows and there are limitations and opportunities in organizational capabilities to obtain knowledge from data, use the knowledge to solve problems, and support complex decisions.

Finally, it is worth to remember what Tapscott and Caston (1993) presented as alignment requirements of technology adoption. The governance of the analytics process might lead to use the technology available in a better way. On the one hand, it is needed to review the scope and shape of the analytics process implementations with the purpose of having more users doing more with existing resources. On the other hand, it is required to foster more involvement between users and owners of the analytics new developments. Users not only need to grow in their capacity to use tools/models but also, and mainly, in the way that they can adopt and adapt the outcomes to the knowledge domain and context of the organization and business processes in particular.

In Section I, we have reviewed some factors that influence the analytics knowledge to be closer to the organizations and with a high potential of adoption. This section has focused on how the analytics process emerges. This renaissance of analytics is because there are changes in the business environment that are converging at the present time. We present in this section, the emerging analytics process that requires to follow similar steps as any technology to be adopted. In Chapter 1, we presented the development of analytics through understanding how the journey for the planning process was, the way of accessing data and understanding of analytic techniques, use of common concepts in management theories, and engagement of people in solving problems using data. In this chapter, we have introduced the analytics process as a technology and from this concept we reviewed the adoption of technology starting with a review of what the analytics knowledge management process should be. This review is followed by a description of steps in the adoption of new technologies based on digital development, as the analytics process is. There are several points to mention such as the need for embedding analytics process into a permanent innovation culture in organizations.

Section II brings the examples of applications of analytics knowledge in Latin America and in emerging economies. We have examples of analytics applications in health care, marketing, manufacture, finance, government, education information and communication technologies (ICT), and in the service industry. All these applications were developed in Chile, Colombia, Mexico, and Peru.

References

Agbatogun, A. O., 2013, Interactive digital technologies' use in Southwest Nigerian universities, *Education Technology Research and Development*, 61(2), 333–357.

Alavi, M. and Leidner, D., 2001, Review: Knowledge management and knowledge management systems: Conceptual foundations and research issues, *MIS Quarterly*, 25(1), 107–136.

Argyris, C., 1994, Good communication that blocks learning, in *Harvard Business Review on Organisational Learning*, Harvard Business Review Paperback Series, Harvard Business School Press 2001, Boston.

Baltzan, P., Detlor, B., and Welsh, C., 2012, *Business Driven Information Systems*, McGraw-Hill Ryerson, Toronto.

Bryenjolfsson E. and Hitt L., 1996, Paradox lost: Firm-level evidence of the returns to information systems spending. *Management Science*, 42(4), 541–558.

Cardwell, D., 1994, *The Fontana History of Technology*, Fontana Press, HarperCollins Publishers, London.

Carroll, J. and Broadhead, R., 2001, *Get a Digital Life*, Stoddart Publishing Co., Toronto.

Charam, R., 2007, *Know-How*, Crown Business, New York.

CNRC, 2016, NRC (National Research Council of Canada) search our success stories, http://www.nrc-cnrc.gc.ca/eng/irap/success/ss_search.html.

Dai, L., Wang, Z., and Yang, Z., 2012, Next-generation digital television terrestrial broadcasting systems: Key technologies and research trends, *IEEE Communications Magazine*, 50(6), 150–158.

Damodaran, L., 2001, Human factors in the digital world enhancing life style the challenge for emerging technologies, *International Journal of Human-Computer Studies*, 55(4), 377–403.

Davenport, T. and Prusak, L., 1998, *Working Knowledge*, Harvard Business School Press, Boston.

Delacruz, E., 2009, Old world teaching meets the new digital, *Cultural Creatives JADE*, 28(3), 261–268.

Diaz, V., 2010, New directions for community colleges, *Web 2.0 and Emerging Technologies*, 2010(150), 57–66.

Dickinson, G., 2001, Enterprise risk management: Its origins and conceptual foundation, *The Geneva Papers on Risk and Insurance*, 26(3), 360–366.

Dutton, W. H., Carusi, A., and Peltu, M., 2006, Fostering multidisciplinary engagement: Communication challenges for social research on emerging digital technologies, *Prometheus*, 24(2), 129–149.

Earl, M., 2001, Regarding the knowledge as a process and KM, *Journal of Management Information Systems*, 18(1), 215–233.

Eppler, M., 2008, Knowledge communication, in M. Jennex (Ed.), *Knowledge Management Concepts Methodologies and Applications*, Hershey, Pennsylvania, pp. 324, 335.

Fitzgerald, M., Kruschwitz, N., Bonnet, D., and Welch, M., 2013, *Digital Transformation Global Executive Study and Research Project*, MIT's Center for Digital Business (CDB) and Capgemini Consulting.

Jin, B. H. and Li, Y. M., 2012, Analysis of emerging technology adoption for the digital content market, *Information Technology Management*, 13(3), 149–165.

Khanagha, S., Henk Volberda, H., Sidhu, J., and Oshri, I., 2013, Management innovation and adoption of emerging technologies: The case of cloud computing, *European Management Review*, 10(1), 51–67.

Kohli, R. and Devaraj, S., 2003, Measuring information technology payoff: A meta-analysis of structural variables in firm-level empirical research, *Information Systems Research*, 14(2), 127–145.

Mougayar, W., 1998, *Opening Digital Markets*, McGraw-Hill, New York.

Mukora, A., Winskel, M., Jeffrey, H. F., and Mueller, M., 2009, Learning curves for emerging energy technologies, *Proceedings of the Institution of Civil Engineers, Energy*, 162(4), 151–159.

Nasbitt, J., Naisbitt, N., and Philips, D., 1999, *High Tech, High Touch*, Broadway Books, New York.

Negroponte, N., 1995, *Being Digital*, Alfred A. Knopf Inc., New York.

Nonaka, I., 1994, A dynamic theory of organizational knowledge creation, *Organization Science*, 5(1), 14–37.

Nonaka, I. and Takeuchi, H., 1995, *The Knowledge-Creating Company: How Japanese Companies Creates the Dynamics of Innovation*, Oxford University Press, New York.

Orlikowski, W. and Thompson, S., 2010, Leveraging the web for customer engagement: A case study of BT's Debatescape, CISR WP No. 380 and MIT Sloan WP No. 4935-11.

Peterson, J., 2006, Ready for ERM: If risk management is new religion, enterprise risk management is its mantra, *ABA Banking Journal*, 98(1), 19–23.

PwC's Global Data and Analytics Survey, 2016, accessed November 12, 2016, http://www.pwc.com/us/en/advisory-services/data-possibilities/big-decision-survey.html.

Quaadgras, A., Taveras, J., and Ross, J., 2012, Transforming supervalu by exploiting scale and becoming hyperlocal, MIT Sloan Center for Information Systems Research WP No. 387.

Rodriguez, E. (Ed.), 2017, *The Analytics Process: Strategic and Tactic Steps*, CRC Press, New York.

Rodriguez, E. and Edwards, J., 2012, Transferring knowledge of risk management to the board of directors and executives, *Journal of Risk Management in Financial Institutions*, 5(2), 162–168.

Ross, J. and Beath, C., 2010, USAA: Organizing for innovation and superior customer service, MIT Sloan Center for Information Systems Research WP No. 382.

Samoff, J. and Stromquist, N., 2001, Managing knowledge and storing wisdom? New forms of foreign aid?, *Development and Change*, 32(4), 631–656.

Scheer, D., 2013, Risk governance and emerging technologies: Learning from case study integration, *Journal of Risk Research*, 16(3), 355–368.

Stehr, N., 2002, *Knowledge & Economic Conduct: The Social Foundations of the Modern Economy*, University of Toronto Press, Toronto.

Tanriverdi, H. and Ruefli, T., 2004, The role of information technology in risk/return relations of firms, *Journal of the Association for Information Systems*, 5(11), 421–447.

Tapscott, D. and Caston, A., 1993, *Paradigm Shift*, McGraw-Hill, New York.

The Economist IU, 2014, *Gut & gigabytes*, Capitalising on the art & science in decision making is an Economist Intelligence Unit report, sponsored by PwC.

Uzzi, B. and Lancaster, R., 2001, Social capital and the cost of business loan contracts, in J. L. Blanton, A. Williams, and S. L. Rhine (Eds.), *Changing Financial Markets and Community Development*, Federal Reserve Bank of Richmond, Richmond, Virginia, pp. 237–261.

Weill, P. and Broadbent, M., 1998, *Leveraging the New Infrastructure*, Harvard Business School Press, Boston.

Wixon, B. and Ross, J., 2012, The US Securities and Exchange Commission: Working smarter to protect investors and ensure efficient markets, MIT Sloan Center for Information Systems Research WP No. 388.

Zhu, K., Kraemer, K. L., and Dedrick J., 2004, Information technology payoff in e-business environments: An international perspective on value creation of e-business in the financial services industry, *Journal of Management Information Systems*, 21(1), 17–54.

ANALYTICS KNOWLEDGE APPLICATIONS IN LATIN AMERICA AND EMERGING ECONOMIES

II

Chapter 3

Analytics Knowledge Application to Healthcare

Esteban Flores and Isabel Rodríguez

Contents

Summary..54
Introduction to Healthcare Data Analytics 54
   How Healthcare Analytics Could Improve Decision Making?.........................55
   Components of Healthcare Analytics..55
   Motivating Examples 56
      Fraud Prevention...56
      Workflow 57
      Support for Clinical Decisions 57
Introduction to Healthcare Data Management.......................................57
   Healthcare Data..57
   About Data Quality...58
   About Data Sources 60
      Electronic Health Records..60
      Biomedical Imaging 61
      Sensor Data...61
Data Description through Statistical Measures and Indicators 62
   Types of Data 62
   Analyzing Data...63
Application: Fraud Detection in the Mexican Healthcare System 66
   Fundamentals of Healthcare Fraud 66

Fraud Identification Using Healthcare Data...68
Solutions to Prevent Frauds Based on Different Statistics Techniques..............70
References 70

Summary

Currently health institutions generate large volumes of data inherent both to clinical and administrative activities. The Healthcare Data Analytics methodology provides tools for the collection, storage, analysis, and interpretation of data. It is a valuable tool that transforms data into useful knowledge for those responsible for decision making within these organizations. This chapter is divided into four parts: the first part describes the theme of Healthcare Data Analytics in general; how it has evolved; and the current needs that institutions and decision makers have in this area. In the second, an introduction to the management of healthcare data and the desirable characteristics required for these data before any analysis is given. The third part describes how to study data through statistical measures and indicators. Lastly, the methods for detecting and mitigating fraud in health systems are established, particularly in Mexico.

Introduction to Healthcare Data Analytics

Currently institutions involved in health care are concerned with improving the quality of the service they provide to patients and families. However, despite new operational and administrative approaches few health institutions in the world have achieved it. A tool with great potential for helping these institutions achieve the goal is to adequately use the health information systems, which provide evidence to reduce and prevent medical errors through the collection of information about each meeting with the patient in different medical situations.

Sometimes due to constant use these information collection systems can generate data overload. For example, in a radio frequency identification device for diabetes care data are captured quickly because they are sent to the server every minute, collecting information such as the location and blood sugar levels, blood pressure, age, weight of the patient, etc.

Therefore, institutions must have methodologies to benefit from the data available to them and thus improve clinical and administrative attention. Healthcare Analytics has the specific methodology to collect, explore, analyze, and interpret clinical phenomena of health data and to turn them into sustainable information in order to improve health institutions.

The challenge for these institutions is to take advantage of the advancement of medical devices technology as well as of information systems in order to create and sustain improvements in the quality, performance, security, and efficiency of health administration.

Healthcare Analytics technique can also be used to identify new opportunities and to suggest innovative ways to address old challenges. It even gives managers and administrators of healthcare institutions decision-making criteria to undertake optimal actions at the appropriate time and with the appropriate technology.

It has recently been demonstrated in different hospitals worldwide that the incorporation of these methodologies reduces mortality rates, healthcare costs, and medical complications.

How Healthcare Analytics Could Improve Decision Making?

Decision makers need information about the global functioning of the healthcare institution. Besides the information of accomplished facts, they need information on what may happen and the possible consequences of this in order to establish priorities for the improvement process of the organization.

Healthcare Analytics methodology provides health institutions tools and data management techniques capable of generating a comprehensive overview of the organization and to understand and perceive the quality and operational performance of the institution through the information obtained.

The objective of Healthcare Analytics is to help those responsible for clinical and administrative decisions to perform rational actions supported by transparent, verifiable, and robust reporting procedures.

Components of Healthcare Analytics

Healthcare Analytics exists to optimize the quality of the care provided to the patient and to reduce service management costs.

The basic components or layers of this analysis system are described in Figure 3.1. The layer of business contexts is the base of the Analytics system, it represents the

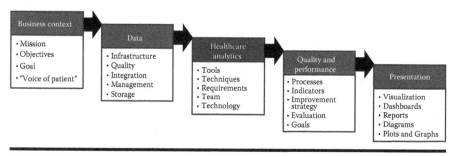

Figure 3.1   Components of healthcare analytics.

"voice of the patient" and provides value to the delivery of effective and safe medical care; however, we must not forget that each organization has its own mission, objectives, and goals (Stromes 2013).

The second layer refers to any action related to health data, where it is essential to have reliable and high-quality data in order to achieve an efficient analysis. The third element consists in the tools and methodologies used by the analysis teams to generate information and knowledge about the health phenomena that can support proper decision making in both clinical and administrative areas. At this stage the active participation of all stakeholders to improve service and medical attention is required. In the fourth component, the processes that need to be optimized in order to achieve the objectives laid out through indicators, and to evaluate the results of the project in order to achieve long-term improvements are identified. The last layer is called the "user interface" because it is the stage in which information is given to those responsible for making decisions and it can be composed of reports, charts, diagrams, maps, specialized graphics, tables, and summary tables. This component the most important one because the information communicated to those responsible must impact from its usefulness in clinical and administrative areas in order to meet the objectives laid out.

The analysis of clinical data requires the participation of everybody involved in the healthcare system: physicians, patients, administrators, and families so that they can define together the necessary measures to achieve the objectives and goals laid out by healthcare institutions.

Motivating Examples

The benefit to those responsible for health and administration areas through the different methodologies of Healthcare Analytics is that decision making is supported by information that yields robust evidence. Given below are some examples in which this benefit can be seen.

Fraud Prevention

Fraud covers a wide range of illicit practices, intentional deceptions, or illegal acts, which do not depend on threats, violence, or physical force. As fraud can be committed by any employee within the organization or by people external to it, it is important to have an effective fraud management program in order to protect the assets and reputation of the organization. Frauds in healthcare contribute to the costs of medical care increment and to improper billing of health insurance. Healthcare Analytics provides hope for a radical transformation of the payment systems of medical claims, thereby reducing erroneous or fraudulent claims for improper procedures. It is possible to prevent fraud because there are computer routines able to find patterns and to pinpoint irregularities and fraudulent activities. This case is illustrated in detail in the section "Application: Fraud Detection in the Mexican Healthcare System."

Workflow

In this process, the multidisciplinary teams must identify what must be improved and how to do it. It is necessary that these multidisciplinary teams have a global vision of the healthcare institution, because this way they will be able to discover the needs of the personnel in different departments to avoid shortages in the personnel assigned to treat patients during critical days and hours; or on the contrary a shortage of patients for the assigned medical personnel, which would generate higher administrative cost. It is important to consider that the patient must receive efficient attention in his or her moment of need and to avoid inefficient quality and performance during medical attention.

Support for Clinical Decisions

The Analytics methodology supports clinical decision making through suggestions and tests for one or several patients. For example, there are now databases with clinical information about patients who suffer chronic illnesses and who have taken specific drugs to alleviate certain ailments. In these databases, the doctor can consult how many people around the world has reacted to these drugs, useful information that will help him make the right decisions for the treatment he will give to his patient, avoiding thus medical mistakes due to the lack of clinical evidence.

Introduction to Healthcare Data Management

Healthcare Data

Health data management cannot be seen only as the process of feeding big databases in the information systems used by clinics and hospitals. Data are a very valuable dynamic asset for every institution since being rightly managed with the right analysis tools they yield sound evidence for decision making.

The activities related to data administration of Healthcare Analytics are

Activity 1. Data Modeling: Data modeling is a technique to formalize and document the processes produced during the design and development of an information system or software application; it takes on account methods and tools to capture the data and the needed technical requirements for the management and administration of the data. Through flux diagrams and data processes, data modeling allows to interpret complex systems as systems easy to understand for users.

Activity 2. Data Creating: Data are created, gotten, or generated through the activities inherent to healthcare institutions such as consultations, laboratory tests, medical devices, etc. Other sources of data are those gathered

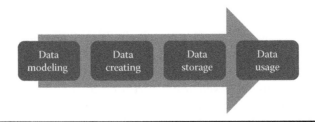

Figure 3.2   Activities associated with the management and administration of data.

by other healthcare institutions and by international organizations such as Food and Agriculture Organization the United Nations (FAO), United Nations Educational, Scientific and Cultural Organization (UNESCO), United Nations (UN), etc. Data is considered the raw material of Healthcare Analytics.

Activity 3. Data Storage: Data must be stored in a manageable database accessible to the users that must work with it. Data must be protected to avoid nonauthorized accesses and the privacy of the people whose information is stored must be respected.

Activity 4. Data Usage: Once data is created and stored the objective is to use it. Healthcare Analytics is one of the ways in which this data can be used to improve decision making in various areas of healthcare institutions.

In Figure 3.2, we can see that these activities must not work in isolation; they must complement each other in order to achieve an effective data management.

The information systems of clinics and hospitals generate immense data volumes, which represent an opportunity for institutions to improve service quality and to reduce operational costs; nevertheless to assure that the data are available and used for these ends is not a trivial task.

These data must meet the following criteria in order to be used in Analytics:

■ To be of high quality, in order to assure that the information generated through the analysis is valid and useful.
■ To be well documented, since the analyst must know about the context in which the data was collected when using it.
■ To be readily accessible and available.

About Data Quality

Data generated by the institutions must comply basically with being useful, since generating and storing unnecessary data generate costs for the organizations. Healthcare institutions must impose strict policies for the management and administration of usable data and never forget that as owner of the data the institution is

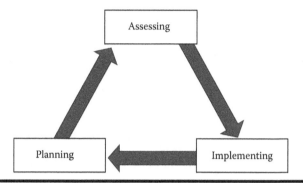

Figure 3.3   Data quality work cycle used by the CIHI.

responsible for the quality of the data, their privacy and safe storage, their availability at the moment they are required, and that they must be periodically updated.

When looking to improve the quality and performance of an institution, solid knowledge of past and current performance is required, as well as a great capacity to detect changes in data pointing to an improvement or a decline in performance. Bad quality data makes it more difficult to detect changes in performance and may lead to wrong interpretations that may yield erroneous conclusions. It is for this reason that every healthcare institution must establish its own requirements for data quality.

For example, in Canada data and its quality are the responsibility of the Canadian Institute for Health Information (CIHI). This institute is involved in rigorous activities to guarantee that the data gathered by the institutions is always of the highest level.

The data quality work cycle used by the CIHI includes three kinds of activities that are illustrated in Figure 3.3. These activities must be repeated as many times as it is necessary to reach the data quality objectives.

During the planning phase all the necessary tasks to prepare and prioritize the processes to exploit the data are included, as well as those for the design of the changes required. The implementation includes the development of the necessary processes and their utilization, which can be data input monitoring and reporting. Assessing is the activity and involves the quality evaluation processes and data exploitation in order to determine if it is necessary to modify procedures. This data quality cycle is iterative and continuous and yields quality products.

A wider definition of data quality according to the CIHI involves five dimensions, which are described below:

1. Accuracy: refers to how well information from the data reflects the reality of the phenomenon it was designed to measure.
2. Timeliness: a dimension that measures the gap between the end of the reference period to which the data pertains and the date on which the data becomes available to users.

3. Comparability: refers to the extent to which databases are consistent over time and with the agreed standard conventions.
4. Usability: reflects the ease with which data may be understood and accessed.
5. Relevance: reflects the degree to which a database meets the current and potential future needs of users.

The holding of good data by an institution does not guarantee that effective analyses of the data are made. This will depend on the tools and techniques of Healthcare Analytics at the disposal of the specialist in the institution to make effective analyses in order to improve processes in any area. Nevertheless, bad quality data will imply a lack of confidence and a shortage in the analyses made and in the results obtained (CIHI 2009).

Generally, the bad quality of the data results from the way in which the users introduce them to the clinical systems. Poorly designed user interfaces generate errors in the inputs. The bad quality of the data may also be due to an erroneous design of the storage structure or to data importation–exportation under different platforms. A common cause generating bad data quality takes place when the data is nonexistent and the user responsible for the input of the patient's data assigns no value to the missing data; that is to say, the user inputs false data about the patient which yields nonreliable information. There are statistical methodologies that can better deal with the missing information.

About Data Sources

Information systems in the healthcare area produce various and large data sources. Some of the most important ones are described below.

Electronic Health Records

Electronic health records (EHR) is an electronic version of the patient's clinical history and includes data related to his care such as demographic information, birth conditions, problems, medications, vital signs, laboratory results, radiology reports, progress notes, medical history, immunizations, and billing.

EHR automates access to information in real time and has the potential to streamline the workflow of medical personnel, in addition to providing an effective and efficient way for organizations to share clinical records between specialists.

EHR is also able to support other activities related directly or indirectly to patient attention through different interfaces, including support for evidence-based decisions, quality management, and results reporting. By using EHR the storage and retrieval of health-related data have become more efficient, since it helps to improve the quality and comfort of patient care; diagnoses are more accurate and coordination in health care is optimized (Figure 3.4).

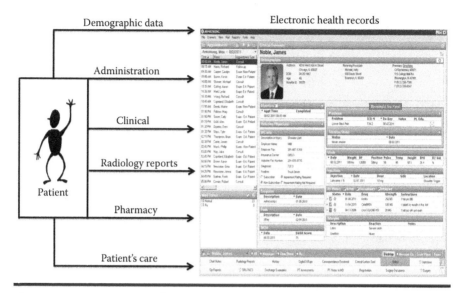

Figure 3.4   Components of EHR.

Biomedical Imaging

The analysis of biomedical imaging involves the measurement of signals from biological sources that originate in various physiological processes. Examples of such images include x-rays, computed tomography (CT) scans, ultrasound, magnetic resonance imaging (MRI), nuclear medicine such as positron emission tomography (PET) and more. The aim for analyzing these biomedical imaging is to generate quantitative information and from it make inferences about the medical condition of a patient. These analyses are meaningful since they are very important to understand the biological systems and to provide solutions to health problems. However, these analyses are not easily interpreted and require great skills to recognize patterns or similarities because the images consist of various complex and irregular shapes.

Sensor Data

Data generated by sensors are always present in the medical field; clinical studies such as electrocardiograms, for example, yield information collected by sensors placed in different parts of a human being's thorax.

One of the most important applications of the data generated by real-time sensors is that patient monitoring is more controlled and efficient in intensive care units or at hospitals in remote locations.

These devices generate large volumes of data, so the use of database processors and specialized hardware for storage is required. As the quantity of these data increases, it provides an alternative to healthcare improvement, but it is also risky to exceed data accumulation. Owing to this it is important to develop new analytical tools able to handle large amounts of data in order to make them meaningful and to interpret them under different clinical contexts.

Data Description through Statistical Measures and Indicators

Data in the health sector is more complex than in other industries due to its nature. It represents the essential component of Healthcare Data Analytics. Therefore, prior to any analysis it is helpful to thoroughly understand the data and the way it is related to the business in the context it is gathered.

The main objective of the analysis is to turn the data into useful information in order to understand the operations of the healthcare institution. The information should be available to physicians, administrators, and other users. Those responsible for carrying out the analysis must be in contact with the data-generating sources, since this is helpful to relate the data in real situations and conditions.

The analyst must take into account, before any analysis, the types of data and which variable they represent in the operating flow of the organization. He or she must also recognize the format and the way data is collected.

Types of Data

Health data has been recently classified into three types: classification, count, and continuous. The attributes associated with the classification data are recorded in one of the two options, for example admitted/not admitted, sick/healthy, stable/serious, etc. The count data is used to document the number of occurrences of events, such as the number of people infected in an epidemic or the number of injured people in an accident, the number of beds available in the emergency room, and other events related to administration and costs. Finally, continuous data are associated with the productivity of a team, information such as the time a patient waits for treatment in an emergency room, the number of studies made to arrive at a diagnosis, and some other performance measurements.

Once real-life data is gathered the data types must be identified as well as the way in which it was stored.

Data in information systems is classified as numeric, character, and binary. In the case of numerical data the system must take into account the number of digits before and after the decimal point and the number of characters allowed as "character" or "string." This classification ensures the right management and storage of data, because through it the arithmetic and logical operations that can be applied to different data types are determined.

Sometimes numeric data are entered as text, for example the weight of a patient can be entered as "192" which can be recognized as numeric data, or "192 pounds" that is recognized as character data since it includes a measurement unit, in this case pounds. Considering the former it is very important to correctly define data attributes, if in the example above the measurement unit is important for the analyst a numerical variable that measures the weight must be created as well as another that specifies the measurement unit for the patient's weight.

Nominal measurement level: These data correspond to names, categories, or labels, they lack an implicit numerical order and meaning and their categories are mutually exclusive. For example, the marital status of a patient, "yes" or "no" answers on a survey of service quality, gender, the number of the health insurance policy, and others.

Ordinal measurement level: Data have an ordered structure of their underlying factors, but it is not possible to determine the differences between the values and the data since these differences are meaningless. For example, the education level of the patients, the degrees of satisfaction in a survey about service quality, etc.

Interval measurement level: These data are similar to those of ordinal measurements; it is possible to determine the distance between one measurement and the other. These data lack an absolute zero point, for zero does not imply the lack of characteristics. For example, a temperature of 0°C does not mean an absence of temperature or the lack of a starting point.

Ratio measurement level: These data are similar to those of the interval measurement level, though they have the additional property of having a starting point or inherent zero (where zero indicates that none of the quantity is present). For values in this level, differences and proportions are meaningful. Examples: number of children, speed, distance, time.

In Analytics, the measurement level of the data determines which statistical procedures are correct for each kind of data.

Analyzing Data

Data analysis is the process that describes and understands data trends in order to generate information that may be used for decision making. Data analysis is the main objective of Healthcare Analytics.

Notwithstanding the way data are used the added value of Analytics is the compilation and analysis of large amounts of data in order to generate a meaningful summary that should help physicians, administrators, and analysts to make evidence-based decisions.

A population is a set of individuals (statistical units) that have the same nature and at least one meaningful feature. It is the reference universe; it is complete since it includes all the elements to be studied, whereas a sample is a subset of the individuals or elements of a population.

For example, a population may consist in all the diabetes patients that were treated during the last six months, and a sample would be a randomly chosen group of these patients to represent the whole population.

Healthcare Analytics can generate inferences or conclusions about a population from sample data. Therefore, it is an indispensable tool to describe, understand, interpret, and predict the behavior of a meaningful phenomenon in healthcare institutions.

Dashboards are present in almost every healthcare institution in order to manage clinics and hospitals since they offer techniques for effective global visualization. The methodological designs used for the creation of the dashboards yield elementary summaries ranging from basic counts to frequencies or to averages.

The most used data summaries in the healthcare area are given in Table 3.1.

Counting is the easiest operation to analyze data and in the healthcare sector serves to answer common questions such as "How many patients are in intensive

Table 3.1 Data Summaries

Summary	Description	Applies to
Count	The count of values of a variable in a data sample	Nominal, ordinal, interval, and ratio
Percentiles	Values of the variable that are ordered from lowest to highest divide the distribution into parts in such a way that each of them contains the same number of frequencies	Ordinal, interval, and ratio
Mean	The sum of the values observed in a variable in a data sample divided by the number of values	Interval and ratio
Median	The middle value of data when they are ordered after their increasing or decreasing magnitudes	Ordinal, interval, and ratio
Mode	Is the value of the data that appears most often	Nominal, ordinal, interval, and ratio
Minimum	The minimum value observed for a variable	Ordinal, interval, and ratio
Maximum	The maximum value observed for a variable	Ordinal, interval, and ratio
Standard deviation	A measure to quantify the amount of variation of the values around the mean, it is a kind of average variation of the values in respect to the mean dispersion of a set of data values	Interval and ratio
Variance	A measure of the variation equal to the square of the standard deviation	Interval and ratio

Table 3.2 Example of Frequency Distribution

Age	Number of Patients	Percentage (%)
0	10	3
1	34	11
2	67	23
3	88	30
4	62	21
5	36	12

care?" or "How many children have the same illness?" Data counting appears in most dashboard applications such as histograms and frequency distributions.

A frequency distribution is the grouping of data into categories mutually exclusive showing the number of observations in each category, for example the number of children between 0 and 5 years that were treated in the emergency room for traumas during the last year can be illustrated in a summarized way, see Table 3.2.

These distributions are very useful to determine the percentage of lost values and invalid inputs in a data sample; they are also very flexible, since they can be used at any level of data measurement.

A histogram is a graphic representation of the distribution of data grouped into classes. It is composed of a series or rectangles and it is a type of frequency table. Each value for the data is ordered and placed in an appropriate class interval. With a histogram it is possible to detect atypical data (Figure 3.5).

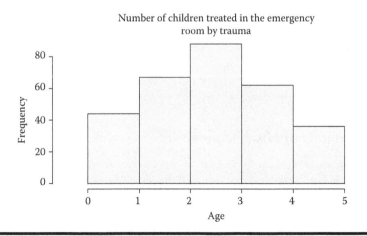

Figure 3.5 Example of a histogram.

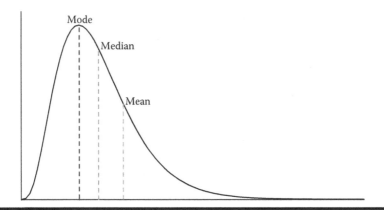

Figure 3.6   Measures of central tendency.

The measures of central tendency are the values located at the core of a data set; the most common measures of central tendency are the mean, the median, and the mode (Figure 3.6).

Application: Fraud Detection in the Mexican Healthcare System

Fraud covers a wide range of illicit practices and illegal acts perpetrated through intentional deception, which impact institutions in several areas, including even the psychological, financial, and operational areas. Fraud can be perpetrated by anyone inside or outside the organization; therefore, it is important that health institutions have an effective fraud management program to protect the assets and reputation of the organization.

Fraud in healthcare institutions has been a major problem faced by most countries, for example, in the United States the cost of fraud in 2015 was of tens of billions of dollars. The rise in healthcare costs is attributed to the risks of fraud in clinics and hospitals; therefore, acquiring an effective fraud detection program will diminish the costs in healthcare services.

Fundamentals of Healthcare Fraud

Health systems are different in every country; nevertheless, there are always three main players: beneficiaries, providers, and insurance agencies.

Beneficiaries are the people who receive some form of health care through medication, special equipment, and medical care. In the United States, more than 84% of the population is covered by some kind of health insurance, while in countries like Mexico it is reported that by the end of 2012 less than 36% of the working population had access to healthcare institutions.

Providers are the organizations that provide health care, such as hospitals, clinics, laboratories, and distributors of medical equipment; human resources such as nurses, doctors, technicians, and administrators who work or serve in an institution are also considered providers.

Insurance agencies are organizations that pay providers for the medical services that the beneficiaries receive. These agencies offer policies with specific coverages that meet the different medical needs of the beneficiaries. In Mexico, less than 5% of the population has a private health insurance, which means that only 6 million people from a population of more than 120 million have insurance coverage (AMIS 2012). In the United States nearly 28% of the population, 83 million people, are covered by government health insurance. In that country, the two largest health insurance agencies are Medicare and Medicaid (Reddy and Aggarwal 2015).

There is also a fourth player, regulatory organizations responsible to verify compliance with the established health institution's laws that exist in each country.

Among the three groups of players most healthcare fraud is committed by organized crime groups and by dishonest healthcare providers.

Under HIPAA (1996), "fraud is committed when an individual or a group of individuals acting together or an organization, knowingly and willfully executes or attempts to execute a scheme to defraud any healthcare benefit program or to obtain by means of false or fraudulent pretenses, representations, or promises any of the money or property owned by any healthcare benefit program."

The approaches used in other domains such as credit card fraud are not applicable for health care, since the users in the medical environment are the beneficiaries who are not guilty of wrongdoing. Therefore, a more sophisticated analysis using Analytics techniques for the health sector is required in order to identify the causes originating fraud.

In some countries, fraud and abuse in the healthcare sector can be attributed to the following: the payment model for the services supplied by the providers, since many insurance agencies pay the claim first and investigate afterwards, which is attractive for fraudsters. Owing to the lack of collaboration between the various insurance agencies for business reasons or competition, fraudsters move from one health system to another without being recognized. The payment model followed by various insurance agencies, in which the providers are paid for individual medical services supplied to the beneficiaries, encourages fraud since the providers can charge for more expensive and unnecessary services.

The most common types of fraud in the healthcare sector include

- Billing for services that were not provided to the beneficiary
- Diagnosis of patients with more severe disease than the actual ones in order to justify more expensive treatments by providers

- Unnecessary medical billing services for the sole purpose of generating insurance payments
- Turnover of each step of a procedure as if they were separate incidents
- Accepting bribes for patient referrals
- Illegal acquisition of prescription drugs for personal use or gain, also known as prescription fraud
- Allocation of financial resources to specialized medical equipment that is never bought by the health institution
- Resource allocation for service delivery contracts which are never carried out

In the following, a fraud case discovered in the state of Guanajuato in Mexico is exemplified.

Example: Officials of the Emergency System of the State of Guanajuato (SUEG) paid in advance almost 17 million pesos for radio communications equipment. These payments were made in April and June 2010; however, on reviewing the inventory of assets of SUEG, the auditors did not locate the equipment and confirmed that 100% of the amount of equipment and service contracts was paid. Furthermore, they found that in some cases used equipment that did not meet the adjudged technical specifications had been delivered. The auditors reported the incident as a fraud in which officials of the Public Health Institute of the State were involved. These officials were fired (Romo 2015).

Fraud Identification Using Healthcare Data

Different types of fraud may be identified through various analytical methods based on data. Federal governments as well as experts in Analytics are deeply interested in studies comprising large volumes of information in order to deal with problems in the healthcare sector, such as frauds.

Most fraud detection methods are based on the construction of user profiles considering deviations from historical data and monitoring user behavior after their profiles. In the healthcare sector such approaches are not applicable, because users in the medical environment are the beneficiaries, who are not guilty of fraud. Therefore, in the healthcare sector a more specialized analysis is required to identify fraud.

Fraud in health care involves premeditated elements and actions, identity theft, and organized crime. Large amounts of money disappear in minutes so it is very important to timely detect fraud through analytical detection methods and the use of data sources which include not solely claims.

For the detection of fraud in the healthcare sector, insurance agencies operate with the following data:

1. Information about the claim, including the amount and nature of the claim.

2. Patient recruitment and eligibility data, consisting of demographic information about patients and their eligibility for the various services.
3. Registration of providers gathering information about medical service suppliers such as hospitals, doctors, laboratories, etc.
4. Blacklists, which provide information on suppliers that, have been fraudulent.

The statistical methods used for the detection of fraud in health care can be divided into two types: supervised and unsupervised.

Among the supervised statistical methods most often used to detect fraud in health care are neural networks, decision trees, and Bayesian networks. Different options combining supervised methods in order to optimize the detection of fraud have been used recently.

Neural networks are systems that perform parallel processing of information inspired by the way the neural networks of the brain process information. These networks are used for the detection of fraud because they have the ability to handle complex data structures and relationships of nonlinear variables. This method has been used to detect fraudulent providers by discriminating characteristics. In Chile (Mesa et al. 2009), they were used to identify fraudulent medical claims submitted to a health insurance company. In Australia, neural networks have been used to classify the care practices of general practitioners and to detect inadequate actions leading to the discovery of frauds: doctors who regularly send their patients to a specific laboratory or doctors visiting a patient more than it is necessary, for example.

The advantage of neural networks is that they are a tool for solving complex problems, which lack a specific algorithm; they are very useful when handling large volumes of data and great uncertainty about the way in which these data are produced. Another advantage is that the neural computations may be performed in parallel and are easily inserted. However, the disadvantage of this statistical method is that it requires to define many parameters before being able to apply the methodology; besides, the processes are very long.

Decision trees have also been used for fraud detection in health care. A decision tree algorithm was used in Taiwan to identify fraud by service providers. This methodology is also used to train auditors in the planning of audit strategies to detect fraud. Through various classifiers a policy for audit planning was promoted, which includes minimizing false positives and thus minimizing waste costs, false negatives, and, maximizing detectability, having therefore the possibility to establish relationships between false positives and false negatives.

The technique of decision trees for detecting fraud in health insurance subscription was used in Australia, where there were about 40,000 subscribers. The decision tree was very complex and had thousands of rules, so the task of interpreting it turned out to be very complex. To solve this difficulty three procedures were posed. First a clustering algorithm whose aim was to divide the profiles of all insurance subscribers into groups was applied. Then a decision tree for each group was built, which turned into a set of rules. Finally, each rule was evaluated by establishing a mapping of the rule to a measurement of its importance using summary statistics such as averages and sizes of the claim.

The advantages of using decision trees for detecting fraud in health care is that they provide good interpretations of the results; they also have the ability to handle lost or missing values. One of their disadvantages is that their interpretability relays on the size of the data and that few adjustable parameters are available.

Among the unsupervised statistical methods for detecting fraud in health care is the heuristic method, which is supported by analysis indicators. This method combines financial information, provider data, medical logic elements, and operational logistics. The electronic method of fraud detection is a heuristic method capable of analyzing requests for reimbursement of medical expenses in an insurance agency in order to compare them with previous fraud statistics and with the behavior of providers who have at some point committed fraud. In the United States, the behavior of providers was classified with 27 indicators grouped into five categories: the financial aspects of the application, medical logic, frequency of treatment, logistics, and insurance provider identification for fraud detection. It was found that some indicators of insurance reimbursement allowed to predict fraud and to produce models that can avoid forecast errors (Mesa et al. 2009).

Solutions to Prevent Frauds Based on Different Statistics Techniques

A high-quality and profitable healthcare system needs effective means to detect fraud.

Sometimes Healthcare Analytics methods for detecting fraud are very rewarding as they provide enormous benefits to healthcare institutions.

In any healthcare institution, it is important to classify the fraudulent events committed by any of the three players of the system: beneficiaries, insurance agencies, and suppliers. Besides, the sources and characteristics of healthcare data must be identified in order to improve their processing: how they are collected, summarized, analyzed, and compared with different methods of Analytics in Health care.

Currently, there are research directives in this area to develop methods and scalable, accurate, and manageable algorithms capable of performing effective and fast fraud detection.

References

AMIS, 2012, *Reporte Asociación Mexicana de Instituciones de Seguros*, México D.F.

CIHI, 2009, *The CIHI Data Quality Framework Canadian*, Institute for Health Information, Ottawa, Ontario.

HIPAA, 1996, Health Insurance Portability and Accountability Act of 1996 (*HIPAA; Public.Law*. 104–191, 110 Stat. 1936).

Mesa, F. R., Raineri, A., Maturana, S., and Kaempffer, A. M., 2009, Fraudes a los sistemas de salud en Chile: un modelo para su detección. *Revista Panamericana de Salud Publica*, 25(1), 56–61.

Reddy, C. K. and Aggarwal, C. C., 2015, *Healthcare Data Analytics*, CRC Press, New York.

Romo, P., 2015, AM Descubren otro fraude en salud, accessed January 14, 2015, http://www.am.com.mx/leon/local/descubren-otro-fraude-en-salud-21272.html.

Stromes, T. L., 2013, *Healthcare Analytics for Quality and Performance Improvement*, John Wiley & Sons, Hoboken, New Jersey.

Chapter 4

Diffusion of Adoptions on Dynamic Social Networks: A Case Study of a Real-World Community of Consumers

Mauricio Herrera, Guillermo Armelini, and Erica Salvaj

Contents

Summary..74
Introduction..74
Datasets...76
    Network Data..76
    Adoption Data..77
Exploratory Data Analysis and *SVM* Classification 77
    Vertex-Based Centrality as an Explanatory Variable...........................78
    Degree Distribution Function...80
    Network Heterogeneities: The Effect of Being a Professional..............80
SIS with Rewiring 82

Conclusions and Discussion 84
   Some Practical Implications 84
   Limitation and Future Work 85
Appendix A: SIS Model with Rewiring 85
Appendix B: *SVM* Classification Prior to Modeling 86
References 88

Summary

The purpose of this study is twofold: first, we intend to understand how the social dynamics on evolving real-world (non-simulated) social networks affects the diffusion of adoptions of new products and services, and second we assess the predictive ability of individual traits and network effects in the diffusion of these adoptions. We take a novel approach closely related to data-driven methodologies based on mining a rich and detailed longitudinal dataset, consisting of records of phone calls between community members in a small town (approximately 4000 inhabitants) over a span of 10 years as a proxy for its social network, together with the follow-up on Internet service subscriptions among customers over the same time.

Our method can be used to estimate the potential effect of social contagion on the adoption of new products. If firms can access their customers' social network data (which is relatively easy, considering the availability of free public information stored in social networking sites), they can simulate the expected diffusion of their new products through social contagion and test, for example, if the first adopters are hubs or regular consumers, if firms should substantially increase their marketing effort at the beginning of the release campaign and target hubs directly, and so on.

Introduction

Marketers can track as to when customers buy products or subscribe services, but it is more difficult to assess the social influence on customers before their decisions, or when and how they pass recommendations on to other customers favoring the diffusion of a product. Solving these issues has meaningful managerial implications. Indeed, traditional marketing instruments have become less effective, prompting marketers and managers to develop approaches that can help entrepreneurs and corporations leverage innovative marketing strategies and replace traditional tools with word of mouth (WOM) tactics for reaching consumers. In this context, the increasing availability of detailed and massive network data has triggered interest in exploiting customers' social networks in order to improve response rates for these WOM marketing campaigns.

Some previous seminal studies have addressed social contagion using *network theory* to manage relational data on diffusion of innovation research. Networks have enabled addressing issues such as heterogeneities in human relations (Burt 1987, Iyengar et al. 2011), the role of opinion leaders (Iyengar et al. 2011) and regular consumers (Watts and Dodds 2007) in the diffusion of innovations, in finding out how to encourage the right people to get the word out (Hinz 2011), and whether there is a complementary effect between social influence and traditional marketing (e.g., advertising) (Iyengar et al. 2011, Risselada et al. 2014).

However most of these studies, on one hand, are limited to small-scale datasets and/or simulated data, besides the use of only macro-level observations, partly because of the lack of high-quality longitudinal data on highly dynamic social networks, and on the other hand assume that social interactions do not change over time. As a result, using social contagion as a tool for diffusion of innovations may not be properly validated, mostly due to the lack of consideration for the inherently dynamic character of social relations. To the best of our knowledge, these issues remain open, despite its important implications for marketing and diffusion of innovation theory.

In this study, we combine a well-structured methodology different tools rooted in physics, epidemiology, and machine learning theories, in order to correctly describe the diffusion of innovations on evolving real-world social networks.

The purpose of this study is twofold: first we intend to understand how social dynamics on evolving real-world (non-simulated) social networks affects the diffusion of adoptions of new products and services, and second we assess the predictive ability of individual traits and network effects in the diffusion of these adoptions.

We take a novel approach closely related to data-driven methodologies based on mining rich and detailed longitudinal dataset, consisting of records of phone calls between community members in a small town (approximately 4000 inhabitants) over a span of 10 years as a proxy for its social network, together with the follow-up on Internet service subscriptions among customers over the same time. The diffusion of Internet service subscriptions among customers is studied using data (right censored) of the time of adoption (subscription to the service).

Owing to the large window of observation for this study, the contact pattern among individuals does not have a static architecture, but rather coevolves together with the diffusion process. Thus, we study social contagion by accounting for social dynamics over time, as well as for the multiple state changes from adoption to disuse that occur over the years. These considerations are critical, because actors in a social network exhibit different likelihoods of being influenced during the diffusion process, and this probability changes over time.

Additionally to network and adoption data, we register attributes that characterize individual traits related to professions, to be or not to be owner of a farm field, and to be an expert on technology according to self-declaration.

We apply two different approaches or models to extract knowledge from our dataset. The first one is a recently published *Susceptible Infected Susceptible* (SIS) model that considers both adoption and network dynamics (see Herrera et al. 2015, for a detailed derivation of this model). In this model, link rewiring simulates the role of individually driven network dynamics in social contagion. Link or connection rewiring is independent of the diffusion process on the network and is described with two closely related parameters—attachment and detachment rates—that are estimated directly from network data.

The second approach is a classification method using *Support Vector Machine* (*SVM*). The aim of this classification is to infer what determines the adoption and what are the conditions negatively/positively correlated with adoption.

We explore the datasets to develop appropriate knowledge and understanding of the data and to deal with the main research questions and hypothesis. Some examples of questions we address with this exploratory analysis: (i) Do owners of farm fields adopt first than traders, professionals, or other people in general? (ii) Is it advantageous for adoption to have experts on technology, hubs, or early adopters as neighbors? (iii) Does closeness centrality, betweenness centrality, or other network centrality measures play any role for an early adoption? (iv) Does exposure of a susceptible individual not yet adopter to neighbors who have previously adopted has any impact on a decision to adopt, and if so, is it different for different professions, field ownership status, or other individual attributes?

Question (i) has to do with *selection*, which indicates that people tend to create relationships with other people who are similar to them adopting similar behavior as a group. Questions (ii) and (iii) are more related with social *influence*. It refers to the behavioral change of individuals affected by others in a network. The social influence effect leads people to adopt behaviors exhibited by their neighbors. The strength of social influence depends on many factors such as the strength of relationships between people in the network, network distance between individuals, temporal effects, characteristics of networks, and individuals in the network. Question (iv) mixes both kinds of phenomena.

Our results indicate that (1) both social contagion and contextual factors matter for the diffusion of innovations. The effect of either single factor alone cannot drive diffusion by itself, (2) considering a static social network in order to study diffusion of innovations might overestimate the effect of social contagion. Indeed, our results confirm that social contagion works, but we also find that constant turnover of neighbor vertices in the network could effectively reduce the rate of contagion, (3) our data-driven model shows a way to simplify network data, by studying the dynamics of the vertex connectivity classes instead of following the dynamics of individual vertices. This approach reduces computation complexity for estimates of social contagion through social networks, which is relevant considering the size of the networks for most customers, and (4) the diffusion of innovation quickly advances into the group of professionals (usually, highly connected vertices in the network), but the rapid detachment from hubs and non-preferential attachment to other vertices reduces the "closeness" of this group putting obstacles to ulterior diffusion into the whole network.

Datasets

Network Data

The dataset consists of records of telephone calls between community members in a small town. We have data on monthly registered telephone calls among customers (corresponding to 1147 households) of a particular phone service between 1998 and 2007. To build the community social network, we used the phone numbers as labels for network vertices and calls as proxies for contacts or edges between these vertices. Phone networks previously have been used to depict the communication and social network contact among members of a community (e.g., Haythornthwaite 2005, Onnela et al. 2007).

The raw data are lists of the total phone calls between vertices in a given month for a span of 10 years. These lists are directed (i.e., i calls j differs from j calls i) and aggregated monthly (monthly sum of all calls from i to j). The graphs and the corresponding adjacency matrices created from these lists are weighted and directed. Next, we discard all links that are not bidirectional from the original graph and treat the remainder as undirected edges. Yet not all directed links correspond to a real social tie: For example, i might consider j her friend, but j may not have that same consideration of i. Before performing any analysis, we must therefore make the graphs undirected. If the relationship between two vertices is not mutual in a given month, the edge is removed from the graph. Thus, two vertices are connected with an undirected edge if there was at least one pair of reciprocated phone calls between them (i.e., i calls j and j calls i).

Adoption Data

We studied the diffusion of Internet service subscription using (right censored) data on the time of adoption of this service from 1998 to 2007. The raw adoption data for Internet service subscription is given as matrix Y with dimension $N \times T$, where $N = 1147$ is the number of vertices and $T = 118$ is the number of months in the observation period. If a vertex has Internet service in a given month, the corresponding matrix entry is equal to 1; a 0 would denote no Internet service.

Exploratory Data Analysis and *SVM* Classification

One of the goals of our investigation is to assess the predictive ability of individual traits and network effects. To this end, we choose explanatory variables or covariates that encode these traits and effects. Individual traits are related to the profession (professionals, agriculture professionals, traders, others), ownership of a farm field (owner of field or farmer), and to be an expert on technology according to self-declaration (expert). These attributes are relatively few and fixed over time. On the other hand, there is a wide variety of metrics and indicators characterizing the network effects that may be relevant in describing the process of adoption. One question immediately arises—which of these metrics we should use and how to estimate their relevance? While there are many network metrics, some of them are strongly correlated and interdependent. To choose a set of representative and relevant metrics for modeling the adoption, reducing biases of that choice we will use a classification based on *SVM*.

Among the existing machine learning methods, *SVM* has demonstrated superior performance in several domains. Its appealing characteristics, such as the absence of local minima and an adequate generalization of new samples, thanks to the structural risk minimization principle (Vapnik 1998), made *SVM* one of the preferred classification approaches among the researchers and practitioners.

The aim is to determine a set of explanatory variables (or characteristics in the language of machine learning), which allow providing a satisfactory data classification (based on quantitative criteria) into two classes—*A*dopters and *S*usceptible individuals (see Appendix B for the results of applying *SVM*).

Feature selection is a very important topic. Finding the adequate subset of relevant variables for a given machine learning task reduces the risk of overfitting, improving the model's predictive performance; and provides important insight into the process that generates the data, enhancing the interpretability of the model (Guyon et al. 2006).

This feature selection allows for less biased judgment about merit or relevance of a particular set of variables for describing the adoption process. We found that variables that contribute more to the classification with *SVM* were the previously mentioned attributes characterizing individual traits—*professional, agriculture professional, trader, owner of field, expert,* and *early adopter*—network centrality metrics—*closeness, betweenness, degree, hubs,* and *structural holes*—and some metrics quantifying influences or exposition to other adopter neighbors—Exposition to *adopter neighbors, expert neighbors, hub neighbors, early adopter neighbors.*

The variables related to individual attributes are binary variables, which take the value 1 if the individual has the corresponding attributes and 0 otherwise. While the variables characterizing network exposition of a vertex are calculated using the mean value of the number of neighbors with the corresponding attribute in the neighborhood of the vertex, right before the adoption takes place. Explanatory variables with a good performance in classification tasks are presented in Table 4.1. These variables can capture the subtleties of the diffusion process of innovation in this community and can be used for ulterior modeling.

Vertex-Based Centrality as an Explanatory Variable

Centrality has attracted a lot of attention as a tool for studying social networks (Freeman 1979, Borgatti and Everett 2006). Vertex-based centrality is defined in order to measure the importance of a vertex in the network. A vertex with high centrality score is usually considered more highly influential than other vertices in the network. The simplest and most popular centrality measure is that of *degree centrality*. Vertex degree is defined as the number of edges that enter or exit from it. From the exploratory data analysis we can see that vertex degree play an important role in diffusion. In fact, as is shown in Figure 4.1a the mean degree centrality in the adopter class is greater than the mean degree centrality for individuals in the susceptible class.

Table 4.1 Characteristics in *SVM* Model after Feature Selection

X	Variable Name (Type)
x_1	Professional (binary)
x_2	Agriculture professional (binary)
x_3	Trader (binary)
x_4	Owner of field (binary)
x_5	Expert (binary)
x_6	Early adopter (binary)
x_7	Mean closeness (continuous)
x_8	Mean betweenness (continuous)
x_9	Mean degree (continuous)
x_{10}	Hubs (binary)
x_{11}	Mean structural holes or Burt constraint (continuous)
x_{12}	Exposition to adopter neighbors (continuous)
x_{13}	Exposition to expert neighbors (continuous)
x_{14}	Exposition to hub neighbors (continuous)
x_{15}	Exposition to early adopter neighbors (continuous)

Closeness centrality measures the centrality by computing the average of the shortest distances to all other vertices $d_i = e_i^T S\mathbf{1}$. Here, e_i is a column vector the ith element of which is 1, and all other elements are 0. S is the matrix whose element (i, j) contains the length of the shortest path from vertex i to j, and 1 is the all one vector. If N is the number of network vertices, then the normalized closeness centrality is defined by $x_i^{(C)} = d_i/(N-1)$.

From Figure 4.1b, we can see that the mean closeness centrality in the susceptible class is greater than for individuals in the class of adopters.

Betweenness centrality measures how much a given vertex lies in the shortest paths of other vertices. The betweenness centrality $x_i^{(B)}$ of vertex i is defined as follows: $x_i^{(B)} = \Sigma_{j,k}\, d_{jik}/d_{jk}$. Here d_{jk} is the number of shortest paths from vertex j to k, and d_{jik} is the number of shortest paths from vertex j to k that pass through vertex i. Vertices of high betweenness occupy critical positions in the network structure, and are therefore able to play critical roles. This is often enabled by a large amount of flow, which is carried by vertices, which occupy a position at the interface of tightly knit groups. Such vertices are considered to have high betweenness. The concept of betweenness is related to vertices that span structural holes.

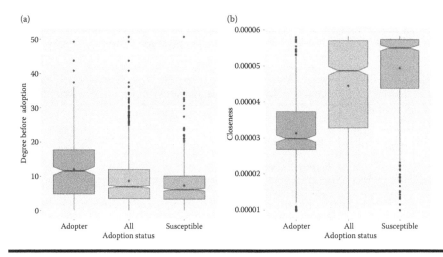

Figure 4.1 **(a) Box plot of mean degree before adoption. (b) Box plot of closeness centrality before adoption. Adopters show greater mean degree than susceptible individuals. On the contrary, susceptible vertices show greater closeness centrality than the adopters.**

Structural holes—in a network, we call a vertex a structural hole if it is connected to multiple local bridges. By removing such an individual, an "empty space" will occur in the network. This is referred to as a structural hole, a vertex that can interconnect information originating from multiple noninteracting parties (Burt 1992).

Degree Distribution Function

Degree distribution function $P_k(t)$ is computed using fraction of vertices in the network with degree k at time t. Figure 4.2 depicts the degree distribution functions, calculated over several months. Despite large observation window for registering data (118 months), the degree distribution function, on average, retains the same shape over time. Empirical evidence indicates that the monthly degree distribution function fluctuates around an average degree distribution function. This is a characteristic feature of a stable community. Thus, for the purpose of simplifying data modeling, the degree distribution function $P_k(t)$ of a particular month t is replaced by the average degree distribution function P_k, taken over all the months in the observation window. In addition, the mean degree $\langle k \rangle$, defined as $\langle k \rangle = \sum_k k P_k$, remains almost constant over time (a line of best fit has a slope of 0.01).

Network Heterogeneities: The Effect of Being a Professional

Professionals and agriculture professionals adopt the technology at a higher rate. Individuals who do not have a definite profession (indicated in Figure 4.3a, as "others") are less likely to adopt new technologies. The curves in the figure represent

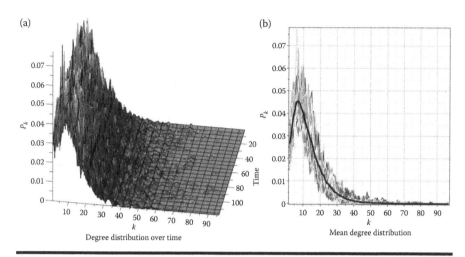

Figure 4.2 (a) Degree probability function of the social network over time. (b) The average probability distribution function (PDF) is in black. This PDF came from fitting by $P_k = k^a \cdot \exp(-b \cdot k)$ the coefficients (95% confidence bounds) are as follows: $a = 0.8199(0.7873, 0.8525)$, $b = 0.1548(0.1506, 0.1589)$; goodness of fit (SSE [sum of squares error]) $= 0.777 \times 10^{-4}$; R-square $= 0.9975$, adjusted R-square $= 0.9975$, RMSE (root mean square error) $= 0.9141 \times 10^{-3}$.

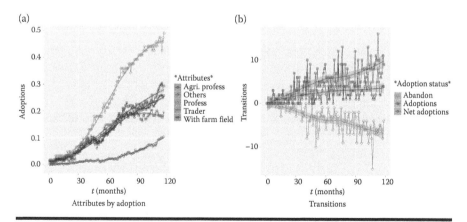

Figure 4.3 (a) Adoption by fixed individual attributes. (b) Transitions per month. The top line (with "□" marker) indicates the number of people who transitioned from susceptible state to adopter ($0 \rightarrow 1$), bottom line (with marker "◇") shows the number who transitioned from adopter to susceptible state ($1 \rightarrow 0$), and the line in the middle (with "○" marker) is the net change in the total number of adoptions for the given month.

proportions and not absolute numbers. For instance, there are 64 professionals, of which approximately 50% become adopters at the end of this study. In the case of agriculture professionals their number is 147 and adopts approximately 32% of them. Field owners are 310 and 25% end up adopting and so forth. It is not surprising that all recognize that proportionally, professionals adopt more (Figure 4.3a).

SIS with Rewiring

In this model, we consider the vertex degree as the main network attribute to be used for explaining observed adoption data. Such a degree-based approximation was first proposed by Pastor-Satorras (Pastor-Satorras and Vespignani 2001a,b, 2002, Pastor-Satorras et al. 2001), under the basic assumption that all vertices in a given degree class (vertices with the same degree) can be considered to be statistically equivalent. That is, all vertices of the same degree have the same probability of contagion at any given time. This approach takes its simplest form when applied to a network with a given degree distribution function, as in our case. The main idea is studying the dynamics of the vertex connectivity classes instead of following the dynamics of individual vertices.

In the SIS model with rewiring (see Herrera et al. 2015 to find details), those individuals who have adopted the innovation are considered *infected*. Fraction or density of the population in an infected state at time t is represented by $x(t)$. Individuals at risk of adopting are in the *susceptible* state $s(t)$.

We consider that the adoptions might occur for two reasons: (1) nonsocial factors such as firm advertising, diffusion of the product in other countries, pricing, and so forth and (2) contact with an infected infectious vertex through the links of a social network.

Individuals can subscribe to the Internet service (adopt), but can also leave the subscription to resume later. This process can be repeated several times as shown in Figure 4.3b. This is why we use an SIS model that includes the possibility that the individual does not remain "recovered" after infection.

We denote by $s_k(t)$ and $x_k(t)$ the densities of susceptible and infected vertices with exact degree k, respectively. These variables are related by

$$s(t) = \sum_k P_k s_k(t)$$

$$x(t) = \sum_k P_k x_k(t)$$

Furthermore, these variables obey the normalization condition

$$s_k(t) + x_k(t) = 1$$

So, we only consider the equation for $x_k(t)$ (see Appendix A).

The model also takes into account changes in the densities $x_k(t)$ due to the rewiring dynamics. Network rewiring is modeled with the detachment rate d_k, which can be directly estimated from the network data, specifically from the degree distribution function P_k. Fitting a parametric model for detachment rate using the network data we have (Herrera et al. 2015)

$$d_k = (1 - 1/k)^a \exp(b \cdot k)/N$$

where the coefficients (95% confidence bounds) are as follows: $a = 0.8199(0.7873, 0.8525)$, $b = 0.1548(0.1506, 0.1589)$. We obtain an important consequence from this formula; the detachment rate d_k increases with the degree k.

The result of applying the SIS model is shown in Figure 4.4. The SIS model with rewiring indicates that the diffusion of innovations is not necessarily enhanced by the social dynamics. This may seem counterintuitive, but there is a plausible explanation for this fact. Indeed, we have modeled social dynamics using network rewiring. Link's rewiring is described by the detachment rate d_k. From data analysis, we found more intensive detachment rates from vertices with higher degree or hubs. On the other hand, hubs are more likely to adopt. Once the contagion of hubs is complete, the contagion spread has more difficulty to reach regular vertices, due to the constant detachment of ties between hubs and vertices with fewer links. This is a feature of this network. Not all networks should have the same behavior and may occur

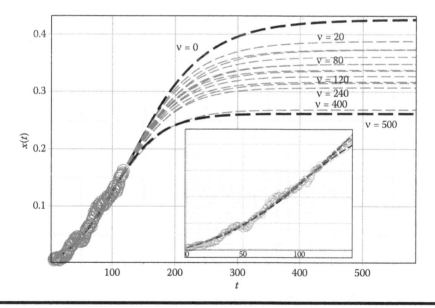

Figure 4.4 **SIS model long-term prediction for the adoption with different rewiring rates v. The fitting of available adoption data is replotted on a finer scale and is given in the inset. Note that increasing the rewiring reduces the prevalence of adoption.**

in other networks that social dynamics contribute positively in promoting diffusion. As a practical implication, we should note that in our particular case of study the strategy to encourage hubs to spread the word out is ineffective and appears doomed to failure. Instead, encouraging regular consumer seems to be a better strategy.

Conclusions and Discussion

The SIS with rewiring model has isolated the important role of the *degree* as an explanatory variable, considering that connectivity in the social contagion is important (as shown in Figure 4.1a). It has also considered as statistically equivalent those vertices with equal degree, which implicitly means that vertices with the same degree have the same hazard to adopt.

One important finding of this study is that classification using automated *SVM* on datasets (adoption data, network data, and individual attributes) is feasible. Moreover, we found that feature selection is a valuable procedure for reducing dataset complexity and, therefore, facilitating the interpretation of the mined patterns in the adoption process.

The *SVM* classification for the adoption process has deepened into the social contagion considering other explanatory variables different from degree (network metrics and attributes of the individual). In particular, the structure of the community of adopters according to the professional status and other attributes is analyzed.

Data analysis has shown that individuals that adopt technology are somehow isolated from the rest of the network, in the sense that they possess less closeness centrality than the rest of susceptible individuals not yet adopters. This happens indistinctly as adopters usually have higher degree centrality (Figure 4.1a), because closeness and degree highlight different aspects of the network centrality.

The detachment rate estimated in the SIS with the rewiring model indicates that connections with hubs–adopters, including professionals–adopters are not maintained over time because individuals quickly detach links with hubs. This it is consistent with the fact that average closeness for hub–adopters in the network is less than for the rest of susceptible individuals. Simply, the paths to hubs–adopters are frequently broken. This hierarchical structure in the community could be considered as an obstacle to the diffusion of new technologies and explain why so few consumers in this particular community have subscribed to Internet service in such a large interval of time.

The *SVM* analysis highlights the significance of the structure or heterogeneity of the community and exposure to contagion spreading, while the SIS model highlights the importance of the dynamics of social relations and the balance between social contagion and external factors or context.

Some Practical Implications

Our method can be used to estimate the potential effect of social contagion on the adoption of new products. If firms can access their customers' social network data (which is relatively easy, considering the availability of free public information stored in social network sites), they can simulate the expected diffusion of their new products through social contagion and test, for example, if the first adopters are hubs or regular consumers, if firms should substantially increase their marketing effort at the beginning of the release campaign and target hubs directly, and so forth. Using this simple model, managers can assess whether grassroots marketing campaigns are likely to work for the launching of their newest product, even before its release. It is worth noting that the model suggests some implications according to network dynamics. For instance, if network rewiring were too high, the strategy of targeting hubs would not work as expected because the social contagion would be lower since the rewiring tends to homogenize the network. So, in this case maybe a more convenient strategy is to focus directly on regular consumers.

Limitation and Future Work

We acknowledge some limitations in this study and thus some avenues for further research. First, our approach models social contagion as a single parameter, but social contagion might be explained by several factors, such as selection or peer influence. We only started in this work the first steps in order to understand the complex role of social heterogeneities and to test the effect of different sources of social contagion on the diffusion of innovations. We also model nonsocial factors as a single parameter, yet the weights of the different factors in the adoption process might differ. Additional research could address this problem by incorporating as many parameters as there are nonsocial issues that the research aims to test.

Third, the simplicity of our model relies on the assumption that the empirical data match the conditions required for mean field theory and that the vertex degree follows a given distribution. If these conditions were not met, the data analysis techniques still work but the researchers would need to use another model. In addition, future research might explore what-if scenarios in which simulation-based and empirical approaches are merged.

Appendix A: SIS Model with Rewiring

$$\frac{dx_k(t)}{dt} = -\vartheta s_k(t) - \gamma x_k(t) - \beta k \Theta(t) s_k(t) - \nu \left(d_k + \frac{1}{N} \right) x_k(t) + \nu \left(\frac{x_{k+1}(t)}{N} + d_k x_{k-1}(t) \right)$$

$$s_k(t) = 1 - x_k(t)$$

We use the term $\vartheta s_k(t)$, for spontaneous contagion due to nonsocial factors. With a probability β per unit time, infected vertices spread the contagion to their

Table 4.2 Parameters and Variables of the SIS Model with Rewiring

Model Parameters	
β	Transmission rate due to social influence
ϑ	Spontaneous adoption rate due to external influences or nonsocial factors
γ	Recovery rate
ν	Overall time scale of rewiring, compared with that of the contagion
d_k	Detachment rate
Model Variables	
$s_k(t)$	Density of susceptible individuals (non-adopters) with degree k
$x_k(t)$	Density of infected individuals (adopters) with degree k
$\Theta(t) = \sum_k kP_k x_k/\langle k \rangle$	Probability that an edge from a vertex of degree k points to an infected vertex

susceptible neighbors. $\Theta(t)$ is the probability that an edge emanating from a vertex of degree k points to an infected vertex. So, the probability per unit time that a susceptible vertex will become infected is $\beta k\Theta(t)s_k(t)$. The factor k stems because each vertex admits the transmission from each of its contacts. Parameter γ represents recovery rate from the infected state.

If an edge from a vertex of degree k is detached, or else when an end of an edge attached by the other end to an infected vertex attaches to a vertex of degree k, the number of infected vertices with degree k decreases. This loss is described by the term $\nu(d_k + (1/N))x_k(t)$, where d_k is the detachment rate. On the other hand, the gain term $\nu((x_{k+1}(t))/N + d_k x_{k-1}(t))$ reflects infected vertices of degree $k-1$ that get an edge and the infected vertices of degree $k-1$ that lose an edge. Both cases arrive at a state with k edges. The parameter ν describes the overall time scale of the rewiring, compared with that of the contagion.

The parameters and variables of the model are summarized in Table 4.2.

Appendix B: *SVM* Classification Prior to Modeling

Given a set of instances with their respective labels (x_i, y_i), where $x_i \in \mathbb{R}^n$, n is the number of characteristics (covariates or explanatory variables), $i = 1, \ldots, m$; m is the number or individuals and $y_i \in \{S, A\}$ (*S* represents the class of *S*usceptible individuals and *A* denotes the class of *A*dopters); the soft-margin *SVM* (Cortes and

Vapnik, 1995) is aimed at finding a hyperplane of the form $f(x) = w^{\top} x + b$ by solving the following quadratic programming problem (QPP):

$$\min_{w,b,\xi} (1/2) \| w \|^2 + C \sum_i \xi_i$$
$$\text{s.t. } y_i (w^{\top} x + b) \geq 1 - \xi_i, \quad \xi_i \geq 0, \quad i = 1, \ldots, m \; (*)$$

where ξ_i is the soft-margin error of the ith training point in the form of a slack variable, and $C > 0$ is a regularization or cost parameter.

A nonlinear classifier can be obtained via the kernel trick. The dual of formulation allows the use of kernel functions, which define an inner product in a higher dimensional Hilbert space, where a hyperplane with maximal margin is constructed. The kernel-based *SVM* formulation (Schölkopf and Smola 2002) is

$$\max_a \sum_i \alpha_i - (1/2) \sum_{i,s} \alpha_i \alpha_s y_i y_s K(x_i, x_s)$$
$$\text{s.t. } \sum_i \alpha_i y_i = 0, \quad 0 \leq \alpha_i \leq C, \quad i = 1, \ldots, m; \quad s = 1, \ldots, m$$

where α are the dual variables corresponding to the constraints in (*). A common choice for the kernel is the *Gaussian kernel*, which usually leads to better results and has the following form:

$$K(x_i, x_s) = \exp\left(\frac{-\| x_i - x_s \|^2}{2\sigma^2} \right)$$

Here, σ is a positive parameter that controls the width of the kernel.

A classification model classifies each instance into one of the classes *A* or *S*. The confusion matrix (see Table 4.3) shows how the model makes the predictions. The rows correspond to the class labels in the dataset. The columns show the predictions made by the model. The value of each element in the matrix is the number of predictions made with the class corresponding to the column. Thus, the diagonal elements show the number of correct classifications made for each class, and the off-diagonal elements show the errors made. There are four possible classifications for each instance, that is, true positive (t_p), true negative (t_n), false positive (f_p), and false negative (f_n).

Table 4.3   Confusion Matrix for Gaussian Kernel SVM Model

Real	Adopter	Susceptible
Adopter	235	39
Susceptible	22	715

Gaussian kernel function $K(x_i, x_s) = \exp(-\|x_i - x_s\|^2/(2\sigma^2))$

Parameter: cost $C = 100$

Hyperparameter: $\sigma = 0.185693614959772$

Number of support vectors: 205

Objective function value: -7308.346

Training error: 0.033946

Overall error: 6%

Averaged class error: 8%

◼ Accuracy is the overall correctness of the model and is calculated as the sum of correct classifications divided by the total number of classifications:

Accuracy $= (t_p + t_n)/(t_p + t_n + f_p + f_n)$.

Accuracy$_{SVM} = 0.9396636993$

◼ Precision is a measure of the accuracy provided that a specific class has been predicted. From the confusion matrix it is calculated that: Precision $= t_p/(t_p + f_p)$.

Precision is 1 when f_p is 0, which indicates there were no spurious results.

Precision$_{SVM} = 0.8576642336$

◼ Recall is referred to as the true positive rate or sensitivity and is given by Recall $= t_p/(t_p + f_n)$.

Recall becomes 1 when f_n is 0, and it indicates that 100% of the t_p were discovered.

Recall$_{SVM} = 0.9143968872$

References

Borgatti, S. P. and Everett, M. G., 2006, A graph-theoretic perspective on centrality, *Social Networks* 28(4), 466–484.

Burt, R. S., 1987, Social contagion and innovation: Cohesion versus structural equivalence, *American Journal of Sociology*, 92(6), 1287–1335.

Burt, R. S., 1992, *Structural Holes: The Social Structure of Competition*, Harvard University Press, Cambridge, MA.

Cortes, C. and Vapnik, V., 1995, Support-vector networks, *Machine Learning*, 20(3), 273–297.

Freeman, L. C., 1979, Centrality in social networks: Conceptual clarification, *Social Networks*, 1(3), 215–239.

Guyon, I., Gunn, S., Nikravesh, M., and Zadeh, L. A., 2006, *Feature Extraction, Foundations and Applications*, Springer, Berlin.

Haythornthwaite, C., 2005, Social networks and Internet connectivity effects, *Information Communication and Society*, 8(2), 125–147.

Herrera, M., Armelini, G., and Salvaj, E., 2015, Understanding social contagion in adoption processes using dynamic social networks, *PLoS One*, 10(10), e0140891. doi:10.1371/journal.pone.0140891.

Hinz, O., Skiera, B., Barrot, C., and Becker, J. U., 2011, Seeding strategies for viral marketing: An empirical comparison, *Journal of Marketing*, 75(6), 55–71. doi:10.1509/jm.10.0088.

Iyengar, R., Van Den Bulte, C., and Valente, T., 2011, Opinion leadership and social contagion in new product diffusion, *Marketing Science*, 30(2), 195–212.

Onnela, J. P., Saramäki, J., Hyvönen, J., Szabó, G., Lazer, D., and Kaski, K., 2007, Structure and tie strengths in mobile communication networks, *Proceedings of the National Academy of Sciences*, 104(18), 7332–7336.

Pastor-Satorras, R. and Vespignani, A., 2001a, Epidemic dynamics and endemic states in complex networks, *Physical Review*, E 63(6), 066117.

Pastor-Satorras, R. and Vespignani, A., 2001b, Epidemic spreading in scale free networks, *Physical Review Letters*, 86(14), 3200.

Pastor-Satorras, R., Vazquez, A., and Vespignani, A., 2001, Dynamical and correlation properties of the Internet, *Physical Review Letters*, 87(25), 8701.

Pastor-Satorras, R. and Vespignani, A., 2002, Epidemic dynamics finite size scale-free networks, *Physical Review*, E65, 035108.

Risselada, H., Verhoef, P. C., and Bijmolt, T. H. A., 2014, Dynamic effect of social influence and direct marketing on the adoption of high-technology products, *Journal of Marketing*, 78(2), 52–68.

Schölkopf, B. and Smola, A. J., 2002, *Learning with Kernels*, MIT Press, Cambridge, MA.

Vapnik, V., 1998, *Statistical Learning Theory*, John Wiley & Sons, New York.

Watts, D. J. and Dodds, P., 2007, Influentials, networks and public opinion formation, *Journal of Consumer Research*, 34(4), 441–458.

Chapter 5

Prescriptive Analytics in Manufacturing: An Order Acceptance Illustration

Federico Trigos and Eduardo M. López

Contents

Summary 92
Introduction...92
    About the Background of This Work 93
    What Is the Scope of This Work? 93
    Definition of the Key Concepts 94
    What Is the Work Performed in This Field? 94
    Theories Used for Approaching the Problem Business Analytics and
    Modeling..95
    Mathematical Programming 95
Description of the Model That Is Studied...95
Project Objectives...96
Methodology for Solving the Problem..96
Models and Concepts Used in the Study 97
How Can the Problem Be Extended to Include Make-to-Stock
Manufacturing Environments? 98
Results and Their Meaning to Managerial Decision Making: A Numerical
Example 99
Results and Their Interpretation 100
Why Is This Approach of the Solution Valuable? 101

Conclusions and Recommendations...101
    Are the Objectives of the Research Achieved?..101
    How Are These Meaningful for Organizations and for Future Research?.......101
        Strategic..102
References...102

Summary

Often times, technical and technological resource limitations do not allow companies to meet their market demand within a fixed period of time. Consistently, they fall short and there is a gap in the production order catalogue so the unfulfilled demand has to be deferred to a future operating period or be lost.

Objectives such as profit maximization had not been widely considered under general operating conditions in the traditional decision models bringing up an opportunity to develop a scheme that leads to a decision, taking into account all possible revenues and costs involved.

In this chapter, two main management decisions are studied. The first decision that management requires is as to which orders to accept ($P_{i1} > 0$). The operation assumption is that the clients accept partial orders as long as this is negotiated at the beginning of the period. Thus, a second management decision deals with whether the accepted orders are going to be produced partially or completely.

Introduction

Decision making is an important management function that has to be performed through an improved process. There are inputs needed and they include historical and recent operating data, business and clients' expectations and priorities, physical and economic constraints, as well as resource limitations and datelines. All of them are combined and manipulated in a decision model the processing of which yields a business decision of what, when, how, and where to do a specific action of economic interest. Owing to global competition, constant change in market needs, and other influencing factors acting on an enterprise, decision-making processes have become crucial and condition the financial success of a business firm.

Manufacturing environments are not exempt of decision-making processes improvement. In fact, some of them are even more sensitive to reach their economic objectives to the quality of the decision-making process adopted and the actions derived from it. Often times, technical and technological resource limitations do not allow companies to meet their market demand within a fixed period of time. Consistently, they fall short and there is a gap in the production order catalogue, so the unfulfilled demand has to be deferred to a future operating period or be lost. This brings up a management dilemma: What criteria should be applied in order to decide which orders are to be presently manufactured and which ones will be negotiated to be produced later on or be lost? This decision-making process and the corresponding decision models used give rise to an area of research known as Order Acceptance.

Classical industrial engineering has focused order acceptance models on achieving cost minimization, maximizing the number of orders accepted, and/or lead-time optimization. However, other economic objectives such as profit maximization had not been widely considered under general operating conditions in the traditional decision models bringing up an opportunity to develop a scheme that leads to a decision, taking into account all possible revenues and costs involved. The final decision might even consider the possibility of breaking up an order into fractions of it (batches), if necessary. After all, financial measures are best understood at executive levels; thus, maximizing profit will bring a healthier economic performance to the business firm and, in the long run, a stronger positioning.

About the Background of This Work

Since the early 1990s, order acceptance has had considerable attention in the literature. Slotnick (2010) published a taxonomy of research papers related to order acceptance and scheduling where chronological developments and contributions to the field are reviewed.

A classification is given dividing problems between single and multiple machines involved, deterministic and stochastic order arrivals, due dates versus producing in a fixed period of time; the objectives to be achieved are economical in nature and they are obtained either by mathematical programming models, computer simulation models, or procedures known as "heuristics" which are easier to implement when programming them in a computer but may not always reach an optimal solution. By analyzing the information published, the level of complexity involved in such decision models is clearly identified, forcing business decisions to be highly dependent on the specific manufacturing environment involved (Pinedo 2012).

What Is the Scope of This Work?

When a company has a single highly specialized machine, it is common that demand exceeds capacity. Deciding what to produce and what to reject or defer for the future is not necessarily simple. First, the type of manufacturing that the family of products has to follow needs to be considered: make-to-order or make-to-stock. Each of them has unique features that influence the decision. Moreover, the lot size of each product ordered may not only need a machine setup, but periodic re-setups such as machine calibration, addition of coolant and lubricant, etc. This is common when tooling and other similar products are manufactured. They all consume time and cost money, so they have to be incorporated into the decision-making process. Finally, the total amount of time available to manufacture the orders becomes the limiting factor. To be able to evaluate, compare, and discriminate alternatives in a systematic and consistent way, overall profit (expected revenue minus total costs involved) will be the objective to be maximized in the decision model so a final strategy of order acceptance can be reached. For each type of manufacturing, there is an optimization model to be built and used.

Definition of the Key Concepts

Catalogue of products: Refers to the set of stock keeping units that a company can produce by order request from a client.

Binary programming model: Mathematical model (objective function and constraints) the decision variables of which can only take one of two values: zero or one.

Integer programming model: Mathematical model the decision variable of which can only take nonnegative integer values.

Make-to-order: The demand is defined by the client's request.

Make-to-stock: The company forecasts the demand.

Manufacturing batch: the fraction of the total demand defined by the manufacturer.

Manufacturing order: the total number of units required for a specific product.

Marginal contribution: Revenue per unit minus its variable cost; in this chapter the variable cost does not include setup or re-setup costs.

Mixed integer programming model: Mathematical model that includes nonnegative real and integer decision-making variables.

Profit: Refers to the total revenue minus total cost.

Re-setup: The preparation previous to a manufacturing batch after the first batch has been produced.

Setup: Initial machine preparation prior to the manufacturing of a particular order.

What Is the Work Performed in This Field?

Most of the modeling developed and reported in Slotnick's article did not contemplate re-setups in the decision-making process. Trigos and López (2015) introduced such possibility extending order acceptance theory to a wider manufacturing universe. In their article, make-to-order environments are described, modeled, and solved, searching for a solution that maximizes the overall profit. The theoretical foundation is based on a network flow optimization model whose equivalence to make-to-order situations yields a mathematical programming problem, which can be solved by a commercial software. If the need arises due to the unavailability of the software, a couple of heuristics are also provided to obtain a good practical solution. This chapter reviews make-to-order order acceptance for a single machine and develops the corresponding make-to-stock modeling under the same circumstances. Decision models will be presented and illustrated with numerical examples so that the decision makers can apply them as often as they need to.

Theories Used for Approaching the Problem Business Analytics and Modeling

Modeling a real situation is an art but it has a scientific basis. A model can be defined as an abstraction of reality where the most important features that need to be studied for a particular problem have been included. If it is used for decision making, all feasible alternatives need to be covered within the model to use it with confidence. Business Analytics in Management Science needs real data and decision models to be effective. Often times, a company collects a large amount of data and has to build up the appropriate model to describe the behavior and to understand the environment. In other cases, there is an existing model (in the industry or the literature) that can provide strategic advantages to a company and the corresponding data have to be gathered appropriately. Both situations can be applied for prescriptive analytics which can tell an organization what, when, how, and where to do something of economic value and competitive advantage. The reader is referred to Asllani (2015) for more details on modeling and business analytics theory.

Mathematical Programming

In the 1940s, a discipline was born under the name of Operations Research. It aids decision makers in describing, improving, and whenever possible, optimizing business activities. One of the most used tools of Operations Research is known as Mathematical Programming the main purposes of which are to represent the goal to be achieved and the existing constraints in symbolic expressions using mathematics, and to develop a procedure or "algorithm" to solve it. This field of knowledge has been used since the 1950s in business decision-making processes, but with the emergence of Business Analytics it has become one of the most important techniques to obtain a competitive advantage. It is composed of an objective function or strategy to follow and will be subject to a set of equations and/or inequalities that characterize the "feasible region" or constraints to be satisfied. The correct application of mathematical programming can help processing large amounts of data in a periodic basis allowing an organization to be constantly in the right track of business success. More information can be found in Dantzig (1963), Hillier and Lieberman (2006), and Taha (2012).

Description of the Model That Is Studied

Let us consider a single machine manufacturing process facing a demand of c orders. Each order represents a unique part number; the ith order requests d_i units to be processed. To manufacture the ith order, a setup is required at the beginning of the order; additional re-setups are required after machining M_i units of the same order. The marginal contribution (MC_i) is defined as the unitary price (revenue) minus the variable manufacturing cost (without including setup costs). Since after M_i manufactured units the machine has to stop and a re-setup has to be performed, the complete order has to be divided into batches, where l_i is the number of batches to satisfy the complete ith order:

$$l_i = \left\lceil \frac{d_i}{M_i} \right\rceil$$

where $\lceil \ \rceil$ is the mathematical ceiling function. Note that if d_i is not a multiple of M_i, the last batch is a fraction of M_i. Let P_{ij} be the number of units to be manufactured for the ith order at the jth batch.

Project Objectives

The first decision that management requires is which orders to accept ($P_{i1} > 0$). The operation assumption is that clients accept partial orders as long as this is negotiated at the beginning of the period. Thus, a second management decision deals with whether the accepted orders are going to be produced partially or completely.

Methodology for Solving the Problem

In a make-to-order environment it is important to negotiate in advance how to handle incomplete orders. In this section, we are going to assume that partial orders have to be delivered as multiples of M_i, although this constraint will be relaxed later on. So,

$$P_{ij} = \begin{cases} M_i & \text{for } j = 1, 2, \ldots, l_{i-1} \\ d_i - (l_i - 1)M_i & \text{for } j = l_i \end{cases}$$

To compute profit and keep record of the manufacturing time, an additional notation is required. Let π_{ij} be the profit of the ith order when j batches are manufactured:

$$\pi_{ij} = \sum_{k=1}^{j} (MC_i P_{ik} - SUC_{ik})$$

where SUC_{ij} represents the cost of the jth setup for the ith order. To track the manufacturing time, let us define t_i as the standard manufacturing time per unit of the ith order and SUT_{ij} as the setup standard time at the beginning of the jth batch of the ith order. Thus, the manufacturing time to produce j batches of the ith order is defined as τ_{ij}:

$$\tau_{ij} = \sum_{k=1}^{j} (t_i P_{ik} + SUT_{ik})$$

Models and Concepts Used in the Study

Let us assume that T units of time are available in this manufacturing period. To solve the problem, Trigos and López (2015) proposed the following binary programming model:

$$\text{Max} \sum_{i=1}^{c} \sum_{j=1}^{l_i} \pi_{ij} y_{ij}$$

subject to

$$\sum_{j=1}^{l_i} y_{ij} \leq 1, \quad \text{for } i = 1, 2, \ldots, c \tag{5.1}$$

$$\sum_{i=1}^{c} \sum_{j=1}^{l_i} \tau_{ij} y_{ij} \leq T$$

where $y_{ij} = 0$ or 1

where each decision variable y_{ij} is defined as

$$y_{ij} = \begin{cases} 1 & \text{if } j \text{ batches are accepted to be produced for the } i\text{th order} \\ 0 & \text{otherwise} \end{cases}$$

Note that the binary programming model has ω binary variables where

$$\omega = \sum_{i=1}^{c} l_i$$

Depending on the magnitude of ω, the binary programming model presented could be difficult to solve. Trigos and López (2015) present alternative methodologies for problems with large ω.

How Can the Problem Be Extended to Include Make-to-Stock Manufacturing Environments?

In make-to-stock environments the manufacturing company cannot keep the constraint of batches size at M_i and the previous binary programming model is no longer valid. In fact, this extension also applies to a large number of make-to-order manufacturing environments in which the customer accepts batches of size less than M_i (flexible batch size). The following decision variables are proposed:

$$x_{ij} = \text{total units to be produced of order } i \text{ using } j \text{ batches}$$

$$a_{ij} = \begin{cases} 1 & \text{if } x_{ij} > 0 \\ 0 & \text{otherwise} \end{cases}$$

The following mixed integer programming model covers the situation just explained:

$$\text{Max} \sum_{i=1}^{c} \sum_{j=1}^{l_i} \left(MC_i x_{ij} - \left[\sum_{k=1}^{j} SUC_{ik} \right] a_{ij} \right)$$

subject to

$$x_{ij} \leq \left(\sum_{k=1}^{j} P_{ik} \right) a_{ij}$$

$$\sum_{i=1}^{c} \sum_{j=1}^{l_i} \left(t_i x_{ij} + \left[\sum_{k=1}^{j} SUT_{ik} \right] a_{ij} \right) \leq T \qquad (5.2)$$

$$\sum_{j=1}^{l_i} a_{ij} \leq 1,$$

where $x_{ij} \in Z^+$ and $a_{ij} = 0$ or 1

The objective function represents the total profit of all the orders accepted (an order i is accepted if $\sum_{k=1}^{l_i} a_{ik} = 1$). The first constraint coordinates the size of x_{ij} with the number of batches to be manufactured. The second constraint limits the manufacturing time of the period, and the last constraint makes sure that at most one x_{ij} is positive for a given i. This model has ω binary variables a_{ij} and ω nonnegative variables x_{ij}, making model in Equation 5.2 more extended and flexible than the binary model in Equation 5.1. Note that an additional implicit condition is embedded in model in Equation 5.2: A jth batch can be a fraction of M_i if and only if the previous $j-1$ have already been completed with M_i units each. This applies to all orders i.

Results and Their Meaning to Managerial Decision Making: A Numerical Example

Let us consider a manufacturing company, which receives three orders ($c = 3$) to be considered within a manufacturing period of 300 time units ($T = 300$). The problem data are contained in Table 5.1.

Using the notation described earlier the problem parameters are computed in Table 5.2.

Form the data shown in Table 5.2, it can be observed that in order to complete the three orders, $\tau_{11} + \tau_{23} + \tau_{32} = 511$ time units are required to obtain a complete profit of $\pi_{11} + \pi_{23} + \pi_{32} = \$6895.00$. However, since only $T = 300$ time units are available we need to apply the models to solve the order acceptance problem for

1. A make-to-order manufacturing environment in which complete order batches are required.
2. A make-to-stock manufacturing environment.

Table 5.1 Data for Numerical Example, Where $o > 1$

Order (i)	d_i	SUT_{i1}	SUT_{io}	MC_i	M_i	SUC_{i1}	SUC_{io}	t_i	l_i
1	130	20	3	$20.00	150	$12.00	$3.00	1	1
2	59	15	2	$50.00	25	$14.00	$5.00	4	3
3	40	50	6	$35.00	23	$17.00	$2.00	6	2

Table 5.2 Numerical Example Problem Parameters

i, j	P_{ij}	$MC_iP_{ij} - SUC_{ij}$	π_{ij}	$t_iP_{ij} + SUT_{ij}$	τ_{ij}
1, 1	130	$2588.00	$2588.00	150	150
2, 1	25	$1236.00	$1236.00	115	115
2, 2	25	$1245.00	$2481.00	102	217
2, 3	9	$445.00	$2926.00	38	255
3, 1	23	$788.00	$788.00	188	188
3, 2	17	$593.00	$1381.00	108	296

Results and Their Interpretation

Using model in Equation 5.1 for (1), the binary programming model for a make-to-order manufacturing environment is

$$\text{Max } 2588y_{11} + 1236y_{21} + 2481y_{22} + 2926y_{23} + 788y_{31} + 1381y_{32}$$

subject to

$$y_{11} \leq 1$$
$$y_{21} + y_{22} + y_{23} \leq 1$$
$$y_{31} + y_{32} \leq 1$$
$$150y_{11} + 115y_{21} + 217y_{22} + 255y_{23} + 188y_{31} + 296y_{32} \leq 300$$
$$y_{11}, y_{21}, y_{22}, y_{23}, y_{31}, y_{32} = 0 \text{ or } 1$$

the optimal solution of which is given by one batch of order 1 with 130 units and one batch of 25 units each of order 2 ($y_{11} = y_{21} = 1$) using 265 time units in total and yields an optimal objective function value of \$3824.00.

Using model in Equation 5.2 to solve (2), the mixed integer programming model for a make-to-stock manufacturing environment is

$$\text{Max } 20x_{11} - 12a_{11} + 50x_{21} + 50x_{22} + 50x_{23} - 14a_{21} - 19a_{22} - 24a_{23} + 35x_{31}$$
$$+ 35x_{32} - 17a_{31} - 19a_{32}$$

subject to

$$x_{11} - 130a_{11} \leq 0$$
$$x_{21} - 25a_{21} \leq 0$$
$$x_{22} - 50a_{22} \leq 0$$
$$x_{23} - 59a_{23} \leq 0$$
$$x_{31} - 23a_{31} \leq 0$$
$$x_{32} - 40a_{32} \leq 0$$
$$x_{11} + 20a_{11} + 4x_{21} + 4x_{22} + 4x_{23} + 15a_{21} + 17a_{22} + 19a_{23} + 6x_{31} + 6x_{32}$$
$$+ 50a_{31} + 56a_{32} \leq 300$$
$$a_{11} \leq 1$$
$$a_{21} + a_{22} + a_{23} \leq 1$$
$$a_{31} + a_{32} \leq 1$$
$$x_{11}, x_{21}, x_{22}, x_{23}, x_{31}, x_{32} \in Z^{+}$$
$$a_{11}, a_{21}, a_{22}, a_{23}, a_{31}, a_{32} = 0 \text{ or } 1$$

the optimal solution of which is given by one batch of order 1 of 130 units plus 33 units of order 2 divided into two batches: one batch of 25 (P_{21}) units and the second batch of 8 ($x_{22} - P_{21}$) units only ($x_{11} = 130$, $x_{22} = 33$), using 299 time units in total, with a maximum objective function value of $4219.00.

Both models have been solved using the software LINDO. Model in Equation 5.2 has a profit of $395.00 more than model 1 due to the fact than model in Equation 5.2 is not restricted to full batch loads.

Why Is This Approach of the Solution Valuable?

Often times, production programming decision makers base their manufacturing planning on intuition, common sense and previous experiences accumulated through time. However, real data are overlooked leading to suboptimal decisions. Applying mathematical models as the ones illustrated in this chapter provide confidence that an optimal solution is always achieved.

The models presented are to be applied at the beginning of every operating cycle, so an optimal economic performance can be proved even in financial statements.

Conclusions and Recommendations

Are the Objectives of the Research Achieved?

The research objectives of order acceptance and order completions under profit optimization is achieved for two different scenarios (make-to-order and make-to-stock manufacturing environments) through the solution of the proposed mathematical programming models, which can be solved by a commercial software and, depending on the problem size, by a free-access software.

How Are These Meaningful for Organizations and for Future Research?

Decision-making processes based on scientific tools will lead organizations to a better financial performance through time. Future research is pending when the models are extended to

1. More than one single machine
2. Multiple periods of operating cycles (allowing inventory in between)
3. Combining decisions when the catalogue of products is composed of make-to-order and make-to-stock products at the same time
4. A single product combines make-to-order and make-to-stock decisions

Strategic

This chapter presents a new contribution of order acceptance theory extending the models presented by Trigos and López (2015), from make-to-order only to make-to-stock and make-to-order flexible batch size manufacturing.

References

Asllani, A., 2015, *Business Analytics with Management Science, Models and Methods*, Pearson Education Inc., Upper Saddle River, New Jersey.

Dantzig, G. B., 1963, *Linear Programming and Extensions*, Princeton University Press, New Jersey.

Hillier, F. S. and Lieberman, G. J., 2006, *Introduction to Operations Research*, 8th ed., McGraw-Hill, New York.

Pinedo, M. L., 2012, *Scheduling: Theory, Algorithms, and Systems*, 4th ed., Springer, New York.

Slotnick, S. A., 2010, Order acceptance and scheduling: A taxonomy and review, *European Journal of Operational Research*, 212(1), 1–11.

Taha, H., 2012, *Operations Research*, 9th ed., Pearson, New York.

Trigos, F. and López, E. M., 2015, Maximising profit for multiple-product, single-period, single-machine manufacturing under sequential set-up constraints that depend on lot size, *International Journal of Production Research*, 54(4), 1134–1151.

Chapter 6

A Stochastic Hierarchical Approach for a Production Planning System under Uncertain Demands

Virna Ortiz-Araya and Víctor M. Albornoz

Contents

Summary..104
Introduction..104
Stochastic Optimization 106
A Stochastic Hierarchical Approach..108
    Hierarchical Production Planning Structure...108
Optimization Models for the HPP Strategy 110
    Aggregate Production Plan..110
    First Disaggregation Level: Item Production Quantities for the
    Corresponding Family in the Month 113
    Second Disaggregation Level: MPS..115
Case Study 116
Conclusions and Extensions 127
Acknowledgments 128
References..128

Summary

Hierarchical production planning is a widely utilized methodology for real-world production planning systems, with the aim to establish alternative decision-making levels of these planning issues. For tactical purposes, the methodology considers an aggregated production planning program, the optimal decisions of which are disaggregated into final products considering one or two disaggregation levels, in order to meet the final demand. Frequently, the hierarchical approach utilizes different deterministic optimization models that impose appropriate constraints to keep coherence of the plan on the production system. However, in many situations, a deterministic model is not appropriate for capturing the uncertain demand behavior that is present in some real-world applications. Uncertain demand can be involved in optimization models in which this parameter is represented by a random variable or a set of scenarios. For that purpose, in this chapter, we introduce a hierarchical approach using different stochastic optimization models, in order to determine the optimal allocation of resources at the tactical level, as well as in reference to the most immediate planning horizon, in order to meet uncertain demands. We also present a case study applying the proposed methodology to an industrial company that produces different household electrical appliances, elucidating the relevancy of the adopted methodology.

Introduction

Production can be defined as the process of transforming raw materials into finished products. Effective management of production process ought to provide finished products in appropriate quantities, at the desired times, of the required quality, and at a reasonable cost. Production management encompasses a large number of decisions. Such decisions involve complex choices among a large number of factors. Often, these choices involve the sacrifice of conflicting objectives under the presence of financial, technological, resource availability, and marketing constraints.

Hierarchical production planning (HPP) systems are developed to establish various levels of decision making and information, in order for managers to focus on the most relevant issues that arise in planning. Considerable contributions have been made by Bitran and Hax (1977) in the area of operations research to resolve production planning problems. Different authors have used the classical model for testing the robustness, coherence, and feasibility in the disaggregation process (Axsäter and Jönsson 1984, Erschler et al. 1986, Mercé 1987, Özdamar et al. 1996, Vicens et al. 2001, Aghezzaf et al. 2010). The most important task consists of providing, with HPP, a robust, stable, and feasible plan, accounting for capacity allocation and priority management, at the level of master production scheduling. Other authors have analyzed the advantages and limitations that these systems

(HPP) offer in various applications, such as agroalimentary (Erromdhani et al. 2012), metal parts fabrication (Neureuther et al. 2004, Özdamar et al. 1997), shoe production (Caravilla and de Sousa 1995), furniture construction (Lario et al. 1994), multiproduct and multi-machine environments (Qui et al. 2001), semiconductor wafer fabrication (Bang and Kim 2010), stationery products manufacturing (Ortiz-Araya et al. 2015), among others.

Enterprises seek a method for predicting the weekly timing and quantity of production, while maintaining coherence between usable stock and forecasted monthly demand. To attain these objectives, advanced planning systems (APS) are used to calculate production at the master production scheduling level. In HPP, once the volume of production quantity is calculated per month for each family, the decision to define the best finished product quantity to produce per week is decided according to the consumer demand. In this chapter, we propose a disaggregation approach process to obtain an optimal volume to transform a production plan into a master production schedule (MPS).

Deterministic optimization models are commonly used to analyze production planning problems, these assume the value of each parameter; consequently, the accuracy is unproven until directly applied within the scenario. Furthermore, the use of a deterministic model, which uses an estimated value, can lead to inappropriate decisions. These considerations have compelled the development of alternative methodologies for production planning under uncertain conditions (Mula et al. 2006, Wu and Ierapetritou 2007). Among the strategies, a stochastic programming model with recourse can explicitly include uncertainty by means of random variables, proposing an optimal solution and accounting for feasibility and optimality applied to different realizations of uncertain parameters (Birge and Louveaux 2011).

This chapter formulates a hierarchical structure based on an aggregated production planning model followed by two disaggregation models, where each level has used a stochastic program model with recourse. The objective of this methodology is to optimize decisions regarding production quantity for each item of a corresponding family within the primary weeks of planning horizon. The first step consists in determining the sales and operational planning, using a multistage stochastic linear programming model with recourse. The second step is a two-stage stochastic quadratic programming model with recourse, used for disaggregating products family into items for a corresponding month. In this context, disaggregation applies only to products. In the final step, disaggregation is used to disaggregate the time, that is, months to weeks of item quantities. This methodology is an extension of previous contributions of Ortiz-Araya et al. (2015) in the case of deterministic demand.

The remainder of this chapter is organized as follows: first, a description is provided regarding basic ideas of a stochastic programming model with recourse. Then, a stochastic hierarchical approach is described detailing the HPP structure and stochastic programming models are proposed. After that, a study case and results are shown. Finally, conclusions and future work are presented.

Stochastic Optimization

Optimization is a methodology relevant to advanced analytical methods for decision making; and is commonly applied with deterministic optimization models, such as those provided through linear, nonlinear, or integer programming. However, in many situations, a deterministic model may be inappropriate in the context of identifying uncertain behaviors present in real-world applications. In production planning problems, uncertainty should be factored in, particularly in regard to future prices, yields, and demands, as well as in processing times and supply of raw materials. There are several ways in which uncertainty can be considered. Within recent decades, several different approaches to optimization under uncertainty have been developed. For example, within robust optimization, uncertain parameters are applied using values in a specific interval range (Bertsimas and Sim 2004). Conversely, stochastic programming consists of optimization models in which some parameters are represented by random variables, referred to as *scenarios*. Numerous models and applications have been published since the seminal works of Dantzig (1955) and Madansky (1960). Although these references are decades old, only within the last 15 years has there been a notable advance in algorithms and computer technology. Subsequently, solutions to large size and more realistic models have increased interest in stochastic programming and their applications, see, for example, Gassmann and Ziemba (2012), King and Wallace (2012), and Wallace and Ziemba (2005).

The two-stage stochastic program with recourse is an important class of models widely used in multi-period planning problems. In these models, there are two kinds of decision variables, presumably performed in two consecutive stages. In the first stage there are decisions, generally referred to as *first-stage* or *here-and-now* decision. These values are taken prior to the realization of the uncertain parameters, and therefore not conditioned by the particular realization. Conversely, during the second stage, referred to as *second-stage* or *recourse*, variables represent the reactive decisions made in recourse or response to compensate for decisions made during the first stage, following the discovery of uncertain parameters. In mathematical terms, a two-stage stochastic linear program with fixed recourse is an equation of identifying the following:

$$\text{Min } c^T x + \Xi_\xi [\text{Min } q(\omega)^T y(\omega)] \tag{6.1}$$

$$\text{s.t. } Ax = b \tag{6.2}$$

$$T(\omega)x + Wy(\omega) = h(\omega) \tag{6.3}$$

$$x \geq 0, \quad y(\omega) \geq 0 \tag{6.4}$$

where c and b are known vectors and A and W are known matrices; and where we assume that $\xi(\omega) = (q(\omega), h(\omega); T(\omega))$ is a random variable. Here, first-stage decisions are represented by vector x and, as previously stated, when the random event (scenario) ω is realized, the second-stage problem data q, h, and T become known, subsequently the second-stage decisions $y(\omega)$ must be made.

The final objective of these models is to determine an optimal first-stage policy, which minimizes the total cost of the model: defined as the sum of the first- and second-stage decision costs (Higle 2005). The formulation and numerical solution of these models is extended to general *multistage* stochastic programming models, via the decomposition principle of dynamic programming (Birge and Louveaux 2011). The objective function contains a deterministic term $c^T x$ and the expected value of the second-stage objective $q(\omega)^T y(\omega)$ is taken over all realization of the random variable ξ. Decisions are made that constraints (6.2) through (6.4) hold (almost surely). Constraint (6.3) shows the dependence of the second-stage decision y on a particular realization (scenario) as well as on the value of the first-stage decisions x. To emphasize this fact, models (6.1) through (6.4) is represented by the *equivalent deterministic problem*

$$\text{Min } c^T x + \Xi_\xi [Q(x, \xi(\omega))] \tag{6.5}$$

$$\text{s.t. } Ax = b \tag{6.6}$$

$$x \geq 0 \tag{6.7}$$

where

$$Q(x, \xi(\omega)) = \text{Min}\left\{ q(\omega)^T y / Wy = h(\omega) - T(\omega)x, \quad y \geq 0 \right\} \tag{6.8}$$

being the value of the second-stage or the recourse program. An exceptional case is when ξ corresponds to a finite discrete random variable (a finite number of S scenarios), that is: $\omega^s = (q^s, h^s, T^s)$ occurs with probability p_s, for $s = 1, 2, ..., S$. In this case, the two-stage linear program simply corresponds to

$$\text{Min } c^T x + \Sigma_s p_s Q(x, \omega^s) \tag{6.9}$$

$$\text{s.t. } Ax = b \tag{6.10}$$

$$x \geq 0 \tag{6.11}$$

where

$$Q(x, \omega^s) = \text{Min}\left\{ q^{sT} y / Wy = h^s - T^s x, \quad y \geq 0 \right\}, \quad \text{for all } s = 1, ..., S \tag{6.12}$$

This model can be equally represented by a *deterministic equivalent model* in its *compact form* according to the following program:

$$\text{Min } cx + p_1 q^1 y^1 + p_2 q^2 y^2 + \cdots + p_S q^S y^S \tag{6.13}$$

$$\text{s.t. } Ax \qquad\qquad\qquad\qquad = b \tag{6.14}$$

$$T^1 x + W y^1 \qquad\qquad\qquad = h^1 \tag{6.15}$$

$$T^2 x \qquad\qquad + W y^2 \qquad = h^2 \tag{6.16}$$

$$\cdots$$

$$T^S x \qquad\qquad\qquad + W y^S = h^S \tag{6.17}$$

$$x \geq 0,\, y^1 \geq 0,\, y^2 \geq 0,\, \ldots,\, y^S \geq 0 \tag{6.18}$$

The broad nature of the resulting models usually cannot be solved by the general optimization software. Some kinds of decomposition algorithms are needed and commonly implemented, such as the Benders' decomposition method, the Dantzig and Wolfe decomposition method, the Lagrangean decomposition method, and their extensions (Ruszczynski 2003). Models presented here are the simplistic form in two-stage programs. Extensions are easily modeled if first- or second-stage integer decision variables are included and/or nonlinear first- or second-stage objectives or constraints functions are incorporated. On the other hand, production planning problems involve sequences of decisions made over time, and during these time periods, such decisions must be made prior to the possible realizations of uncertain parameters in future periods. The resulting model for the optimal decision making is then a multistage stochastic program with recourse, as a natural extension of the two-stage programs. The multistage program, with a finite number of scenarios, still has an equivalent deterministic model used for a large number of scenarios and solved with appropriate extensions of aforementioned decomposition methods (Pflug and Pichler 2014). In the next section, we present the scope of applicability of stochastic programs with recourse for hierarchical planning problems, which seems particularly suited to exploit the hierarchical structure of the models, as well as the dynamic structure of problems.

A Stochastic Hierarchical Approach

Hierarchical Production Planning Structure

Hax and Meal introduced the HPP concept in 1975 (Hax and Meal 1975). This method mainly consists of recognizing the differences between tactical and operational decisions. Tactical decisions are associated with aggregate production planning (sales and operations planning [SOP]), whereas operational decisions are the results of the disaggregation process (MPS). The structure HPP allows the differentiation of planning levels by dividing them into sublevels. Hax and Meal proposed three levels of disaggregation: items, families, and groups. The model made by Bitran et al. (1981) uses the convex knapsack problems to disaggregate production. The first level consists of allocating the production capacity among product types using an aggregate planning model. The planning horizon of the resulting linear programming model normally requires a year to properly consider the fluctuations of product demand. Following, on the second level, the disaggregation process takes into account the optimal production discovered in the first level, in order to issue the production of families. In this stage, an objective is to minimize the total setup costs. For the second model, an algorithm is proposed by Bitran and Hax (1981). Finally, the family production allocation is divided into items belonging to each family. An analysis of these models considering consistence, coherence, and robustness were presented by Erschler et al. (1986) and Mercé (1987). They proposed a disaggregation structure composed of two levels: disaggregation decisions for groups monthly, into families, in the same period. The methodology developed by these authors consists of using new constraints in the disaggregation model formulated by Bitran and Hax (1981) for the first level. At this level, the determined decisions are taken into account as constraints for the second level. This procedure aims to establish the coherence of decisions for each level. Many studies in the context of HPP propose to determine the robustness in production volumes dealing with uncertain demands. Laserre and Mercé (1990) have analyzed demand uncertainty under necessary and sufficient conditions to obtain a robust aggregation plan. If demand uncertainty is addressed in the first level (aggregation plan), it was established that the variation of demand in a detailed plan will be controlled, and thus stable MPS can be obtained. Özdamar et al. (1996) propose a heuristic modification to the algorithm of Bitran and Hax (1981) and an alternative filling procedure to improve infeasibilities in the disaggregation stage for family production. Then, the principal problem is to coordinate these different levels in order to determine an optimal, robust, and stable plan of disaggregation. Gfrerer and Zäpfel (1995) continue the analysis of Mercé's proposition (1987) by incorporating other constraints to assure sufficiency and robustness for the disaggregation process. Giard (2003) examines the disaggregation problems in the context of coherence for situations in which the products are not homogeneous in volume or structure to the interior of the family. In every application and methodology developed by the previous authors, the disaggregation procedure is realized for a monthly period. In our study, we proposed to show that the disaggregation procedure allows the prediction of item product quantities per week (per frozen horizon in the study).

Ortiz-Araya et al. (2004) try a disaggregation structure composed of two levels. They determined that in the possibility of obtaining different detailed plans using an HPP procedure from one stable production plan. Nevertheless, the primary results show that the stability present in the aggregation plan is lost in the obtained MPS. Ortiz-Araya (2005) shows the interest of tactical planning and more particularly,

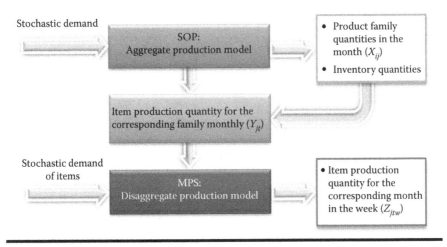

Figure 6.1 Disaggregation structure for the analyzed problem.

the way to determine detailed plans (MPS), by using an HPP structure. In this context, the author proposes a disaggregation methodology at two levels, which allows identification of *stable* MPS, by accounting *robust* and *stable* forecasted plans (SOP). Optimization problems are proposed, as well as constraints which consider decisions relative to each level, in order to insure consistency among them. The author applies a treatment model for the real demand by using the AR (p) process, in order to increase the stability of the different MPS determined. Currently, the disaggregation methodology proposed by Ortiz-Araya et al. (2015) is extended explicitly including various demand scenarios as part of the model formulation.

The proposed disaggregation structure is shown in Figure 6.1. Aggregate production planning problems are optimized to obtain product family and inventory quantities for each month. Optimization procedures are realized according to stochastic demands, represented by a finite set of scenarios. The aggregated decisions (product family, inventory, and unmet demand) are introduced during the first disaggregation level, considered as an intermediate stage for obtaining production quantity of items for the corresponding family, during the month. The second and final disaggregation level of this methodology is obtained by accounting for item stochastic demand scenarios for established master production scheduling, during the weeks of the studied month.

Optimization Models for the HPP Strategy

Aggregate Production Plan

The aggregate production planning problem is one of the biggest problems when making midterm decisions in the operations management of complex manufacturing systems (Buzacott 2013). Typically, a deterministic optimization model for this problem provides an optimal production policy that meets forecasted demands for different product families, within each time period of the planning horizon. This satisfies some capacity constraints, while minimizing total production and inventory costs.

A deterministic model assumes that all parameters of the model are known and certain. In many cases, some are uncertain and simply replaced by their expected values, in order to be included in a deterministic model. However, the optimal solution achieved in this manner may not sufficiently represent the reality and does not account for the variability of these parameters with respect to their expected value. Thus, among the different methodologies for production planning under uncertainty (Mula et al. 2006), we consider a stochastic optimization model with recourse based on Escudero et al. (1993) and Alonso-Ayuso et al. (2005).

Next, a stochastic optimization model with recourse is presented in the context of a production planning problem with uncertain demands. The demands of the entire planning horizon are modeled using a given finite set of scenarios, each with its own occurrence probability. In the application, these scenarios could be defined as simple predictions made by an expert. Alternatively, these scenarios could also be obtained through available historical data, using classical forecasting techniques. To define the aggregated production planning stochastic model, the following notation is considered:

Parameters

T: total number of periods
I: total number of product families
S: total number of demand scenarios
p_s: probability for demand scenario s
d_{its}: demand for family i in period t under scenario s
c_{it}: unit production cost of family i in period t
h_{it}: inventory carrying cost per unit of family i in period t
o_t: cost per man-hour of overtime hours in period t
f_{it}: shortage cost per unit of family i in period t
m_i: hours required to produce one unit of product family i
rm_t: total availability of regular hours in period t
om_t: total availability of overtime hours in period t

Decision variables

X_{it}: number of family units i to be produced in period t
I_{its}: number of inventory units for family i at the end of period t under scenario s
U_{its}: unmet demand of family i in period t under scenario s
O_t: overtime hours used during period t

It is important to note that decision variables X_{it} and O_t have no scenario suffix and must be anticipated within the initial stages of the planning horizon. In such a scenario, the only *recourse* action available is to build an inventory or allow an unmet demand to hedge against the uncertainty. Then, the corresponding stochastic programming model with *recourse* is given by the following minimization problem:

$$\text{Min} \sum_{i=1}^{I}\sum_{t=1}^{T} c_{it}X_{it} + \sum_{t=1}^{T} o_t O_t + \sum_{s=1}^{S} p_s \left[\sum_{i=1}^{I}\sum_{t=1}^{T} h_{it} I_{its} + \sum_{i=1}^{I}\sum_{t=1}^{T} f_{it} U_{its} \right] \quad (6.19)$$

s.t.

$$X_{it} + I_{i(t-1)s} - I_{its} + U_{its} = d_{its}, \quad t = 1, 2, ..., T; \; i = 1, 2, ..., I; \; s = 1, ..., S \quad (6.20)$$

$$\sum_{i=1}^{I} m_i X_{it} \leq rm_t + O_t, \quad t = 1, 2, ..., T \quad (6.21)$$

$$O_t \leq (om)_t, \quad t = 1, 2, ..., T \quad (6.22)$$

$$X_{it}, I_{its}, U_{its}, O_t \geq 0, \quad t = 1, 2, ..., T; \; i = 1, 2, ..., I; \; s = 1, ..., S \quad (6.23)$$

$$I \in N, \quad U \in N \quad (6.24)$$

In this model, the objective function in Equation 6.19 minimizes the total cost, defined as the addition of the costs of production, hours, and recourses, as well as the expected inventory and shortage demand cost, which defines the *recourse* cost. Equation 6.20 establishes that the required demand for each product family must be satisfied by production and inventory, however allowing the eventuality of this demand. In these equations, I_{i0s} denotes the initial inventory level, for each family i and scenario s, for which we naturally assume are identical within all scenarios of a given family. Constraints (6.21) correspond to capacity constraints where the total time requirement for producing the different items, at a rate of m_i hours per unit of family product i, can never exceed the time availability in regular and overtime hours. Constraints (6.22) consider the upper limits in the utilization of overtime hours. Constraints (6.23) are the nonnegativity constraints for the different decision variables. Finally, constraints (6.24) impose *non-anticipativity constraints* that guarantee that the solution obtained by the model does not depend on information that is not yet available, at any given time in the planning horizon. More precisely, if two different scenarios s and s' are identical up to time period τ, on the basis of the available information on them at time period T, then until time period τ the decisions I_{its}, U_{its} and $I_{its'}$, $U_{its'}$ must also be identical for $1 \le t \le T$.

The resulting model is actually a *multistage* stochastic program with simple recourse, where production and overtime hour variables are fixed in nature, and their values are not conditioned by any particular realizations of uncertain demand. On the other hand, the inventory and unmet demand decisions are the *recourse* decision variables that represent the reactive decisions to adjust to each stage in recourse for the decision made by the input value parameters following the realization of the uncertainty.

First Disaggregation Level: Item Production Quantities for the Corresponding Family in the Month

At this level, volumes obtained during each period within the aggregation plan are disaggregated into production plans for each item in the family product, considered important in order to minimize the available inventory levels because of their financial impact on the income balance.

The variables in this model are units of items to be produced, the available inventory, and the unmet demand units for each month. The model considers the demand requirements for each item and the coherence between family decisions in the aggregate plan (inventory levels and product family quantities).

To define first stochastic disaggregated model, the following extra notation is considered:

Parameters

$J(i)$: set of items belonging to product family i
d_{jts}: demand for item $j \in J(i)$ in period t under scenario s

Decision variables

Y_{jt}: number of units to be produced of item j in period t
I_{jts}: number of inventory units of item j at the end of period t under scenario s
V_{jts}: unmet demand level of unit j in period t under scenario s

Following, the optimal production policy obtained in the aggregated plan for each product family is disaggregated separately for each family i, and for every period (one month) t in the more immediate planning period, using a rolling horizon strategy. It is important to emphasize that in the in-house production decision, the variable Y_{jt} has no scenario suffix and must be anticipated at the beginning of each month, defining the *first-stage* decision variable in the proposed model. On the other hand, the *recourse* or *second-stage* action is given by the inventory and the unmet demand to hedge against uncertainties, whose values depend on the corresponding scenario realization in response to the production decision.

Then, a corresponding two-stage stochastic program with *recourse* is given through the following minimization problem:

$$
\text{Min} \sum_{s=1}^{S} p_s \left[\sum_{j \in J(i)} \left[\frac{X_{it}^* + \sum_{j \in J(i)} (I_{j(t-1)s})}{\sum_{j \in J(i)} d_{jts}} - \frac{Y_{jt} + I_{j(t-1)s}}{d_{jts}} \right]^2 \right] \tag{6.25}
$$

s.t.

$$
Y_{jt} + I_{j(t-1)s} + V_{jts} = d_{jts} + I_{jts}, \quad j \in J(i), \quad s = 1, \ldots, S \tag{6.26}
$$

$$
\sum_{j \in J(i)} Y_{jt} = X_{it}^* \tag{6.27}
$$

$$
\sum_{j \in J(i)} V_{jts} = U_{its}^*, \quad s = 1, \ldots, S \tag{6.28}
$$

$$
Y_{jt} \geq 0, \quad I_{jts} \geq 0, \quad V_{jts} \geq 0 \quad j \in J(i), \quad s = 1, \ldots, S \tag{6.29}
$$

$$
I \in N, \quad V \in N \tag{6.30}
$$

In this model, the quadratic objective function in Equation 6.25 minimizes the expected total variation between the available items for each product, with respect to the available units in the corresponding product family. This function is defined by the expected value of the quadratic expressions sum, where each expression corresponds to the difference between two terms. The first term accounts for the ratio between available quantities (family products volumes and used stocks) and the aggregated modified demand for the month. The second term is of the same rate but for the corresponding family. Constraints (6.26) establish that the required demand for each item must be satisfied using production and inventory, however allowing the eventuality of unmet demand units; considering the same production decision variable for each scenario realization. Constraints (6.27) and (6.28) impose that the total number of produced items and the total allowable unmet demands units must be equal to the family level of production and the unmet demand level according to the aggregated plan, respectively. Constraints (6.29) are the nonnegativity constraints for the different decision variables. Finally, constraints (6.30) impose the *non-anticipativity constraints* ensuring that the solution obtained by the model at the first stage must be identical for all the first stage, to define an implementable policy according to the scenario tree used in the aggregated plan.

Second Disaggregation Level: MPS

To achieve the final objective of this proposal, at this level, the second disaggregation model attempts to obtain weekly production quantities for each item, considering the optimal solutions of monthly productions reached in models (6.25) through (6.30) as the input data. This new model includes weekly production decisions, and a decision variable defined by scenarios, not restrained in sign that represents the recourse decision to confront different demand scenarios monthly. The optimal solution takes into account the expected set up incurred in to produce each item (for the respective week) finding weekly balance decisions.

The second level of disaggregation considers the following extra notation:

Parameters

$W(t)$: set of weeks for the corresponding month t
s_{jt}: set up cost for item j during month t
d_{jtws}: demand for item j during week $w \in W(t)$ under scenario s

Decision variables

Z_{jtw}: number of item units j to be produced in week $w \in W(t)$
I_{jtws}: units of inventory/backlogged demand of item j in week $w \in W(t)$ under scenario s

$$\text{Min} \sum_{s=1}^{S} p_s \left[\sum_{w \in W(t)} \frac{(s_{jt} * d_{jtws})}{Z_{jtw}} \right] \qquad (6.31)$$

s.t.

$$Z_{jtw} + I_{jt(w-1)s} - I_{jtws} = d_{jtws}, \quad w \in W(t), \quad s = 1, \ldots, S \qquad (6.32)$$

$$\sum_{w \in W(t)} Z_{jtw} = Y_{jt}^* \qquad (6.33)$$

$$Z_{jtw} \geq 0, \quad w \in W(t) \qquad (6.34)$$

$$I \in N \qquad (6.35)$$

In this model, the convex function in Equation 6.31 minimizes the expected set up cost for each item during a period t (month). Constraints (6.32) establish that the required demand during week $w \in W(t)$ for each item must be satisfied using production and inventory, however allowing the eventuality of backlogging, considering the same unrestricted decision variable I_{jtws}. Constraint (6.33) impose that the total number of items produced during the month t must be equal to the level of production according to the decisions in the first level of disaggregation. Constraints (6.34) are the nonnegativity constraints for the production decision variables. Finally, constraint (6.35) impose the *non-anticipativity constraints* for the inventory/backlogged-demand decision variables.

Case Study

The proposed methodology is applied to a case study using data from an electric appliance manufacturing plant considering three refrigerator families. The items are refrigerators (final products) with specific characteristics such as color, type of door, height, accessories and performance. On the other hand, set refrigerators agree the corresponding families. Each family shares a common setup cost for the manufacturing setup. Scale economies are accomplished by jointly replenishing items belonging to the same family. The proposed models are tested for 10 items that are grouped into three families, according to Figure 6.2.

The planning horizon has 12 months, where the first three are the frozen horizon considered in the disaggregation models. The second disaggregation level is made for 12 weeks, corresponding to the first three months of the frozen horizon (see Figure 6.3).

The different models are solved using AMPL (Fourer et al. 2002) with CPLEX 11.0 linear and quadratic solutions for the first and second model, respectively, and with MINOS 5.5 as a general nonlinear optimization solver for the third model, on a desktop computer with a processor of 1.8 GHz and 1 GB of RAM. The methodology applied to each procedure is showed in the flowchart Figure 6.4.

The stochastic programming problem considers nine scenarios defined through an arborescent tree structure. Figure 6.5 more clearly exemplifies the scenarios resolved in the stochastic model.

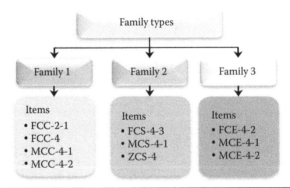

Figure 6.2 Families and items for the disaggregation model.

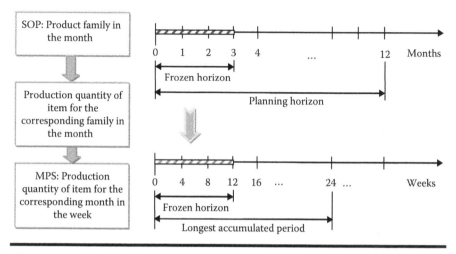

Figure 6.3 Planning horizon and disaggregation structure for the analyzed problem.

Tables 6.1 through 6.3 show the results for the aggregate production plan of family 2 that will input data for the first disaggregation level, that is, inventory, unmet, and family production quantities for the corresponding month. In this case, models (6.19) through (6.24) has a total of 696 decision variables and 375 equality and inequality constraints, without considering the nonnegativity conditions of the different variables. The execution time for determining the aggregated

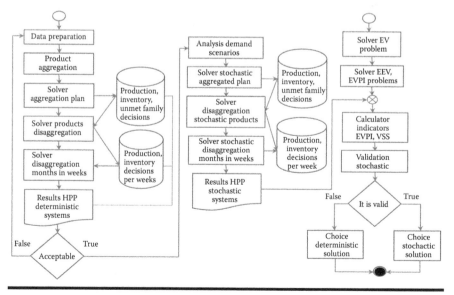

Figure 6.4 Methodology flowchart work.

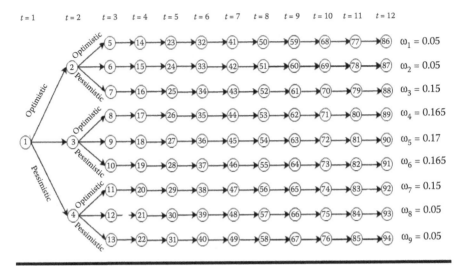

Figure 6.5 Scenario tree used in the stochastic model of hierarchical production.

plan was around 84 seconds. It can be observed that the family production quantities obtained in this example vary from 2.500 to 3.750 approximately.

The following results (Tables 6.4 through 6.6) correspond to models (6.25) through (6.30) of the first disaggregation level, where it only shows the three-month frozen horizon for family 2. In this case, the model has a total of 57 decision variables and 37 constraints, not considering the nonnegativity constraints and the non-anticipativity conditions on the resource variables that are not the same in number depending on the month. The execution time for each instance was approximately 1 second and required approximately 30 iterations using CPLEX 11.0. It is possible to see that constraint (6.27) may be verified as FCS-4-3 + MCS-4-1 + ZCS-4 = 1260 + 1575 + 200 = 3035. Here, 3035 units is the family product quantities for month 1. Then, this constraint is accomplished for the obtained results, that is, coherence between the aggregate production plan and the first disaggregation level.

The disaggregation procedure is made using the demand scenarios (see Table 6.7) for different items per family. This data, along with other decisions obtained in the first level disaggregation model, are introduced in the final disaggregation level according to the tree of the first month (frozen horizon) for families 1 and 3. The simulation model provides the results specified in Table 6.8.

Figure 6.6 shows the behavior disaggregation of item production quantities monthly per week. It is possible to observe that the production levels for the first month of refrigerator ZSC-4 is almost stable however, when production begins during the fifth week, the production level increases to satisfy the demand volumes. This behavior also occurs for other refrigerators. If we look at the production levels for each item of family 1 and 3, respectively (Table 6.8), we can conclude that the

Table 6.1 Data Input of Demand and Results of Production Quantities, Inventory Quantities, and Unmet for Scenarios 1, 2, and 3 of Family 2 in the Respective Months

Scenario	1				2				3			
Month	d_{its}	X_{its}	I_{its}	U_{its}	d_{its}	X_{its}	I_{its}	U_{its}	d_{its}	X_{its}	I_{its}	U_{its}
1	3035	3035	0	0	3035	3035	0	0	3035	3035	0	0
2	3248	2951	0	297	3248	2951	0	297	3248	2951	0	297
3	4182	3484	0	698	3834	3484	0	350	3484	3484	0	0
4	4394	2655	0	1739	4028	2655	0	1373	3661	2655	0	1006
5	3947	3289	0	658	3619	3289	0	330	3289	3289	0	0
6	4641	3154	0	1487	4254	3154	0	1100	3867	3154	0	713
7	3666	2750	0	916	3361	2750	0	611	3054	2750	0	304
8	3464	2599	0	865	3176	2599	0	577	2886	2599	0	287
9	3422	2851	0	571	3137	2851	0	286	2851	2851	0	0
10	3550	2926	0	624	3254	2926	0	328	2957	2926	0	31
11	4182	2591	0	1591	3834	2591	0	1243	3484	2591	0	893
12	4098	3074	0	1024	3757	3074	0	683	3414	3074	0	340

Table 6.2 Data Input of Demand and Results of Production Quantities, Inventory Quantities, and Unmet for Scenarios 4, 5, and 6 of Family 2 in the Respective Months

Scenario		4				5				6		
Month	d_{its}	X_{its}	I_{its}	U_{its}	d_{its}	X_{its}	I_{its}	U_{its}	d_{its}	X_{its}	I_{its}	U_{its}
1	3035	3035	0	0	3035	3035	0	0	3035	3035	0	0
2	2951	2951	0	0	2951	2951	0	0	2951	2951	0	0
3	3834	3484	0	350	3484	3484	0	0	3137	3484	0	0
4	4028	2655	0	1373	3661	2655	0	1006	3296	2655	347	294
5	3619	3289	0	330	3289	3289	0	0	2961	3289	0	0
6	4254	3154	0	1100	3867	3154	0	713	3482	3154	328	0
7	3361	2750	0	611	3054	2750	0	304	2750	2750	0	0
8	3176	2599	0	577	2886	2599	0	287	2599	2599	0	0
9	3137	2851	0	286	2851	2851	0	0	2568	2851	0	0
10	3254	2926	0	328	2957	2926	0	31	2663	2926	283	0
11	3834	2591	0	1243	3484	2591	0	893	3137	2591	546	0
12	3757	3074	0	683	3414	3074	0	340	3074	3074	0	0

Table 6.3 Data Input of Demand and Results of Production Quantities, Inventory Quantities, and Unmet for Scenarios 7, 8, and 9 of Family 2 in the Respective Months

Scenario	7				8				9			
Month	d_{its}	X_{its}	I_{its}	U_{its}	d_{its}	X_{its}	I_{its}	U_{its}	d_{its}	X_{its}	I_{its}	U_{its}
1	3035	3035	0	0	3035	3035	0	0	3035	3035	0	0
2	2657	2951	294	0	2657	2951	294	0	2657	2951	294	0
3	3484	3484	294	0	3137	3484	641	0	2788	3484	990	0
4	3661	2655	0	712	3296	2655	0	0	2929	2655	716	0
5	3289	3289	0	0	2961	3289	328	0	2632	3289	1373	0
6	3867	3154	0	713	3482	3154	0	0	3095	3154	1432	0
7	3054	2750	0	304	2750	2750	0	0	2444	2750	1738	0
8	2886	2599	0	287	2599	2599	0	0	2310	2599	2027	0
9	2851	2851	0	0	2568	2851	283	0	2283	2851	2595	0
10	2957	2926	0	31	2663	2926	546	0	2367	2926	3154	0
11	3484	2591	0	893	3137	2591	0	0	2789	2591	2956	0
12	3414	3074	0	340	3074	3074	0	0	2733	3074	3297	0

Table 6.4 Data Input of Demand and Results for the First Disaggregation Level: Item Production Quantities, Inventory Quantities, and Unmet Demand for Frozen Planning for Scenarios 1, 2, and 3, Respectively, of Family 2

Scenario	1				2				3			
Item	d_{jts}	Y_{jt}	I_{jts}	V_{jts}	d_{jts}	Y_{jt}	I_{jts}	V_{jts}	d_{jts}	Y_{jt}	I_{jts}	V_{jts}
FCS-4-3	1260	1260	0	0	1260	1260	0	0	1260	1260	0	0
MCS-4-1	1575	1575	0	0	1575	1575	0	0	1575	1575	0	0
ZCS-4	1260	200	0	0	1260	200	0	0	1260	200	0	0
FCS-4-3	1082	983	0	99	1082	983	0	99	1082	983	0	99
MCS-4-1	1733	1575	0	158	1733	1575	0	158	1733	1575	0	158
ZCS-4	433	393	0	40	433	393	0	40	433	393	0	40
FCS-4-3	1636	1363	0	273	1500	1363	0	137	1363	1363	0	0
MCS-4-1	1575	1575	0	315	1733	1575	0	158	1575	1575	0	0
ZCS-4	546	546	0	110	601	546	0	55	546	546	0	0

Table 6.5   Data Input of Demand and Results for the First Disaggregation Level: Item Production Quantities, Inventory Quantities, and Unmet Demand for Frozen Planning for Scenarios 4, 5, and 6, Respectively, of Family 2

Scenario	4				5				6			
Item	d_{jts}	Y_{jt}	I_{jts}	V_{jts}	d_{jts}	Y_{jt}	I_{jts}	V_{jts}	d_{jts}	Y_{jt}	I_{jts}	V_{jts}
FCS-4-3	1260	1260	0	0	1260	1260	0	0	1260	1260	0	0
MCS-4-1	1575	1575	0	0	1575	1575	0	0	1575	1575	0	0
ZCS-4	1260	200	0	0	1260	200	0	0	1260	200	0	0
FCS-4-3	983	983	0	0	983	983	0	0	983	983	0	0
MCS-4-1	1575	1575	0	0	1575	1575	0	0	1575	1575	0	0
ZCS-4	393	393	0	0	393	393	0	0	393	393	0	0
FCS-4-3	1500	1363	0	137	1363	1363	0	0	1227	1363	136	0
MCS-4-1	1733	1575	0	158	1575	1575	0	0	1418	1575	157	0
ZCS-4	601	546	0	55	546	546	0	0	492	546	54	0

Table 6.6 Data Input of Demand and Results for the First Disaggregation Level: Item Production Quantities, Inventory Quantities, and Unmet Demand for Frozen Planning for Scenarios 7, 8, and 9, Respectively, of Family 2

Scenario	7				8				9			
Item	d_{jts}	Y_{jt}	I_{jts}	V_{jts}	d_{jts}	Y_{jt}	I_{jts}	V_{jts}	d_{jts}	Y_{jt}	I_{jts}	V_{jts}
FCS-4-3	1260	1260	0	0	1260	1260	0	0	1260	1260	0	0
MCS-4-1	1575	1575	0	0	1575	1575	0	0	1575	1575	0	0
ZCS-4	1260	200	0	0	1260	200	0	0	1260	200	0	0
FCS-4-3	885	983	98	0	885	983	98	0	885	983	98	0
MCS-4-1	1418	1575	157	0	1418	1575	157	0	1418	1575	157	0
ZCS-4	354	393	39	0	354	393	39	0	354	393	39	0
FCS-4-3	1363	1363	98	0	1227	1363	234	0	1091	1363	370	0
MCS-4-1	1575	1575	157	0	1418	1575	314	0	1260	1575	472	0
ZCS-4	546	546	39	0	492	546	93	0	437	546	148	0

Table 6.7 Demand Scenarios for Item FCS 4-3 in the Corresponding Weeks

Month	Week No	Scenario								
		1	2	3	4	5	6	7	8	9
1	1	441,0	441,0	441,0	441,0	441,0	441,0	441,0	441,0	441,0
	2	378,0	378,0	378,0	378,0	378,0	378,0	378,0	378,0	378,0
	3	252,0	252,0	252,0	252,0	252,0	252,0	252,0	252,0	252,0
	4	189,0	189,0	189,0	189,0	189,0	189,0	189,0	189,0	189,0
2	5	378,7	378,7	378,7	344,05	344,05	344,05	309,75	309,75	309,75
	6	324,6	324,6	324,6	294,9	294,9	294,9	265,5	265,5	265,5
	7	216,4	216,4	216,4	196,6	196,6	196,6	177	177	177
	8	162,3	162,3	162,3	147,45	147,45	147,45	132,75	132,75	132,75
3	9	572,6	525	477,05	525	477,05	429,45	477,05	429,45	381,85
	10	490,8	450	408,9	450	408,9	368,1	408,9	368,1	327,3
	11	327,2	300	272,6	300	272,6	245,4	272,6	245,4	218,2
	12	245,4	225	204,45	225	204,45	184,05	204,45	184,05	163,65

Table 6.8 Results of the Second Disaggregation Level for the First Three Months of Families 1 and 3

	Family 1			Serial No		Family 3	
Week No	FCC-2-1	FCC-4	MCC-4-1	MCC-4-2	FCE-4-2	MCE-4-1	MCE 4-2
1	110,4970	472,2640	110,4970	566,677	314,9090	200,7140	131,7780
2	102,2260	437,1580	102,2260	524,567	291,4750	185,7510	121,9280
3	83,2841	356,7540	83,2841	428,124	237,8050	151,4820	99,3705
4	71,9921	308,8240	71,9921	370,632	205,8110	131,0530	85,9234
5	117,9110	394,6300	117,9110	632,113	262,1580	210,9050	138,6710
6	109,0900	365,2820	109,0900	585,149	242,6370	195,1860	128,3110
7	88,8880	298,0680	88,8880	477,588	197,9290	159,1850	104,5820
8	76,8453	258,0000	76,8453	413,470	171,2770	137,7240	90,4364
9	139,8700	513,0270	84,1216	822,342	350,4200	281,9630	185,0970
10	129,4210	474,8960	77,8073	761,266	324,3520	260,9730	171,2920
11	105,4880	387,5680	63,3459	621,388	264,6490	212,9000	139,6760
12	91,2212	335,5090	54,7252	538,004	229,0590	184,2430	120,8290

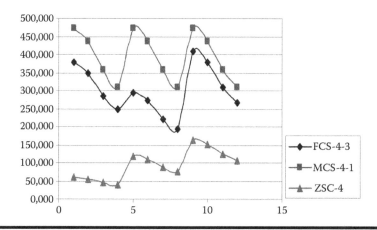

Figure 6.6   Behavior of MPS for family 2 (item FCS-4-3, MCS-4-1, and ZSC-4) in the first 12 weeks once the disaggregation process is applied.

production levels change and the production volumes for the first week of each corresponding month are always higher when compared with other weeks.

A stochastic program is usually much more difficult to solve than a deterministic model obtained by simply replacing the random variables with their expected value, or by a particular scenario realization, such as the worst case or most probable scenario. For that reason, it is important to know if the solution obtained from the mentioned deterministic models are nearly optimal or totally inaccurate. From a mathematical point of view, there are two measures that clarify this question: the expected value of perfect information (EVPI) and the value of the stochastic solution (VSS) (Birge and Louveaux 2011). In this case study, we obtain the EVPI that measures the maximum amount a decision maker would be prepared to pay in return for complete and accurate information regarding the future. The EVPI is, by definition, the difference between the optimal value of the recourse problem (RP), also referred to as the here-and-now solution, and the expected value of the objectives value function of models (6.19) through (6.24) solved for each scenario realization separately, usually referred to as the wait-and-see solution (WS). Table 6.9 shows the optimal values necessary to compute the EVPI measure.

According to EVPI = RP−WS = USD 322.838, the firm would greatly benefit from perfect information regarding future demand, and the obtained amount is how much the firm would be prepared to pay during the 1-year planning horizon.

Conclusions and Extensions

We proposed a methodology to disaggregate a production plan into an MPS. The structure utilized, and the models formulated, ensure coherence between aggregated production planning into two disaggregation levels, allowing to obtain a

Table 6.9 Optimal Values Models (6.19) through (6.24)

Scenario	USD
Scenario 1	12,976,072
Scenario 2	11,694,569
Scenario 3	10,449,980
Scenario 4	11,617,461
Scenario 5	10,374,813
Scenario 6	9,261,384
Scenario 7	10,300,499
Scenario 8	9,193,745
Scenario 9	8,247,766
Wait-and-see (WS)	10,426,907
Recourse model (RP)	10,749,745

different detail plan per week. Moreover, it is shown to be suitable to deal with the uncertainty present in future demands by using a stochastic programming model with recourse that provides an optimal production decision for the immediate time horizon (frozen horizon), which does not depend on every particular scenario considered within the problem.

The study case shows that for small and medium instances, the proposed models could be easily solved by commercial optimization solvers. However, if one intends to use this methodology considering the large number of scenarios, it would require development of more suitable numerical strategies in order to solve the resulting stochastic program with recourse, which is beyond the scope of this chapter.

The methodology used in this study may be applied directly to supply chain management.

Acknowledgments

The authors acknowledge the financial support from the Dirección General de Investigación y Postgrado of the Universidad del Bío-Bío, Grant No 060609 3/R, and from the Dirección General de Investigación, Innovación y Postgrado of the Universidad Técnica Federico Santa María, Grant USM 28.15.20.

References

Aghezzaf, El. H., Sitompul, C., and Najid, M., 2010, Models for robust tactical planning in multi-stage production systems with uncertain demands, *Computers & Operations Research*, 37(5), 880–889.

Alonso-Ayuso, A., Escudero, L., and Ortuño, M. T., 2005, Modelling production planning and scheduling under uncertainty, in S. W. Wallace and W. T. Ziemba (Eds.), *Applications of Stochastic Programming*, SIAM Publications, Philadelphia.

Axsäter, S. and Jönsson, H., 1984, Aggregation and disaggregation in herarchical production planning, *European Journal of Operational Research*, 17(3), 338–350.

Bang, J. and Kim, Y., 2010, Hierarchical production planning for semiconductor wafer fabrication based on linear programming and discrete event simulation, *IEEE Transactions on Automation Science and Engineering*, 7(2), 326–336.

Bertsimas, D. and Sim, M., 2004, The price of robustness, *Operations Research*, 52(1), 35–53.

Birge, J. R. and Louveaux, F., 2011, *Introduction to Stochastic Programming*, 2nd ed., Springer, New York.

Bitran, G. R. and Hax, A. C., 1977, On design of hierarchical production planning systems, *Decisions Sciences*, 8(1), 28–55.

Bitran, G. R. and Hax, A. C., 1981, Disaggregation and resource allocation using convex knapsack problems with bounded variables, *Management Science*, 27(4), 431–441.

Bitran, G. R., Haas, E. A., and Hax, A. C., 1981, Hierarchical production planning: A single stage system, *Operation Research*, 29(4), 717–743.

Buzacott, J. A., 2013, Then and now—50 years of production research, *International Journal of Production Research*, 51(23–24), 6756–6768.

Caravilla, M. A. and De Sousa, J. P., 1996, Hierarchical production planning in a Make-To-Order company: A case study, *European Journal of Operation Research*, 86(1), 43–56.

Dantzig, G. B., 1955, Linear programming under uncertainty, *Management Science*, 1(3), 197–206.

Erromdhani, R., Eddaly, M., and Rebai, A., 2012, Hierarchical production planning with flexibility in agroalimentary environment: A case study, *Journal of Intelligent Manufacturing*, 23(3), 811–819.

Erschler, J., Fontan, G., and Mercé, C., 1986, Consistency of the disaggregation process in hierarchical planning, *Operations Research*, 34(3), 464–469.

Escudero, L., Kamesan, P., King, A., and Wets, R., 1993, Production planning via scenarios modelling, *Annals of Operations Research*, 43(6), 311–335.

Fourer, R., Gay, D. M., and Kernigham, B. W., 2002, *AMPL: A Modeling Language for Mathematical Programming*, 2nd ed., Cengage Learning, Boston.

Gassmann, H. I. and Ziemba, W. T., 2012, *Stochastic Programming. Applications in Finance, Energy, Planning and Logistics*, World Scientific Publishing Company, Singapore.

Gfrerer, H. and Zäpfel, G., 1995, Hierarchical model for production planning in the case of uncertain demand, *European Journal of Operational Research*, 86(1), 142–161.

Giard, V., 2003, *Gestion de la production et des flux*, 3rd ed., Economica, Paris.

Hax, A. C. and Meal, H. C., 1975, Hierarchical production planning systems, in M. A. Geisler (Ed.), *Studies Management Sciences, Vol. I, Logistics*, North Holland-American Elsevier, New York, pp. 53–69.

Higle, J. L., 2005, *Stochastic Programming: Optimization When Uncertainty Matters*, Tutorial in Operations Research, INFORMS, New Orleans.

King, A. J. and Wallace, S. W., 2012, *Modeling with Stochastic Programming*, Springer, New York.

Lario, E. F. C., Vicens, S. E., and Ros, L., 1994, Application of an MRP matrix-based hierarchical planning model to a furniture Company, *Production Planning and Controll*, 5(6), 562–574.

Laserre, J. B. and Mercé, C., 1990, Robust hierarchical production planning under uncertainty, *Annals of Operations Research*, 26(1), 73–87.

Madansky, A., 1960, Inequalities for stochastic linear programming problems, *Management Science*, 6(2), 197–204.

Mercé, C., 1987, Cohérence des décisions en planification hiérarchisée, *Thèse de Doctorat d'Etat*, Université Paul Sabatier, Toulouse.

Mula, J., Poler, R., García-Sabater, J. P., and Lario, F. C., 2006, Models for production planning under uncertainty: A review, *International Journal of Production Economics*, 103(1), 271–285.

Neureuther, B., Polak, G., and Sanders, N., 2004, A hierarchical production plan for a make-to-order steel fabrication plant, *Production Planning & Control*, 15(3), 324–335.

Ortiz-Araya, V., 2005, Proposition d'un modèle de désagrégation pour un plan tactique stable dans le contexte de Chaîne Logistique et de l'usage d'un APS, *Thèse de Doctorat*, Université Henri Poincaré, Nancy I. France.

Ortiz-Araya, V., Albornoz, V. M., and Bravo, D. A., 2015, A hierarchical production planning in a supply chain with seasonal demand products, *DYNA Management*, 3(1), 1–15.

Ortiz-Araya, V., Thomas, A., and Hutt, C., 2004, Proposition of a disaggregation method for robust tactical planning, in G. Lefranc (Ed.), *Proceeding Third Conference on Management and Control Production and Logistics*, pp. 291–296, Universidad de las Américas, Santiago de Chile.

Özdamar, L., Atli, A. Ö., and Bozyel, M. A., 1996, Heuristic family disaggregation techniques for hierarchical production planning systems, *International Journal of Production Research*, 34(9), 2613–2628.

Özdamar, L., Yetis, N., and Atli, A. Ö., 1997, A modified hierarchical production planning system integrated with MRP: A case study, *Production Planning & Control*, 1(1), 72–87.

Pflug, G. Ch. and Pichler, A., 2014, *Multistage Stochastic Optimization*, Springer, New York.

Qui, M., Fredendall, L., and Zhu, Z., 2001, Application of hierarchical production planning in a multiproduct, multi-machine environment, *International Journal of Production Research*, 39(13), 2803–2816.

Ruszczynski, A., 2003, Decomposition methods, in A. Ruszczynski and A. Shapiro (Eds.), *Stochastic Programming*, pp. 141–211, Elsevier Science, Amsterdam.

Vicens, E., Alemany, M. E., Andres, C., and Guarch, J. J., 2001, A design and application methodology for hierarchical production planning decision support systems in an enterprise integration context, *International Journal of Production Economics*, 74(1), 5–20.

Wallace, S. W. and Ziemba, W. T. (Eds.), 2005, *Applications of Stochastic Programming*, MPS-SIAM Series on Optimization, Philadelphia.

Wu, D. and Ierapetritou, M., 2007, Hierarchical approach for production planning and scheduling under uncertainty, *Chemical Engineering and Processing*, 46(1), 1129–1140.

Chapter 7

Big Data and Analytics for Consumer Price Index Estimation

Patricio Cofre and Gerzo Gallardo

Contents

Summary..131
Introduction..132
Methodology...133
Results...135
Conclusions and Recommendations..137
Reference 139

Summary

This chapter will walk you through the methodology and experiment results that allow one to be confident in using the consumer price index based on scraped price data, by showing how the mathematical models can address the method weaknesses, and what new opportunities this new method offers. The technology to periodically record online prices on a large scale is now becoming widely available. The methodology of data scraping provides an opportunity to improve statistical data and its quality, with the reduction of the overall workload for data collection.

Introduction

Inflation is one of the economic phenomena that receive particular attention from public policy actors, because of its effects in the allocation of resources, the distribution of income, economic development, and thus on the well-being of the population. Therefore, having an early and reliable vision of the inflation allows one to define appropriate anti-inflationary policies, achieving stability in the purchasing power of the currency.

In the financial planning of countries, companies, and even individuals, inflation represents a subject of paramount importance. At the level of nations, many of its main indicators are indexed to inflation, such as the estimate of annual real growth. At the level of companies, there are several industries for which accurate and current prices information is critical for decision making. This is the case in the financial markets, real estate, and retail sectors, among others. Investment banks require forecasts of changes in the consumer price index (CPI) to decide positions with respect to different investment instruments. The real estate industry needs to know the variations in the values per square meter of real estate in different areas in planning their next projects. In the retail, prices are crucial to monitor the competition, to take more aggressive positions (either upward or downward) or maintain their prices. Finally, at the individual level, inflation represents the deterioration of the yield of our income to obtain goods or services in the market.

The indicator for measuring inflation is the CPI, which quantifies the evolution of the prices of a set of goods acquired by households in the urban area.

CPI is traditionally estimated through a complex process of field and phone-based price collection of goods and services, commonly found in an urban family market basket. These prices are weighted according to their importance in the basket, and then the index is calculated.

This chapter covers a method to use Big Data to estimate the index, by using high-frequency scraped prices data from a broad number of online retails.

The strengths of the traditional method are that it can capture prices of goods and specially services that are hard to find online. One weakness is that the method is highly manual, so it can only cover the goods of the basket, and the frequency is rarely higher than monthly.

The strengths of the scraped data method are that it can cover exhaustively all the goods available online, allowing to further calculate the CPI for different groups of the population, such as the rural population, the elderly, and the poor, among others, and not only the average urban family. Moreover, the frequency of data gathering allows one to calculate the index more often, and thus better supporting decision making. A known weakness of this method is the difficulty to include services prices, since they usually require a quotation process.

Halfway between these two methods are the scanner data, or data capturing services, such as ACNielsen (Cavallo, 2016), that can cover a range of goods larger than

Table 7.1   Different Data Sources

	Traditional Method	*Scraped Data*	*Scanner Data*
Collection frequency	Monthly	Daily	Weekly
All products in retail	No	Yes	No
Real-time availability	No	Yes	No
Services availability	High	Low	Low
Collection cost	High	Low	High
Geo-localized results	No	Yes	Yes

those available in the basket, or startups such as Premise* that aggregate prices collaboratively collected by individuals that snapshot price tags throughout the world.

A drawback of this last method is that it still requires a decent amount of manual operations that might present some of the following problems:

1. The delivery of the information is not timely
2. The solutions are not scalable when required to generate analysis of historical price fluctuations
3. The data may contain errors by the way they are captured
4. More time is required to clean and prepare the data analysis

The main differences between scraped data and the two other sources of price information commonly used in studies of price dynamics, CPI, and scanner data, are summarized in Table 7.1.

This chapter will walk you through the methodology and experiment results that allow us to be confident in using the CPI based on scraped prices data, by showing how the mathematical models can address the method weaknesses, and what new opportunities this new method offers.

Methodology

A large and growing number of retails are posting prices online all over the world, either to sell online or to advertise prices for potential customers during their online research.

Since there is no historical record of these prices, they need to be continually collected over time.

The technology to periodically record online prices on a large scale is now becoming widely available. Using a combination of web programming languages,

---

* http://www.premise.com/

we built automated procedures that scan the code of publicly available webpages every day, identifying the relevant pieces of information, and store the data in a database. This data is commonly called scraped data.

The scraping methodology works in three steps. First, at a fixed time each day, a software downloads a selected list of public webpages where the product and price information are shown. These pages are individually retrieved using the same web address (URL) every day. Second, the underlying code is analyzed to locate each piece of relevant information. This is performed by using special characters in the code that identify the start and end of each variable, and have been placed by the page programmers to give the website a particular look and feel. For example, prices are usually shown with a dollar sign in front of them and enclosed within a <price>and</price> tags. Third, the software stores the scraped information in a database that contains one record per product per day. These variables include the product's price, the date, category information, and an indicator of whether the item was on sale or not (if available).

Other technology widely available that has made this method possible is the processing power of the Cloud that allows to have, for a required time window, of computational capacity rarely found in Latin-American companies.

Given all of this, it is possible to generate indicators and reports, and providing access in real time, enabling them to perform further alerts and predictive analysis.

The methodology of scraping includes a study of the price variation, and how it correlates with the respective components of the CPI; thus it is possible to determine the relevant ones.

Price analyses include a sample of product per category; for example, in the food category, in the so-called meat products and specifically beef, only the varieties of greater representability in the family shopping basket are selected. Scraping methodology collects the census of beef by-products and, given that, in the analysis stage, debugging is performed, by leaving out those by-products that do not show real correlation with the variations in the prices of beef. This can be extrapolated to the entire range of activities and products that the methodology of scraping considers.

In the debugging process described above, simple correlation tests are performed, where it is possible to get positive or negative results. For our analysis, in a first stage we seek for high positive correlations, since it would indicate that the variations between the by-product picked up by the scraping register a direct relation in comparison with the category CPI. On the contrary, if the by-product collected through scraping has negative correlation, variation on it would be contrary to the CPI variation, and therefore would be initially discarded as an essential by-product.

From the above, it is possible to separate items that do have high positive correlation from those that do not, and therefore track those prices that include a real approach to what has been officially published.

Once debugging is complete, one of the analyses that we perform is the daily volatility measurement, to identify the possible peak in a few specific days, in order to perform additional purge stages.

Finally, it is possible to make predictions based on the varieties of products that register high and robust correlation with the category CPI. Then, through time series algorithms such as ARIMA, SARIMA, and ESARIMA it will be possible to extrapolate monthly fluctuations based on daily prices.

Results

The solution has managed to obtain better information and focus more on the analysis, identifying opportunities for improvement in their forecasts and providing feedback to the system to have new indexes online automatically. Price data from 98 items, comparable to those in the basket, were considered, processing since November 2013 more than 100 GB of raw data during the first 18 months of operation.

Scraped data, so far, has allowed us to generate projections of CPI calculation with errors less than 5% compared with the official source. In Figures 7.1 through 7.4, comparative results between scraped data and the official source for four products of the market basket are given.

Ground transportation represents a critical item for the families in Latin America, since it gives large coverage in the region in affordable prices. As shown in Figure 7.1, all the directions of change are captured correctly, and fitted with decent precision; the amount of the month to month change is in the index.

The difficulty, in this case, is to select routes and hours of greater representability. For this, we selected sets of routes and schedules of higher demand (peak hours) in order to investigate the correlation of that series of scraping and the CPI. The

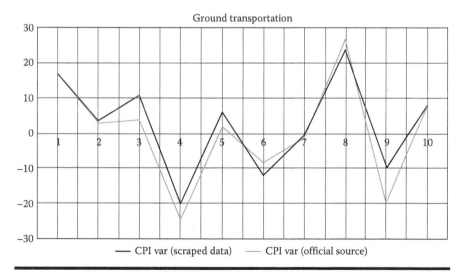

Figure 7.1   Comparison of ground transportation and CPI variation.

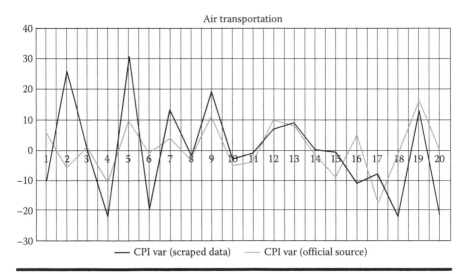

Figure 7.2 Comparison of air transportation and CPI variation.

process of debugging gave us the relevant routes and optimal schedules with which it was possible to obtain a high and positive correlation.

Air transportation also represents an important item in Latin America, since it has been an industry that has led the revenue management movement, the prices are changing with high frequency. As shown in Figure 7.2, in more than half of the cases the directions of change are captured correctly, and fitted with good precision; the amount of the month to month change is given in the index.

In the same way as in ground transportation, the difficulty of the scraping air transportation process is to select the routes and timetables of higher representability. In addition, some currency transformation is necessary in the case of international flights.

Chicken meat is an excellent representative of the customer basket of goods, transversally purchased by many households in Latin America. As shown in Figure 7.3, in most of the cases the directions of change are captured correctly, and fitted with reasonably good precision; the amount of the month to month change is given in the index.

Pork meat is also a good transversally purchased by households. As shown in Figure 7.4, in most of the cases the directions of change are captured correctly, and fitted with good precision, the amount of the month to month change in the index.

Housing rent prices is one of the largest expenses of families, and therefore a good analysis of price variation is critical at all levels. An interesting use of the scraped data method is the geo-localization of results. In Figure 7.5, rent prices are shown over a map in a heat scale of colors, depicting the zones that have experienced the highest valuation and devaluations, allowing nations, companies, and individuals to take better public policy and investment decisions.

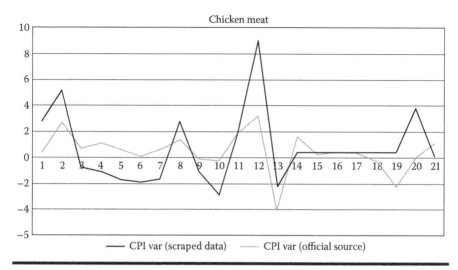

Figure 7.3   Comparison of chicken and CPI variation.

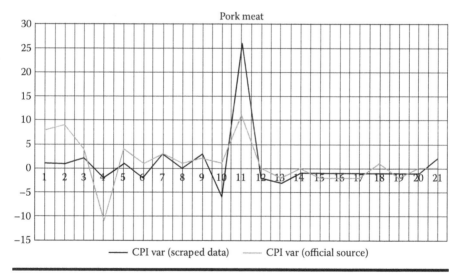

Figure 7.4   Comparison of pork meat and CPI variation.

Conclusions and Recommendations

The conducted experimental results allow us to gain confidence in the value of scraped data to predict on a daily basis the CPI of the month, allowing to timely support decision making for nations, companies, and individuals.

The solution shows small differences with the official source, and also an excellent prediction of the direction of change (rise or fall).

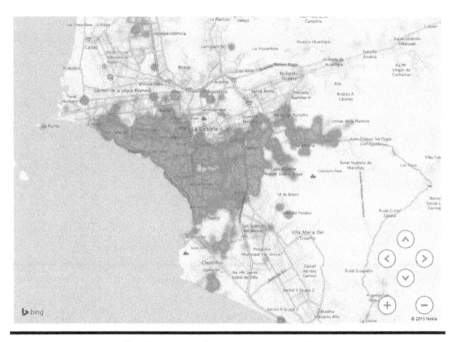

Figure 7.5   Geo-localized square mile rent price variation.

The solution has generated the following benefits:

1. Timely and online data access and pricing information, having, for example, a process that took more than four hours of work to be online early every day.
2. Costs reduction compared with traditional processes for capturing and processing of such data. The measurements have been identified to affect cost savings of more than 80% compared with traditional methods of capturing and processing data.
3. Increased focus on internal analysts' teams in analytical work itself, and not in capturing and preparing data, which allows companies to react in a more timely manner to changes in the market. In this sense, we detected savings of 40%–60% working time analysts.
4. Access rates and continuously updated forecasts.
5. Increase in quality and relevance of the information, which has allowed decision makers to have greater confidence indicators and predictions, validated from the ongoing work of other analysts.

As a first experiment, we have developed a tool to predict CPI daily, in a manner similar to the traditional monthly index of the official source; however, a huge amount of value can be added by generating thematic CPIs such as different baskets for different segments of the population, or industry-specific CPIs, even if the category do not belong to the market basket of goods.

The methodology of scraping provides an opportunity to improve statistical data and its quality, with the reduction of the overall workload for data collection. Using prices scraping to cope with the growing number of sources of data on the Internet requires careful planning in various fields, such as legal and privacy rights that must be addressed at the beginning of the project. Some countries such as Australia, the Netherlands, and Germany had already begun to use the methodology given all the benefits described above. Latin America should begin to study the feasibility of the use of Big Data at the disposal of the measurements of economic indicators as relevant as the CPI.

Reference

Cavallo, A., 2016, Scraped data and sticky prices, Working paper, MIT & NBER Review of Economics and Statistics, Posted Online November 2, 2016.

Chapter 8

Prediction and Explanation in Credit Scoring Problems: A Comparison between Artificial Neural Networks and the Logit Model

---

Edgardo R. Bravo, Alvaro G. Talavera, and Michelle Rodriguez Serra

Contents

Summary..142
Introduction..142
Background...145
  Logit Model...145
  Artificial Neural Networks..146
Application...149
  Data 149
  Results with the Logit Model..150
  Neural Network Results..152
  Comparison of Results..154

Conclusions and Recommendations.. 155
References 156

Summary

This chapter focuses on the quantitative solution, through mathematical models, of the credit scoring problem, or classifying good or bad payers. There are multiple approaches for credit risk classification. The chapter shows comparatively, both in the predictive and explanatory phases, two techniques—one parametric and directly interpreted, and the other black-box and nonparametric—that solve the problem of credit scoring.

The problem of credit scoring is defined, and the logit model (direct interpretation parametric technique) on the one hand and the artificial neural network (nonparametric black-box technique), on the other, are explained in the theory section. This framework is used to develop an application using data from a Latin American financial institution. Finally, both models are compared in the predictive and explanatory phases.

Rather than being seen as alternative techniques, both may be used in a complementary manner. In the predictive phase, though the results point to the predictive capacity of the neural network being greater than that of the logit model, the information provided by each can contribute to a more consistent prediction. In the explanatory phase, although the results show that the importance of the variables for each of the techniques may not entirely overlap; again the information they provide can be helpful in reaching a deeper analysis of the behavior of the variables.

Management requires tools in order to make decisions about whether or not to grant credit to applicants; data mining has several techniques available to this end. Our study shows the advantages and disadvantages of each and how the information each provides can help management to improve both its predictions and the justification for its decisions (explanatory phase). The comparison of techniques to solve the problem of credit scoring has focused primarily on the predictive phase (which technique has the greater predictive capacity), but there is a paucity of studies that make the comparison for the explanatory phase, particularly in the context of Latin America. This chapter aims to contribute to closing that gap.

Introduction

The financial crises in recent years have highlighted the importance for money-lenders, banks, and regulators in assessing the credit risk. According to the Basel Committee, credit risk is the most serious problem in banking. That is why credit scoring systems have been important tools for credit risk evaluation and monitoring (Doumpos and Zopounidis 2014, Anagnostopoulos and Abedi 2016).

Taking into account this issue in business, the study of credit risk assessment is of particular interest in academia and has been the subject of ongoing study (Abdou et al. 2008).

Credit risk refers to the probability that a borrower fails to make the payments he owes. Credit risk assessment can be classified into two types. In the first, the process classifies the credit applicant as good or bad based primarily on the applicant's attributes. In the second, the process evaluates a client with a credit granted to weigh the risk of nonpayment, including among other aspects the payment history (Laha 2007, Khashman 2010). This study focuses on the first of these.

An applicant can be classed based on the judgment and experience of the credit analyst and/or on automated credit rating techniques. Techniques based on judgement are founded on the personal reputation of the applicant, ability to repay the loan, guarantees, and so on. Automated credit rating is based on data-mining techniques to recognize the patterns that help in the rating (Abdou and Pointon 2011).

The financial markets are becoming increasingly complex (new clients, new preferences, new risks, etc.) and more dynamic (changing components). Also, decision makers demand more and more quantitative indicators to back up their decisions. This greater complexity, dynamism, and demand for quantitative support make it necessary to incorporate computer-based data-mining techniques. This study focuses on said techniques.

It must be said that there can be two aims in rating the applicant. The first aim is to use the rating for predictive purposes. That is, a function established under a given technique is used to predict whether new applicants will be "good" or "bad" payers. A key indicator for comparison is thus the predictive capacity of the model (i.e., the extent to which it predicts correctly).

The second aim is to use the rating for explanatory purposes. On the basis of the technique used, it must be able to show which independent variable is significant in explaining the dependent variable and the relative importance between dependent variables.

From the point of view of management, it is important to predict the clients who may default on payment, but it is also of interest to understand which factors (independent variables) may have a greater relative weight in explaining the possibility of payment or nonpayment (dependent variable). Thus, management can take special care in monitoring or in establishing policies for critical variables.

The classification techniques that data mining offers can be formulated in various ways; however, in this study, the following taxonomies are relevant. In the first place, techniques can be classed as parametric or nonparametric (West 2000, Abdou and Pointon 2011).

Let us first consider that

$$Y = F(X_1, X_2, X_3, \ldots X_n) + \varepsilon$$

where Y is the dependent variable relating to the quality of the payer (good or bad); X_i are the independent variables (e.g., income level, age, etc.); and ε is the error term (the random part). F is the function—including the parameters—that describes the behavior of Y on the basis of X_i.

Parametric techniques (e.g., discriminant analysis, logit model) require the prior specification of a function (or model) that relates the independent variables to the dependent variable. In practical terms, this function may be known—grounded in theory—or assumed. These techniques use observations of Y and X_i to estimate the parameters of the function. Once the parameters have been estimated, they can be used for prediction with new applicants. There are many examples of these techniques in the credit scoring literature (e.g., Greene 1998, Banasik et al. 2001). One disadvantage of the parametric techniques is that they have a rigid structure (the mathematical function does not change and only allows for estimating the parameters). These techniques may thus not be appropriate to represent the phenomena that do not follow the known mathematical functions.

The nonparametric techniques, on the other hand (e.g., artificial neural networks), do not assume a function a priori but instead approximate the function based on observations. Once the function has been approximated, it can be used predictively for the new applicants. Neural networks have also been extensively used in the credit scoring literature (Cimpoeru 2011, Khashman 2011, Zhao et al. 2015). One relative advantage of these techniques is that they can represent complex nonlinear mathematical functions. This flexibility of nonparametric techniques has demonstrated the superiority, under certain conditions, of its predictive power in comparison to parametric techniques (Altman et al. 1994, Abdou et al. 2008).

A second taxonomy, relating to explanatory purposes, separates direct interpretation techniques from the black-box techniques. The first (e.g., the logit model) provides equations that are relatively easy to interpret, where one can see the relative contribution of each independent variable on the dependent variable. The black-box techniques (e.g., artificial neural networks) can help with prediction but there may be limitations in understanding clearly how the independent variables affect the dependent variable (Albright and Winston 2014, Nettleton 2014). Many researchers reject the use of neural networks precisely because of this limitation (Benítez et al. 1997). However, methods that allow analysis of the effects or significance of independent variables on dependent variables in neural networks have been developed in recent years (e.g., Montano and Palmer 2003, Green et al. 2009).

A review of the literature shows that credit scoring studies that compare parametric techniques and neural networks mainly deal with the predictive aim. In this regard, a number of studies have compared the predictive power of neural networks with parametric techniques such as discriminant analysis, logistic regression, the probit model, or the logit model (Tam and Kiang 1992, Abdou and Pointon 2011, Cimpoeru 2011). However, it is less frequent to find studies that also compare the parametric techniques and neural networks in the context of an explanatory aim.

This study thus aims to show comparatively both the predictive and the explanatory phase of an easily interpreted parametric technique (logit model) and a black-box nonparametric technique (artificial neural networks).

Background

Classification problems such as the credit scoring issue can be faced with a variety of techniques, both parametric and nonparametric, as well as those that offer direct interpretation and those that do not (black box). In this chapter, we will compare the logit model (a direct interpretation parametric technique) with artificial neural networks (nonparametric technique with a black-box interpretation).

Logit Model

This model enables a prediction of the probability whether or not an individual belongs to a group based on a series of independent variables that may be both quantitative and qualitative. It also allows to know the relative weight or effect of the explanatory variables in the model. There are different kinds of logit model: the dichotomous model is used when there are two mutually exclusive alternatives and the multiple choice model is used when there are more than two options to be modeled.

The logit model is defined by the following function, where "X_i" are the independent variables and "Y" is the dependent variable:

$$\text{Prob}(Y = 1) = \frac{1}{1 + e^{-(\alpha + \beta_i X_i)}}$$

This should be read as, the probability of belonging to the group coded as 1 (e.g., a paying client) is given by the mathematical function shown, provided a set of variables X_i are given.

The logit model has some advantages over other parametric models in the financial context. For example, with regard to discriminant analysis, the logit model does not assume restrictions on the normality of the distribution of variables; in financial problems we use qualitative variables that do not meet that assumption (Press and Wilson 1978).

To apply the model for predictive purposes, the following steps are taken:

1. The available observations are randomly divided into two samples (training and testing).
2. The logit model is carried out with the training sample. This phase makes it possible to estimate the logit function parameters.

3. The relevance of the variables is checked by the statistical significance of the parameters. It is possible that not all the variables contribute to improving the estimate.
4. The predictive capacity of the model is checked (number of correct predictions as a proportion of the total number of observations).
5. Using the estimated parameters from the training phase, the prediction is carried out on the test sample.
6. The predictive capacity of the model is reviewed.

For explanatory purposes, it is not yet possible to directly interpret the β_i parameters since they are nonlinear models. Their sign indicates the direction in which probability moves when the corresponding explanatory variable increases, but the size of the parameter does not coincide with the magnitude of variation in probability (as would occur in a linear regression model). To this end, we use the odds ratio the software supplies (a definition and detailed calculation can be found in Jaeger 2008).

Mathematically it can be shown that

$$\text{Odds ratio} = \exp(\beta_i)$$

The odds ratio$_i$ is interpreted as the number of times the preference for option 1 as opposed to 0 varies when X_i increases by one. The following cases may arise:

■ The odds ratio$_i$ = 1 (the value of the parameter $\beta_i = 0$). In this case, the independent variable X_i does not have any effect on the preference for option 1 over 0.
■ The odds ratio$_i$ > 1 (the value of the parameter $\beta_i > 0$). In this case, when the independent variable X_i increases, there is an increase in the preference for option 1 over 0.
■ The odds ratio$_i$ < 1 (the value of the parameter $\beta_i < 0$). In this case, when the independent variable X_i increases, there is a decrease in the preference for option 1 over 0.

Thus, for explanatory purposes, the following steps are followed:

1. The odds ratio values of the logit model are calculated for each variable.
2. The relative importance is interpreted based on the odds ratio.

Artificial Neural Networks

A neural network is similar to a human brain in two main aspects: (1) the knowledge it acquires from its environment through a learning process and (2) the weights

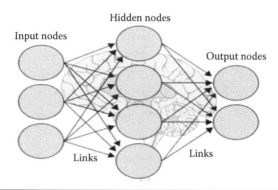

Figure 8.1 Multilevel neural network.

associated with the connections between neurons, known as synaptic weights, which are used to store the knowledge acquired.

Neural networks are by definition approximations of universal functions (Haykin 1994), which approximate a nonlinear function f:A → B, where A and B are the sets of input and output data. Neural networks have hidden nodes between the input and output nodes. Each node consists of neurons or processing units (Figure 8.1).

Neurons carry out simple processes, transmitting their results to neighboring processors. The ability of neural networks in carrying out nonlinear relationship between inputs and outputs makes them useful techniques in pattern recognition and in modeling complex systems (Bishop 1995).

Networks can be distinguished by their topology: feed-forward networks and recurring networks. In feed-forward networks, all the signals go from the input node to the output with no cycles nor connections between neurons in the same node of the neural network. In recurring networks these connections do exist.

Another typology distinguishes between supervised learning networks and unsupervised learning networks. In supervised learning, the network uses a set of observations where the value of the dependent variable is known for each set of independent variables. The learning algorithm consists of minimizing error in relation to the known input and output data. In unsupervised learning, the network uses only a set of input observations. The network must self-organize (or self-train) depending on some kind of existing structure within the input data set.

The neural network used in this work is a feed-forward multilayer perceptron network with supervised learning. This technique can solve a variety of problems with a high degree of complexity (including credit scoring).

This kind of network carries out the processing based on the input. The output obtained is compared with the expected output. A weight adjustment process that seeks to minimize the error is applied on the basis of the error obtained.

Each processing unit is structured with inputs x_i, outputs $\hat{y}_i$, weightings w_i, threshold θ_i, and a differentiable function φ, as shown below (see also Funahashi 1989):

$$\hat{y} = \varphi\left(\sum_{i=1}^{k} w_i x_i - \theta\right) \tag{8.1}$$

In Equation 8.1, weights are calculated according to the learning rule known as back-propagation (Rumelhart et al. 1985), which basically consists of applying a family of optimization methods based on a gradient to find the optimum value of the weights with a view to minimizing the error norm between the desired output ($y \in B$) and the output calculated by the neural network $\hat{y}$, that is,

$$\min\|y - \hat{y}\| \tag{8.2}$$

As in the logit model, not all the variables can contribute to the estimate. In the case of neural networks, global stochastic optimization technique, known as genetic algorithms (Goldberg and Holland 1988), can be used to reduce variables; it chooses the best subset of data using a probabilistic criteria, thus eliminating redundant data. This algorithm has parameters such as population size, number of generations, probabilities of crossover, and mutation (see also Witten and Frank 2005).

To apply the model for predictive purposes, the following steps are taken:

1. The available observations are randomly divided into two samples (training and testing).
2. The model is carried out with the training sample. This phase makes it possible to estimate the network parameters.
3. The relevance of the variables is checked through another heuristic method (e.g., genetic algorithms). It is possible that not all the variables contribute to improving the estimate.
4. The predictive capacity of the model is checked (number of correct predictions as a proportion of the total number of observations).
5. Using the estimated parameters from the training phase, the prediction is carried out on the test sample.
6. The predictive capacity of the model is reviewed.

For explanatory purposes, it must be remembered that neural networks are black-box techniques and the interpretation of results is therefore not direct. The function estimated by the neural network will be very complex because, looking at the structure of the neural network, there are functions in each node of both the visible and hidden layers. In view of this fact, some researchers have suggested sensitivity analysis as an option to be able to estimate the magnitude and sense of impact of the independent variables on the dependent variables (see also Montano and Palmer 2003, Green et al. 2009).

Application

To illustrate credit scoring problem solving comparatively, we will apply both techniques (logit and neural networks) taking as a basis the credit history of a Latin American financial entity.

Data

The database has 10 attributes (Table 8.1). The class attribute (dependent variable) indicates whether or not the client paid off the credit. The other attributes are considered independent variables.

The database was divided into three training samples and three test samples. Table 8.2 shows the number of observations per sample.

Table 8.1 Attributes of the Client Table

Variable	Descriptor	Type
ESCT	Civil status	Categorical
NDEP	Number of dependents	Categorical
RENDA	Family income	Numerical
VBEM	Value of the good acquired	Numerical
NPARC	Number of installments	Numerical
VPARC	Value of the installment	Numerical
TEL	Has a phone	Categorical
IDADE	Client age	Numerical
RESMS	Time of residence (months)	Numerical
INPUT	Value of input	Categorical
CLASS	Classification of payment (1 paid/0 did not pay)	Categorical

Table 8.2   Samples

	Train 1	Train 2	Train 3	Test 1	Test 2	Test 3
Observations	1500	1500	1500	577	577	577

Results with the Logit Model

With this data structure and sample configuration, the data was processed with SPSS software version 22.

In the training phase, the model was initially carried out with the 10 independent variables available in the database. The results (Table 8.3) have shown that some of these variables increase the probability of payment (e.g., ESCT), while others reduce it (e.g., IDADE).

The results also show (Table 8.4) that in all three training groups the predictive capacity (correct classification) is similar and has an approximate value of 73.7% (average).

However, the results show that of these 10 variables, only four (ESCT, NPARC, IDADE, and RESMS) are statistically significant. This leads us to modify the initial model to four independent variables.

Table 8.3   Ten Variables Model–Training Phase–Coefficients

Variable	Train 1	Train 2	Train 3
ESTC			
ESTC(1)	0.5544	0.7122	0.5687
ESTC(2)	0.6969	0.5794	0.8717
ESTC(3)	0.5142	0.9083	0.6379
NDEP	−0.2828	−0.2370	−0.3918
RENDA	−0.0001	−0.0001	−0.0001
VBEM	0.0003	0.0002	0.0004
NPARC	0.1259	0.1273	0.1041
VPARC	0.0052	0.0053	0.0053
TEL(1)	0.3762	0.3748	0.1709
IDADE	−0.0964	−0.0875	−0.0958
RESMS	0.0120	0.0117	0.0126
ENTRADA	−0.0012	−0.0012	−0.0017

Table 8.4 Ten Variables Model–Training Phase–Predictive Capacity

Descriptor	Train 1 (%)	Train 2 (%)	Train 3 (%)
Correct classification (%)	74.10	73.10	74
Incorrect classification (%)	25.90	26.90	26.00

Results (Table 8.5) show that the ESTC, NPARC, and RESMS variables increase the probability of payment whereas IDADE reduces it.

The results also show (Table 8.6) that in all three training groups the predictive capacity (correct classification) is similar and is approximately 73.27% (average). If we compare this with the predictive capacity of the model with 10 variables, we can see that the elimination of six nonsignificant variables had practically no impact on the predictive capacity.

We then execute the model with the test samples, keeping the coefficients from the training phase. The results (Table 8.7) indicate that the predictive capacity in this phase is similar to that in the training phase (average 73.27% vs. 72.2%).

For explanatory purposes, in Table 8.5 the sign of the coefficients shows that ESTC, NPARC, and RESMS increase the probability of payment while IDADE reduces it.

Table 8.5 Four Variables Model–Training Phase–Coefficients

Variable	Train 1	Train 2	Train 3
ESTC			
ESTC(1)	0.6354	0.7639	0.6384
ESTC(2)	0.7000	0.5984	0.8895
ESTC(3)	0.6456	0.9804	0.6894
NPARC	0.1016	0.1011	0.0789
IDADE	−0.0959	−0.0867	−0.0951
RESMS	0.0133	0.0127	0.0136

Table 8.6 Four Variables Model–Training Phase–Predictive Capacity

Descriptor	Train 1 (%)	Train 2 (%)	Train 3 (%)
Correct classification (%)	73.40	73.30	73.1
Incorrect classification (%)	26.60	26.70	26.90

Table 8.7   Four Variables Model–Test Phase–Predictive Capacity

Descriptor	Test 1 (%)	Test 2 (%)	Test 3 (%)
Correct classification (%)	70.00	74.00	73
Incorrect classification (%)	30.00	26.00	27.40

Table 8.8   Four Variables Model–Training Phase–Odds Ratios

Variable	Train 1	Train 2	Train 3
ESTC			
ESTC(1)	1.8879	2.1465	1.8934
ESTC(2)	2.0138	1.8191	2.4339
ESTC(3)	1.9071	2.6655	1.9926
NPARC	1.1070	1.1063	1.0821
IDADE	0.9086	0.9170	0.9092
RESMS	1.0134	1.0128	1.0137
Constant	9.3447	6.2722	11.6136

However, as we have stated previously, given that logit is a nonlinear model, the size of the parameter does not coincide with the magnitude of variation in probability.

An overall view of the coefficients (Table 8.5) and the odds ratios (Table 8.8) show that IDADE (negatively) and NPARC (positively) are the variables that most affect the dependent variable. In the case of ESTC, given that it is a categorical variable, a single occurrence has significant impact.

Neural Network Results

With the above-mentioned data structure and samples, the data was processed with SPSS software version 22.

In the training phase, the model was initially carried out with the 10 independent variables available in the database (Figure 8.2).

The results show (Table 8.9) that in all three training groups the predictive capacity (correct classification) is similar and has an approximate value of 76.83%.

The genetic algorithm to reduce variables was then carried out and established that there were three most relevant variables: NPARC, IDADE, and RESMS. For the reduced model and for comparative purposes, we took into account these three variables as well as ESTC, which was proposed as significant by the logit model.

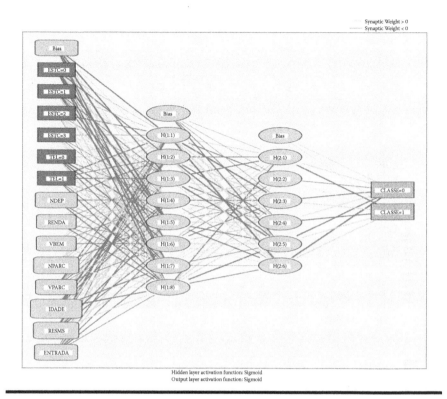

Figure 8.2   Resulting neural network.

The results show (Table 8.10) that in all three training groups the predictive capacity (correct classification) is similar and has an approximate value of 75.8%. If we compare this with the predictive capacity of the model with 10 variables, we can see that the elimination of six nonsignificant variables had hardly any impact on the predictive capacity.

We then execute the model with the test samples, keeping the coefficients from the training phase. The results (Table 8.11) indicate that the predictive capacity in this phase is similar to the training phase (average 74.4% vs. 75.8%).

Finally, Table 8.12 shows the sensitivity analysis that indicates the relative importance of the variables. For all the samples, IDADE and RESMS are the

Table 8.9   Ten Variables Model–Training Phase–Predictive Capacity

Descriptor	Train 1 (%)	Train 2 (%)	Train 3 (%)
Correct classification (%)	76.60	76.10	77.80
Incorrect classification (%)	23.40	23.90	22.20

Table 8.10   Four Variables Model–Training Phase–Predictive Capacity

Descriptor	Train 1 (%)	Train 2 (%)	Train 3 (%)
Correct classification (%)	77.10	74.30	75.90
Incorrect classification (%)	22.90	25.70	24.10

Table 8.11   Four Variables Model–Test Phase–Predictive Capacity

Descriptor	Test 1 (%)	Test 2 (%)	Test 3 (%)
Correct classification (%)	73.70	74.20	75.20
Incorrect classification (%)	26.30	25.80	24.80

Table 8.12   Four Variables Model–Training Phase–Importance of the Variables

Descriptor	Train 1	Train 2	Train 3
IDADE	0.39	0.41	0.36
RESMS	0.32	0.32	0.31
NPARC	0.22	0.21	0.25
ESTC	0.07	0.06	0.08

factors that have the greatest incidence on the dependent variable. It should be noted that the table indicates the importance but not the sign of the impact of the independent variable on the dependent variable. It must be recalled that in the logit model, IDADE had a negative incidence on the dependent variable.

Comparison of Results

For the predictive phase, the overall results of the reduced models show that the predictive capacity of the neural network is greater than that of the logit model both in the training phase ($\Delta2.5\%$; 75.8% vs. 73.3%) and in the test phase ($\Delta2.2$; 74.4% vs. 72.2%). This result is coherent with other studies (e.g., Bonilla et al. 2003). It is possible that predicting whether a credit will be paid off in this financial institution has a more complex behavior than that assumed by the logit model.

On comparing the variables that continue to be used in the reduced models, we can see that the models overlap on three variables (NPARC, IDADE, and RESMS) but differ in one (ESTC). It should be borne in mind that in the logit model the technique for the reduction of variables was statistically significant, and in the neural network it was a heuristic technique (genetic algorithm). This suggests that, with the same input/output data, the use of different approximations can lead to differing predictive models.

For the explanatory phase, both approximations show that IDADE is one of the two variables with the greatest impact. But the other factor with the greatest impact is NPARC in the case of the logit model and RESMS in the case of the neural network. This difference may be due to the approximations used by each technique. We must recall that the neural network builds the function and estimates parameters based on data, whereas in the logit model a function is given and the data is used to estimate the parameters. In the logit model, therefore, the a priori function in some way conditions the relationship between the parameters, whereas this does not occur in the neural network.

Conclusions and Recommendations

The study suggests that for predictive purposes the use of different approximations (a parametric and a nonparametric technique) may help to establish the predictive capacity of a model in relative terms. The neural network, as a universal approximation of the function that links the input and the output data, sets a benchmark for predictive capacity that a parametric model such as logit should aim for.

The study also shows that the use of different approximations can help to establish in relative terms whether the reduction in variables is more or less consistent. For the reduction in variables, in the neural network we used a genetic algorithm which extracted from the data the relevance of variables. In the case of the logit model, assuming an a priori function conditions the significance of the variables (through their statistical significance).

In the explanatory phase, the logit model can be interpreted directly from reading the signs of the parameters and the odds ratios. The neural network requires a sensitivity analysis that is far more complex to understand, although it is now easier to carry out through the SPSS sensitivity analysis.

Interpretation in the logit model enables an explanation of the relative magnitude and the sign of the impact of a dependent variable on the independent variable. In the neural network, the sensitivity analysis shows the relative magnitude but not the sign.

The underlying recommendation from the results is that, rather than alternative approximations, these should be seen as complementary techniques. In the predictive phase, both approximations can give greater information about the predictive capacity in comparison to the logit model. And in the explanatory phase, it can help us to understand the consistency of the impact relative to the variables.

References

Abdou, H. and Pointon, J., 2011, Credit scoring, statistica techniques and evaluation criteria: A review of the literature, *Intelligent Systems in Accounting, Finance and Management*, 18(2), 9–88.

Abdou, H., Pointon, J., and El-Masry, A., 2008, Neural nets versus conventional techniques in credit scoring in Egyptian Banking, *Expert Systems with Applications*, 35(3), 1275–1292.

Albright, S. and Winston, W. L., 2014, *Business Analytics: Data Analysis & Decision Making*, Cengage Learning, Stamford, CT.

Altman, E. I., Marco, G., and Varetto, F., 1994, Corporate distress diagnosis: Comparisons using linear discriminant analysis and neural networks (the Italian Experience), *Journal of Banking & Finance*, 18(3), 505–529.

Anagnostopoulos, Y. and Abedi, M., 2016, Risk pricing in emerging economies: Credit scoring and private banking in Iran, *International Journal of Finance & Banking Studies (2147–4486)*, 5(1), 51–72.

Banasik, J., Crook, J., and Thomas, L., 2001, Scoring by usage, *Journal of the Operational Research Society*, 52(9), 997–1006.

Benítez, J., Castro, J. L., and Requena, I., 1997, Are artificial neural networks black boxes?, *IEEE Transactions on Neural Networks*, 8(5), 1156–1164.

Bishop, C. M., 1995, *Neural Networks for Pattern Recognition*, Oxford University Press, Oxford, UK.

Bonilla, M., Olmeda, I., and Puertas, R., 2003, Modelos Paramétricos Y No Paramétricos En Problemas De credit scoring, *Spanish Journal of Finance and Accounting/Revista Española de Financiación y Contabilidad*, 32(118), 833–869.

Cimpoeru, S. S., 2011, Neural networks and their applications in credit risk assessment. Evidence from the Romanian Market, *Technological and Economic Development of Economy*, 17(3), 519–534.

Doumpos, M. and Zopounidis, C., 2014, *Multicriteria Analysis in Finance*, Springer, New York.

Funahashi, K. I., 1989, On the approximate realization of continuous mappings by neural networks, *Neural Networks*, 2(3), 183–192.

Goldberg, D. E. and Holland, J. H., 1988, Genetic algorithms and machine learning, *Machine Learning*, 3(2), 95–99.

Greene, W., 1998, Sample selection in credit-scoring models, *Japan and the World Economy*, 10(3), 299–316.

Green, M., Ekelund, U., Edenbrandt, L., Björk, J., Forberg, J. L., and Ohlsson, M., 2009, Exploring new possibilities for case-based explanation of artificial neural network ensembles, *Neural Networks*, 22(1), 75–81.

Haykin, S., 1994, *Neural Network: A Comprehensive Foundation*, Prentice-Hall, Upper Saddle River, NJ.

Jaeger, T. F., 2008, Categorical data analysis: Away from Anovas (transformation or not) and towards logit mixed models, *Journal of Memory and Language*, 59(4), 434–446.

Khashman, A., 2010, Neural networks for credit risk evaluation: Investigation of different neural models and learning schemes, *Expert Systems with Applications*, 37(9), 6233–6239.

Khashman, A., 2011, Credit risk evaluation using neural networks: Emotional versus conventional models, *Applied Soft Computing*, 11(8), 5477–5484.

Laha, A., 2007, Building contextual classifiers by integrating fuzzy rule based classification technique and K-Nn method for credit scoring, *Advanced Engineering Informatics*, 21(3), 281–291.

Montano, J. J. and Palmer, A., 2003, Numeric sensitivity analysis applied to feedforward neural networks, *Neural Computing & Applications*, 12(2), 119–125.

Nettleton, D., 2014, *Commercial Data Mining: Processing, Analysis and Modeling for Predictive Analytics Projects*, Elsevier, Waltham, MA.

Press, S. J. and Wilson, S., 1978, Choosing between logistic regression and discriminant analysis, *Journal of the American Statistical Association*, 73(364), 699–705.

Rumelhart, D. E., Hinton, G. E., and Williams, R. J., 1985, Learning internal representations by error propagation, *DTIC Document*. Report No. CS-8506, La Jolla Institute for Cognitive Science, University San Diego, California.

Tam, K. Y. and Kiang, M. Y., 1992, Managerial applications of neural networks: The case of bank failure predictions, *Management Science*, 38(7), 926–947.

West, D., 2000, Neural network credit scoring models, *Computers & Operations Research*, 27(11), 1131–1152.

Witten, I. H. and Frank, E., 2005, *Data Mining: Practical Machine Learning Tools and Techniques*, Morgan Kaufmann, San Francisco.

Zhao, Z., Xu, S., Kang, B. H., Kabir, M. M. J, Liu, Y. and Wasinger, R., 2015, Investigation and improvement of multi-layer perceptron neural networks for credit scoring, *Expert Systems with Applications*, 42(7), 3508–3516.

Chapter 9

A Multi-Case Approach for Informational Port Decision Making

Ana Ximena Halabi-Echeverry, Mario Ernesto Martínez-Avella, Deborah Richards, and Jairo Rafael Montoya-Torres

Contents

Summary...160
Introduction..160
Antecedents..161
Rationale of This Work...162
Methodology to Guide the Selected Multiple Cases...165
    Theory Building from Cases Applied to the Port Informational Integration.......165
    Step 1: Fostering the Proposition for Each Multiple Case..........................167
    Step 2: Linking the Propositions with the BPIs...167
    Step 3: Searching for Patterns Using the Outputs of the DM Workflows......171
    Step 4: Finding Empirical Evidence for Each Proposition..........................175
    Step 5: Mapping the Spatial or Institutional Proximities (Jurisdictions)
    among Pairs or Subsets of Multiple Cases...179
Conclusions...183
References...183

Summary

Informational integration is one of the important challenges and more aggressive strategies toward radical actions, for instance, to protect the environment from unwise long-term decisions. It is essential that port decision makers see the urgency in the formulation and consideration of port decision support in the long term. The strategy of theory building from cases demonstrates its objectivity emphasising the real-world context in which the port informational integration may occur. This chapter weighs the importance of multiple port cases to support informational integration with extant literature, therefore, demonstrating that a multi-case study analysis can accommodate a rich variety of empirical analyses. This chapter presents a novel multi-case approach valuable for informational port decision making. The multiple case consolidates the new knowledge for port informational integration. The argument is that expertise on this matter is served by consistent empirical evidence in a process accounting for data, models and for the corresponding validation of multiple case studies.

The findings suggest that the practitioners should pay attention to the distinct roles and contexts in which port informational integration may take place while deciding on the strategic orientation, that is, to adopt the business process intelligence (BPI). The multi-case presented is a novel contribution to data analytics appropriate for the port study, and also responds to the necessity of introducing more intelligent decision support tools in which experimental data and results for comparison between ports are not available to meet future challenges.

Introduction

The integration of regional infrastructure (physical and informational) is essential for the economic well-being of nations. The lack of exposure, resources, and integrated data faced by the port decision makers shows an absence of a focus on knowledge and experience, currently concentrated on operational and sometimes tactical information systems, but that have not been used with computer-based techniques for higher level managerial decision making. This is particularly true in the case of developing countries where many of the inputs/data needed are either missing or not taken into consideration. Data analytics is therefore an important issue to justify knowledge discovery in cases (i.e., ports and regions) in which the use of data integration, access to information, and experience is highly developed. Emphasis is placed in this chapter on the future focus on the intelligent decision-making support for the informational integration of ports. By studying and comparing cases from diverse port experiences, port decision makers can learn—build a theory of what is going on. Similar business processes can be learnt intelligently even though different algorithms and types of data need to be used.

The inclusion of multiple study objectives provides insights into the building case theory for designing decision support systems involving cooperation among ports. The literature highlights the technological aspects such as the need for more support functions in port information systems and the need to introduce intelligent support tools that can cope with the complexity of global port operations and governance (Murty et al. 2005). Consequently, significant informational decisions let port authorities and relevant stakeholders cover the various aspects of business strategy, in part because shortcomings in reliable data and information exchange often hamper collaborations and partnerships (Henesey 2006, Almotairi et al. 2011). This issue raises the questions dealt with in this chapter:

RQ1: How can an approach to multiple cases be served by consistent empirical evidence expertise on port decision support to promote collaboration and partnership for informational integration among ports?

RQ2: How does Data Analytics justify knowledge discovery in cases (i.e., ports and regions) in which the use of data integration, access to information, and experience must be highly developed?

The methodology in this chapter guides the selected multi-cases for port informational integration, along with some of the advantages of using ports. The multiple cases are located in three regions, that is, United States, Rijn Delta (Belgium and Netherlands), and Colombia to deepen the understanding on identified patterns across cases. Work progresses toward a multi-case for South American port jurisdictions; some of these results are included in the chapter. The multi-cases presented are a novel contribution to data analytics appropriate for port studies. They uncover the necessity of introducing a more intelligent decision support in which the experimental data and the results for comparison between ports are not yet available to meet future challenges.

Antecedents

The multi-case cases dig into the several initiatives for port integration mentioned by Wang et al. (2015). This diversity denotes the significant levels of formality required for port integration, varying from informal agreements of cooperation to advanced strategic alliances, joint ventures, and acquisitions. These authors present a very recent and convenient research on this topic. A first comprehensive definition for port integration is (Wang et al. 2015, p. 612) as follows:

Typically, port integration refers to as an assemblage of potential approaches for utilization by port authorities to increase the operational production capacity and resources in relation to handling and shipping activities, and optimize allocation of coastlines, berths, infrastructures, water and land area, shipping routes within the port system.

An additional definition states (Wang et al. 2015, pp. 615–16) the following:

> Port integration is multileveled in nature, comprising integration between large ports and small/medium-sized ports (with the former merging with the later), between small- and medium-sized ports (with the weaker typically merging the stronger), and between the large ports…consequently, port scale and strength typically determine the mode of port integration.

Wang et al. (2015) have studied the concept of port integration within the context of a port jurisdiction including the scope and administrative rank. Their review allows for a comprehensive understanding and scope of port integration acknowledging the importance for its definition in this chapter; although, Wang et al. (2015) state that to date, a paucity of data relating to port integration strategies exists and very few literature effectively exhibit the potential for the port integration perspective. Table 9.1 extracts the definitions of these initiatives making possible to address some elements that add important meaning to the definition provided for port informational integration in this chapter, such as jurisdictional, regional, and strategic alliances. In the same line, Ducruet (2009) emphasizes "the emergence of new territories of port governance and port development" which makes possible linkages and stimuli for possible mechanisms of comparison among ports. Bichou (2006) and Bichou and Gray (2005) also studied port integration from the supply chain perspective for many years now.

Although the above-mentioned authors explored comprehensively the concept of port integration, little is known in the present about the business processes to promote port informational integration; as per the knowledge of the authors, it might be explained by the sensitive character of information and its competitive grounds, and/or the lack of strategies determining this concept and the interdisciplinary literature covering the topic. The consideration for port informational integration requires an engagement/partnership among ports and also development of capabilities on sharing information, planning, and execution in a collaborative way.

Adding to previous definitions, in this chapter port informational integration is defined by Halabi-Echeverry (2016) as

> a higher perspective of port cooperation in which development of capabilities on sharing information, planning and execution allows two or more ports to make progress and deliver benefits among the partners

Rationale of This Work

As mentioned, informational integration among ports is a new decisional perspective in the port domain. The recognition of this decision-making situation targets strategies requiring a comprehensive study on factors that enable port integration.

Table 9.1   Initiatives for Port Integration

Initiatives for Port Integration	Definition
(a) *Government-driven* perspective of port integration (p. 617)	Is typically undertaken via the creation of regional or national development strategies, whereby, the government in question mergers two or more ports, thus establishing a new port authority for the implementation of unified port planning, construction, operation, and management.
(b) *Market-driven* perspective of port integration (p. 618)	Is characterized by an aggressive growth strategy based on acquisition of existing terminal assets or construction of new terminals via the sharing of both capital benefits and investment risks.
(c) *Government/ market* perspective of port integration (p. 619)	Typically applies to capital investment or mutual shareholding in the presence of governmental support, for the integration of ports across administrative areas, with only slight changes to the existing patterns of port administrative structure.
(d) *Strategic alliance* perspective of port integration (p. 619)	In order to counteract a shortage of port resources... [ports set up a] regular scheduling of alliance conferences, and the formulation of organizational treaties in order to create and maintain an orderly market.
(e) *Port internal* perspective of port integration (p. 621)	Individual owners may integrate resources characterized by the same location but diverse ownership, thus developing integration relationships between separate terminals and/or operators located within the same individual port.
(f) *Jurisdictional* perspective of port integration (p. 621)	Refers to instances of ports characterized by differing locations but within the same prefectural region and their establishment of a new united port authority, integrated resources, and one overarching port name.
(g) *Port integration across neighbor region* perspective (p. 621)	Refers to ports belonging to different prefectural regions, are located within the same bay, and share navigation channel and hinterland... [it] focuses on the integration of port resources within one jurisdictional location owned by two or more port authorities and is based on several factors including not only regional regulatory and social networks but also the scientific and rational utilization of shoreline resources.

(Continued)

Table 9.1 (*Continued*) Initiatives for Port Integration

Initiatives for Port Integration	Definition
(h) *Regional port integration* perspective (p. 622)	Refers to ports located within two or more jurisdictional areas regardless of that separating distances are integrated cross-regionally...they are typically characterized by diverse objectives and dynamics, such as the optimization of shoreline resources or the elimination of unhealthily aggressive competition.
(i) *Hub-feeder port* perspective (p. 622)	Is categorized by inter-port cooperation in terms of the logistical chain and the development of feeder shipping networks.

Source: Extracted from Wang, C., Ducruet, C., and Wang, W., 2015, *Chinese Geographical Science*, 25(5), 612–628.

Linking these strategies with the potential necessities for port integration raises directions to BPI. "BPI builds on techniques such as data mining and statistical analysis…, and adapts them to the requirements of business process management." Davenport et al. (2006) and Genrich et al. (2008) further explain the scope for BPI as "an emerging, interdisciplinary area that aim at developing models, techniques and tools to improve different aspects of how business processes are modeled and conducted." Thus, it is not only an application of business intelligence (BI), but it also integrates contributions from other disciplines.

This chapter refers BPIs as data-driven decision support systems (DSSs) as being related interchangeably with the analysis of data and its transformation into the potential knowledge for port informational integration. Three BPIs support this rationale and are published elsewhere. Here, those are mentioned to provide the motivation to answer "how" to promote port integration; which to the knowledge of the authors lacks sufficient business strategies and interdisciplinary literature to address its challenges (Lam and Notteboom 2014). Therefore, a multi-case study analysis can accommodate empirical analyses to promote BPIs such as (Halabi-Echeverry 2016)

1. The BPI to promote port informational integration in cooperative decision making on environmental and ecological sustainability (BPI-COSEDAM).
2. The BPI to promote port informational integration in collaborative decision making on transport or (inter) organizational networks (BPI-COLSETAM).
3. The BPI to promote port informational integration through port logistics performance in terms of economics (BPI-POFEDAM).
4. The BPI to promote port integration in monitoring and controlling security processes susceptible to or restricted by legal and ethical factors (BPI-SELTIDAM).

The context of each BPI can be executed by a port decision maker whose function enables its usage. More importantly that ports depend on the concept of territory as a source of power, that is, region, jurisdiction, proximity to neighbors, hinterland, and internal boundaries (Wang et al. 2015). It is proposed the organizational context for port informational integration as determined by the spatial boundaries and/or the surrounding environment at which each BPI can participate in and develop. As suggested by Brennan and Martin (2012), a spatial proximity is more than just a distance measure; it distinguishes the basic notion of an influenced area and its impact area. Two organizational contexts become important in understanding the proximities/linkages in which a BPI for port informational integration is developed:

1. Institutional/jurisdictional proximity, namely ecosystemic and normative
2. Spatial proximity, namely local, neighboring, and regional

Methodology to Guide the Selected Multiple Cases

Inherently different contexts of ports, within specific spatial dimensions, control areas or jurisdictions, and strategic priorities, among others, are used in the chapter to support the methodology to guide the selected multiple cases. First, it is presented the theory building from cases applied to the port informational integration. Then, the methodological steps are proposed in justifying the multiple cases for port informational integration.

Theory Building from Cases Applied to the Port Informational Integration

Woodside (2010) cites a formal definition of a case study:

> A case study is an empirical inquiry that investigates a contemporary phenomenon within real life context, especially when the boundaries between phenomenon and context are not clearly evident.

Hiranandani (2014) distinguishes case studies by their focus on a particular case. When there are several research focuses, several cases are used; these studies are named "multiple case studies." The seminal work of Eisenhardt (1989) and Eisenhardt and Graebner (2007) reveal the research strategy of theory building from cases, particularly multiple cases (Eisenhardt and Graebner 2007, p. 25):

> Building theory from case studies is a research strategy that involves using one or more cases to create theoretical constructs, propositions

and/or midrange theory from case-based empirical evidence. Case studies are rich empirical descriptions of particular instances of a phenomenon that are typically based on a variety of data sources. The theory is emergent in the sense that is situated in and developed by recognizing patterns of relationships among constructs within and across cases and their underlying logical arguments.

The theory building from cases demonstrates its objectivity emphasizing the real-world context in which the phenomena occur. Moreover, theory building from cases is more likely to answer "how" and "why" questions over unexplored research areas, which ratifies its proper use to promote port informational integration. The port cluster environment serves as interesting phenomena in which intensive flow of information may occur for the analysis of port informational integration. In particular, De Langen (2004, 2006, 2015) contributes to a great discussion on the factors driving the development of ports in clusters. Central to this notion is the acknowledgment that clusters are mainly produced by common economic interests; however, other perspectives are equally important such as clusters developed on common interests for knowledge and information creation, better known as regional learning systems (De Langen 2004). Recently, the work of De Langen (2015) also draws on the notion of governance in ports in clusters providing an extensive empirical framework to cluster success.

In building theory from case studies, "cases are selected because they are particularly suitable for illuminating and extending relationships and logic among constructs [and propositions]. The choice is based less on the uniqueness of a given case and more on the contribution to the theory development within the set of cases." (Eisenhardt and Graebner 2007) Four multiple cases are selected as a result. Figure 9.1 displays the multi-case chaining schema, which explains graphically the organizational context in which port informational integration is developed. The first circle shows the multiple case describing the local spatial proximities of port clusters in the United States. The second circle shows two multiple cases describing the cross-regional port clusters in the context of Nafta corridors in United States and the Rijn–Schelde Delta ports in Netherlands and Belgium. The third circle shows an individual case in the context of port jurisdictional (institutional) proximities in South America (Buenaventura Colombia) and it also presents work in progress for cases in the context of multi-port jurisdictional proximities in the same region.

Five methodological steps are proposed in justifying the multiple cases for port informational integration. The steps are (1) fostering the proposition for each multiple case, that is, statements subject to empirical testing; (2) linking the propositions with the BPIs; (3) searching for patterns using the outputs of the data mining (DM) workflows; (4) finding empirical evidence for each proposition; (5) mapping the spatial or institutional proximities (jurisdictions) among the pairs or subsets of multiple cases. Each step of the methodology is developed next.

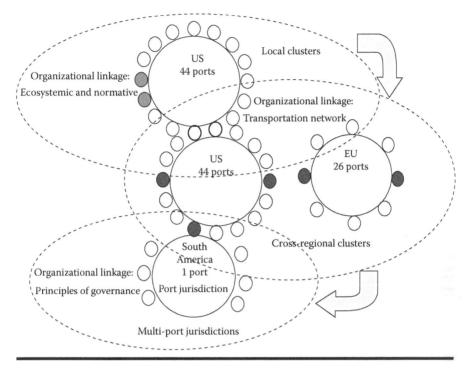

Figure 9.1 Complete multi-case chaining schema.

Step 1: Fostering the Proposition for Each Multiple Case

- Proposition #1: Ports in clusters would integrate informationally if environmental forces and factors of institutional governance (laws, regulations, and standards) may lead to common interests among the members.
- Proposition #2: Ports in clusters would integrate informationally if similarities and differences among the members would determine the use of common resources (physical and nonphysical).
- Proposition #3: Ports in clusters would integrate informationally if the performance of an individual member may influence positively the performance of the whole cluster.
- Proposition #4: Ports in clusters would integrate informationally if ethical and legal principles of governance are important determinants for the quality of the whole cluster.

Step 2: Linking the Propositions with the BPIs

The construct in Figure 9.2 shows the environmental forces and factors of institutional governance that shape the BPI-COSEDAM. Ports depend on the

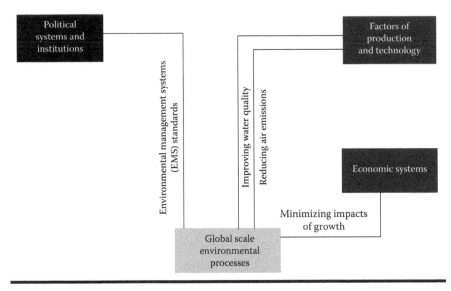

Figure 9.2 BPI-COSEDAM.

environment in which they operate to be sustained. Even if ports compete rather than collaborate in many of their functions, the necessity of ports to collaborate is stronger when the function of the port concentrates on operating under the consideration of climate, water, air, soil, and use of biodiversity as resources (Verhoeven, 2010, Hall et al. 2011). As a result, to integrate the environmental management functions among ports such as plans, documents, policy, normativity, and performance measurements is of extreme importance and requires a systematic approach to enhance its practice in future. Following Lam and Notteboom (2014) and Verhoeven (2010) it is possible to come to the conclusion that ports are able to successfully use environmental management systems (EMS) to identify and manage environmental and ecological challenges, setting standards, and accomplishing international initiatives. The construct in Figure 9.3 shows the relationships within the construct such as (a) the Selection/deviation of routes as a factor including geographical aspects to render a port more competitive (Yeo et al. 2008); (b) the throughput volume of the port; (c) imports and exports of cargo the origin or destination of which is overseas and/or the domestic market in monetary or freight units (Luan et al. 2010); and (d) prompt response as part of the port service component. (It may signify zero waiting time service or another dimension of service perceived for the port partner) (Yeo et al. 2008.); (e) infrastructure demand as related with the concept of urban expansion and demand for infrastructure construction (Han et al. 2009); and (f) land use patterns as the spatial pattern of port expansion affected by physical factors (Han et al. 2009). Additionally, infrastructure demand refers to the demand for port infrastructure construction (Han et al. 2009), such as gas and oil pipeline

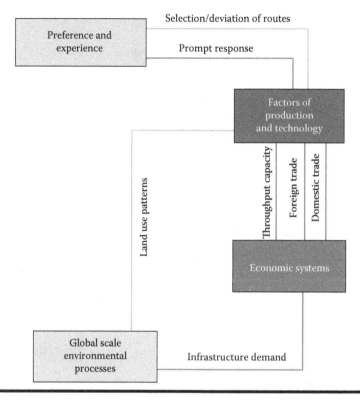

Figure 9.3 BPI-COLSETAM.

connections (GasPipes; OilPipes). Holding closely this notion, land use patterns refer to the spatial pattern of port expansion such as roll-on/roll-off, containers, and liquid bulk facilities (FacitityR; FacilityC, FacilityQ) affected by physical factors such as tides which determine the conditions of fixed or floating facilities and its specific services. The construct in Figure 9.4 shows a relationship between the port throughput (by commodity) as a performance standard, and the long-term patterns of international trade (export-oriented commodity) influenced (positively/negatively) by the operation of the port. This approach has challenged other researchers such as Luan et al. (2010) who state that "the social impact of port economy on city economy [in] previous researches mostly [has] considered the unilateral impact of port on city using port-city static models; which [hardly] reflect the dynamic change of the port-city interaction system (p. 399)." The construct in Figure 9.5 combines the concepts related to the principles of legal and ethical governance of port authorities. The outlining scheme are one to enhance maritime, ship, and port facility securities, and another to understand the ethical challenges port authorities may face when implementing them. Most of the factors are conveyed in such a way to ensure successful safety and environmental

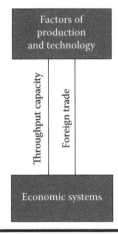

Figure 9.4 BPI-POFEDAM.

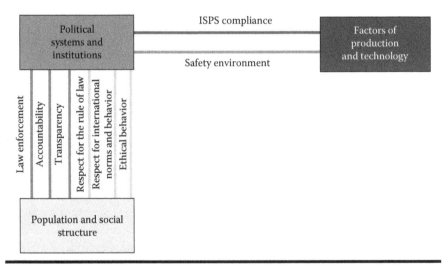

Figure 9.5 BPI-SELTIDAM.

inspections (for a detailed explanation see *Life at Sea*, 1974, as amended [SOLAS PROT 1978] and International Convention on Load Lines, 1966 [LL 1966]). The Code of Security of Ships and of Port Facilities (ISPS Code) can also be associated to security levels occurring in the interface ship/port area. Factors associated with these levels can be vessels inspected (inspections), vessels detained (detentions), vessels detected with deficiencies (deficiencies), and port facilities authorized to issue ship sanitation certificates under International Health Regulations (IHS).

In the quest to address a wide spectrum of corporate social responsibility (CSR) challenges, specifically to make it useful in port clusters, the inclusion of the International Organization for Standardization [ISO] 26,000 as an element of analysis is suggested.

Step 3: Searching for Patterns Using the Outputs of the DM Workflows

Figure 9.6 exemplifies the patterns among ports to enable identification of a partner port in an environmental benchmark context. The assumption is that a port would want to cooperate with other ports who shared their information on standards based on desirable requirements for the port's sustainable development. Some of the main challenges include (1) reduction of air emissions, (2) water quality improvements, and (3) minimization of the growing impacts of port. The classification is used to describe the distinct groups of ports with a special emphasis on the leaders of EMS programs. For example, Rule 5 (R5) identifies 20 out of 28 (average users), 7 out of 9 (followers), and only 1 leader. This might indicate that high concentrations of ozone within the area of the port followed by none historical encountered problems at receiving ozone substances by the seaport, is an important precedent to classify the seaport among those that should meet additional measures and requirements that otherwise are

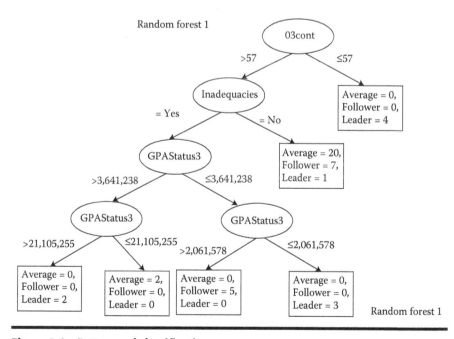

Figure 9.6   Patterns of classification.

appropriate for those classified as leaders in EMS programs. Interesting patterns of classification are

O3: (ordinal)/O3cont (nominal): fourth highest daily maximum 8-hour average of ozone concentrations (O3 air pollutants) measured in parts per billion (ppb) within an area of a port state.

Inadequacies: yes/no historical problems encountered at the port reception facility and informed to International Maritime Organization (IMO).

GAPStatus3: current GIS acres calculated for a U.S. state under the protection laws for conversion of natural land and water cover for the majority of area, according to the GAP analysis program in the U.S. Geological survey (USGS), subject to extractive uses of either broad, low intensity type (i.e., logging) or localised intense type (i.e., mining).

Type: Type of port, that is, deep water, seaport, river-based.

NMS: yes/no existence of national marine sanctuaries (NMS) where the port is relatively close.

LandFarms: land in farms given in acres by state and country where the port is elatively close.

Figures 9.7 through 9.9 exemplify patterns among ports of similar or dissimilar features such as their capacities and geographical location. It also may enable port authorities to form mutually beneficial networks informational integration. Interesting patterns of clustering are

Calls: Records of calls service of vessels of 10,000 DWT (deadweight) or greater

DmTrCg: Domestic trade of cargo in millions of U.S. dollars

FoTrExpCg: Foreign trade of export cargo in millions of U.S. dollars

WtContExp: Waterborne containerized export cargo in TEUs (20-ft equivalent units)

CapacityV: Vessels' capacity served by the port sized in DWT tons

GasPipes: Existence of gas pipeline connections

Tide: Tidal mean current rates (for vessels approaching and/or mooring)

OilPipes: Existence of oil pipelines connections

FacilityQ: Existence of infrastructure and facilities for serving liquid bulk cargo

FacilityC: Existence of infrastructure and facilities for serving containerized cargo

FacilityR: Existence of infrastructure in facilities for serving Ro-Ro cargo

Figure 9.9 exemplifies the patterns of time series and forecast components (i.e., seasonality, forecast horizon, predictors) for individual ports belonging or wanting to belong to specific cluster that share information in order to raise confidence within partner ports about investment, projects, trade facilitation, among others, that allow ports' advancement. Patterns describe the basic trends either emphasizing a random walk with moderate damping or a statistical trend reinforcing the series.

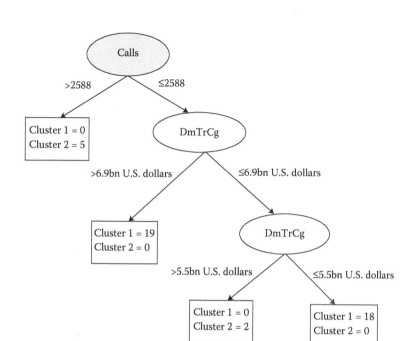

Figure 9.7   Patterns of clustering U.S. ports.

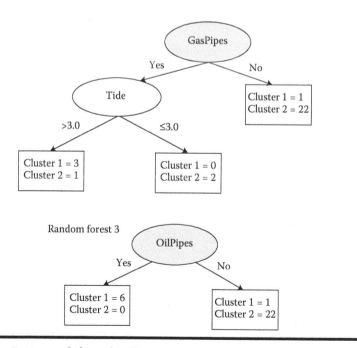

Figure 9.8   Patterns of clustering EU ports.

(a)   Interesting patterns of autocorrelations (ACF) spanned series 2001–2005

Foreign trade of exports commodity cargo (Coffee)
ARIMA (0, 0, 0) (1, 0, 0)

Port throughput by commodity (outgoing cargo) (coffee)
ARIMA (2, 0, 0) (0, 1, 0)

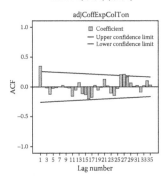
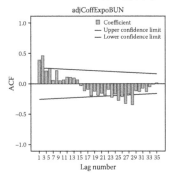

(b)   A weakly cross-correlation at lag 11 is observed to improve the prediction of CoffExpColTon.
A nonsignificant positive lag indicates that the first series specified: CoffOutBUN,
leads the second series thus it can predict the other somehow

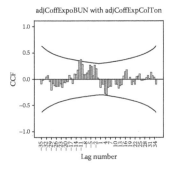

(c)   Analyses for the spanned series 2001 to 2005 encompass part of the trend observed for 1999–2003.
However, this one led to a marked improvement in seaport performance and operations (compared to what
it was before); though the improvement in seaport management and technology has not been quite as
impressive as in other countries around the world, we see how the port performance indicator CoffOutBUN
gains importance in the prediction of CoffExpColTon, thus indicating that the port operation was able
to affect the economy in regards to the exports of coffee somehow in a 78.7%.

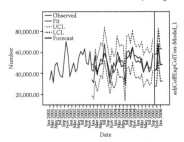

Model description

		Model type
Model ID	adjCoffExpColTon Model_1	ARIMA (0,0,0)(0,1,0)

Model statistics

Model	Number of predictors	Model fit statistics		Ljung-Box Q(18)			Number of outliers
		Stationary R-squared	R-squared	Statistics	DF	Sig.	
adjCoffExpColTon-Model_1	1	.787	.524	16.349	18	.568	2

Forecaset

Model		Jan 2006	Feb 2006	Mar 2006	Apr 2006	May 2006
adjCoffExpColTon-Model_1	Forecast	42,771.32	43,590.45	67,793.49	48,227.89	48,296.82
	UCL	58,036.66	58,855.79	83,058.84	63,493.23	63,562.16
	LCL	27,505.98	28,325.11	52,528.15	32,962.55	33,031.47

For each model, forecasts start after the last non-missing in the range of the
requested estimation period, and end at the last period for which non-missing
values of all the predictors are available or at the end date of the requested
forecast period, whichever is earlier.

Figure 9.9   Patterns of prediction. (a) Patterns of autocorrelation (ACF)—spanned series 2001–2005. (b) Patterns of cross-correlations (CCF)—spanned series 1999–2003. (c) Driving the forecasting model—spanned series 2001–2005.

Patterns of autocorrelation function (ACF), partial correlation function (PCF), and cross correlation function (CCF) give clear indication for prediction model's identification and seasonality behaviors. Patterns in outliers' visualization (if presented) give evidence of the historical events happening in the period of interest. Patterns produced by the forecasting model acquire knowledge in connection with the empirical evidence extracted from the domain. Interesting patterns of prediction are

> *Series of interest*: National exports of coffee (CoffExpCol) and port throughput in tons for coffee cargo (CoffOutBUN).
>
> *Historical period*: Historical and representative spanned series came out over the historical periods, 1999 through 2003 and 2001 and 2005.
>
> *Causal economic forces*: During the analysis performed to the series causal forces were identified; those that tend to drive the series up and those that drive the series down.
>
> *Series trend patterns*: Two trend patterns are observed: (a) the short-term pattern that relies on random walk processes (latest observation) and (b) the medium-to long-term pattern, which relies more on the historical data, providing an estimate of the series level.
>
> *Seasonality*: Whether the seasonality pattern was identified.
>
> *Forecast horizon*: Forecasts for seven months ahead for each spanned series were validated within the upper and lower ranges with 95% confidence.
>
> *Important event/outlier*: Important events identified through the "outliers" analysis.

Step 4: Finding Empirical Evidence for Each Proposition

The empirical evidence in Tables 9.1 and 9.2 shows the extant literature covering the local spatial proximities of port clusters in the United States. The spatial proximities among the ports are indicated by *if-then* rules obtained from the classification and clustering activity. Los Angeles and Long Beach are characterized by their high capacity to serve vessels and the cargo they are able to move. Unlike, the ports of Seattle and Portland are characterized by a lower capacity and throughput. Table 9.3 shows the extant literature covering the cross-regional spatial proximity—NAFTA Corridors in United States—Ports of New York, Houston, and Oakland. Ports of New York and Houston are characterized by their capacity and spatial extent. They are referred as gateways (container ports) for international trade. Globalization and integration processes, namely The North American Free Trade Agreement (NAFTA), have impacted the nature and function of continental production, consumption, and distribution. For international trade, the gateways of this system are the major container ports along the coastal areas from which long-distance trade corridors are accessed (Rodrigue 2008). The port of Oakland rather differs in its trade capacity but can be considered among the busiest ports reflecting a critical mass

Table 9.2   Empirical Evidence: Multi-Case: Local Spatial Proximity in United States—Ports of Los Angeles and Long Beach

Reducing Air Emissions	Empirical evidence: "The growth of trade and transportation is confronting the physical and organizational capabilities of all but a few. Delays and traffic interruptions are unfortunate features of ports, airports, rail yards, and urban highways everywhere. Ports like Los Angeles and Long Beach suffer from delays that ripple along entire logistics chains. Congestion aggravates environmental problems. Sustainable development strategies is potentially the single most important issue facing the growth, performance and organization of gateways (Comtois and Slack 2009, p. 130)." This point is also compared to port environmental actions in the same ports. "The port of Long Beach implemented the Green Flag Speed Reduction Program. By slowing down ships can reduce airborne emissions ans shipowners in return are granted a discount the following year as an incentive (Lam and Notteboom 2014, p. 173)." Similarly, Los Angeles and Long Beach adopted the Clean Trucks Program. "The port authorise trucking firms to access, the port through offering a limited number of concessions that will be granted to those that can meet certain criteria, including deploying vehicles that meet the 2007 EPA standards (Lam and Notteboom 2014, p. 173)."
Infrastructure Demand	
Minimizing Impacts of Growth	
Environmental Management System Standards	

Table 9.3   Empirical Evidence: Multi-Case: Local Spatial Proximity in United States—Ports of Seattle and Portland

Infrastructure Demand	Empirical evidence: "the capacity of the Pacific Northwest region [Ports of Seattle, Tacoma, and Portland] to handle intermodal freight transportation demand will not be sufficient to satisfy the demand in the future. Also, there is a general sense among stakeholders that intermodal freight transportation brings significant benefits from both sustainability and service points of view as they consider that intermodal transportation reduces gas emissions as compared to using truck when moving freight over long distances and reduces road congestion (Vergara et al. 2015, pp. ii, 67)."
Reducing Air Emissions	
Port Throughput	

Table 9.4 Empirical Evidence: Multiple-Case: Cross-Regional Spatial Proximity—NAFTA Corridors USA

Foreign Trade	Empirical evidence: "Transportation systems are composed of a complex set of relationships between the demand, the locations they service and the networks that support movements. Such
Domestic Trade	conditions are closely related to the development of transportation networks, both in capacity and in spatial extent. Future transportation systems will likely be shaped by the same forces than
Port Throughput	in the past but it remains to be seen which technologies will prevail and what will be their
Selection/Deviation of Routes	impacts on the structure. Ongoing deregulation combined with the North American Free Trade Agreement (NAFTA) concluded in 1991 have had some impact on North American transport corridors (Rodrigue et al. 2013)." "A second consideration relates to the physical infrastructure of
Prompt Response	the geographic location in which NAFTA-related economic activity is concentrated. This are seems the most difficult, since it immediately calls into question the choice, level of
Infrastructure Demand	comparability and aggregation of environmental data (OEDC 2000, p. 58)." "Gateways tend to be dominant markets and this for all the two major maritime facades, the East and the West coasts
Environmental Management Systems Standards	(the Gulf Coast plays a more marginal role particularly for containers) (Rodrigue and Notteboom 2010, p. 499)." "The maritime Port of New York was the nation's second busiest waterborne freight gateway for international trade by value of shipments in 2008 (Bureau of Transportation Statistics (RITA) 2009 p. 24). "The maritime Port of Houston was the nation's third busiest freight gateway for waterborne international trade by value of shipments in 2008 (RITA, 2009, p. 28)." "The maritime Port of Oakland was the nation's 12th busiest waterborne freight gateway for international merchandise trade by value of shipments in 2008 (RITA, 2009, p. 70)."

Table 9.5   Empirical Evidence: Multi-Case: Cross-Regional Spatial Proximity—Rjin–Schelde Delta Ports in Netherlands and Belgium

Land Use Patterns	Empirical evidence: "The Rhine–Scheldt Delta port region is highly dependent on bulk commodities linked to energy production and the oil-based chemical industry. The shift away from fossil fuels to non-fossil fuels is considered as a major challenge and opportunity. The Delta port region should adopt a leading role in this transition to remain competitive as one of the most important energy and chemical clusters in the world. This can be done by further strengthening the linkages between the petrochemical complexes in different ports of the Delta, and by leading the way in innovation in the area of sustainable production methods and "ecologies of scale." It is imperative that these "ecologies of scale" advantages at individual port level (e.g., via co-siting); but also on a regional cross-border scale (e.g., the combined chemical industry in Rotterdam, Antwerp, Moerdijk and Terneuzen and along axes such as the Albert Canal), should be fully acknowledged in environmental policy (Notteboom 2011, p. 9)."
Infrastructure Demand	
Environmental Management System Standards	

for the port cluster. Table 9.4 shows the extant literature covering the cross-regional spatial proximity—Rijn–Schelde Delta Ports of Rotterdam, Antwerp, Moerdijk, and Terneuzen in Netherlands and Belgium. Regarding the cluster similarities among these ports, it can be said that they hold a leading role as one of the most important energy and chemical clusters in the world. The cluster differences indicated mostly for the port of Moerdijk can be explained based on its characteristics as an inland terminal with a limited infrastructure to service liquid bulk cargo (as it was in the year 2008). Tables 9.5 and 9.6 show the extant literature covering port jurisdictional(Institutional) proximities in South America. Taken the individual jurisdictional case of Buenaventura, influences from the port to the local/national economy are observed raising confidence/awareness about investment projects, trade facilitation, among others. The regulatory system attained by each port jurisdiction has its main component in the ships' inspections target and certification. An important distinction on territorial boundaries is relevant to the state's jurisdiction. Maritime zones geneate

Table 9.6   Port Jurisdictional Case: The Port of Buenaventura in Colombia

Port Throughput	Empirical evidence: "The port model prevailing in Latin America and the Caribbean is the result from the major reforms of the decades of the 1990s and 2000s. It allowed for substantial achievements as regards the reduction of foreign trade port costs, but with limitations in terms of adding value to trade facilitation and transport in the supply chains of importers and exporters (Latin American and Caribbean Economic System (SELA) 2015; p. 5)." "In the past, general cargo traffic was less containerisable, regional port competition was less of an issue, and ports comprised a lot of labour intensive activities, generating considerable value-added and a multitude of direct and indirect impacts on the national economy, including of course the facilitation of international trade (Haralambides 2015, p. 226)."
Foreign Trade	
	In countries like Colombia, a crisis is being experienced due to the lack of investment in infrastructure to carry out general improvements particularly to the ports. Kent and Ashar (2010) indicate that ports of Colombia were privatized between 1990 and 1997. The period observed between 1999 and 2003 is thus a post-privatization period. It is therefore feasible to assume that the national economy particularly in regards to the exports of coffee may be unstable. Analyses for the spanned series 2001–2005 encompass part of this trend. Changes in the economy may have been influenced by improvements in port performance and operations; though the improvement in seaport management and technology has not been quite as impressive as in other countries around the world.

those distinctions creating debates around resources' exploitation and use of ecosystems and territorial protection (Table 9.7).

Step 5: Mapping the Spatial or Institutional Proximities (Jurisdictions) among Pairs or Subsets of Multiple Cases

Figures 9.10 through 9.13 graphically illustrates the spatial proximities of multiple cases one and two.

Table 9.7   Multiple-Case Institutional Proximity—Ports in South America

Measures in addressing compliance with the safety environment	Empirical evidence: Guy and Lapointe (2011) suggest that interregional and inter-jurisdictional perspectives are attracting interest into transportation policies and port planning; however, that poses challenges for "integrating different modal, cargo-based and regional segments of the transport industry [due to it also] raises governance difficulties because it involves more than one jurisdiction (p. 161)."
Measures in addressing compliance with the safety environment	
Measures in addressing compliance with law enforcement (LE)	An important distinction on territorial boundaries is relevant to a State's jurisdiction. Maritime zones generate those distinctions creating debates around resources' exploitation, use of ecosystems and territorial protection.
Corporate Social Responsibility	"On 12 December 2014, the Latin American and Caribbean Economic System (SELA) and CAF-development bank of Latin America concluded a Technical Cooperation Agreement initiated in November 2013 and whose purpose was the creation of the Latin American and Caribbean Network of Digital and Collaborative Ports (NDCP) in the first phase, which involved nine ports, namely: Manzanillo and Veracruz (Mexico); Buenaventura and Cartagena (Colombia); Callao (Peru); San Antonio and Valparaiso (Chile), and Balboa and Colon (Panama). This agreement was part of SELA's systematic effort in the area of trade facilitation, supported by information and communications technologies (ICT) and the construction of intra-regional dialogues to undertake concerted actions and participate as a trusted third party in proposals for international cooperation in order to promote regional initiatives on such issues. It also complements SELA's action to boost the implementation of foreign trade single windows in Latin American and Caribbean countries (UNCTAD 2015, p. 24)."

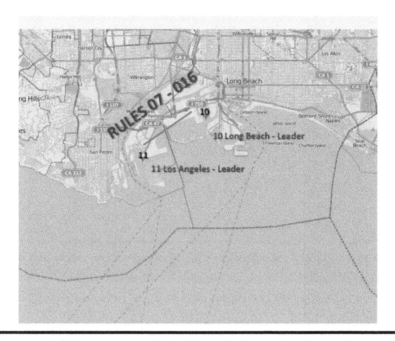

Figure 9.10   Multiple-case: Local spatial proximity in U.S.—Ports of Los Angeles and Long Beach.

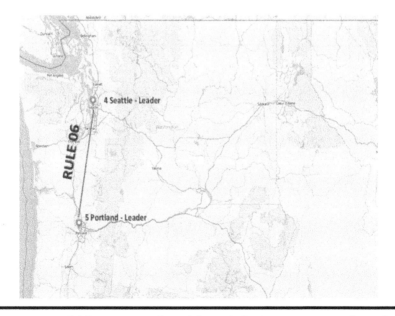

Figure 9.11   Multiple-case: Local spatial proximity in U.S.—Ports of Seattle and Portland.

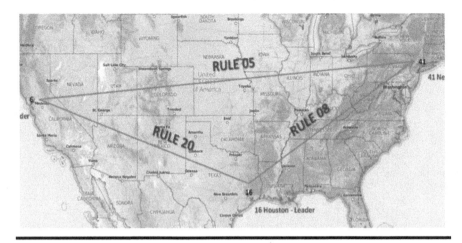

Figure 9.12   Multiple-case: Cross-regional spatial proximity—NAFTA Corridors USA.

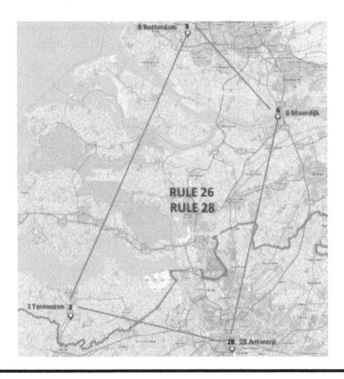

Figure 9.13   Multiple-case: Cross-regional spatial proximity—Rijn–Schelde Delta Ports in Netherlands and Belgium.

Conclusions

This chapter weighs the importance of multiple port cases to support informational integration with extant literature. The theory building from cases demonstrates its objectivity emphasising the real-world context in which the port informational integration may occur, therefore, demonstrating that a multi-case study analysis can accommodate a rich variety of empirical analyses. The argument is that expertise on this matter is served by consistent empirical evidence in a process accounting for data, models and the corresponding validation for multiple case studies. Evidence shall be regarded as clear statements to justify data analytics and a combination of research objectives.

References

Almotairi, B., Flodén, J., Stefansson, G., and Woxenius, J., 2011, Information flows supporting hinterland transportation by rail: Applications in Sweden, *Research in Transportation Economics*, 33(1), 15–24.

Bichou, K., 2006, Review of port performance approaches and a supply chain framework to port performance benchmarking, *Research in Transportation Economics*, 17(24), 567–598.

Bichou, K. and Gray, R., 2005, A critical review of conventional terminology for classifying seaports, *Transportation Research Part A: Policy and Practice*, 39(1), 75–92.

Brennan, J. and Martin, E., 2012, Spatial proximity is more than just a distance measure, *International Journal of Human-Computer Studies*, 70(1), 88–106.

Bureau of Transportation Statistics (RITA), 2009, America's Freight Transportation Gateways, Retrieved from https://www.rita.dot.gov/bts/sites/rita.dot.gov.bts/files/publications/americas_freight_transportation_gateways/2009/pdf/entire.pdf accessed July 2016.

Comtois, C. and Slack, B., 2009, Competitiveness of green gateways: A blueprint for Canada, in P. W. D. Langen, C. S. Ducruet, and T. Notteboom (Eds.), *Ports in Proximity: Competition and Coordination Among Adjacent Seaports.*, pp. 128–133, Ashgate, Farnham, England.

Davenport, T., Mansar, S., Reijers, H., and Rosemann, M., 2006, Preface, in J. Eder, and S. Dustdar (Eds.), *Business Process Management Workshops: BPM 2006 International Workshops*, BPD, BPI, ENEI, GPWW, DPM, semantics4ws, Vienna, Austria , September 4–7, 2006. Proceedings. pp. 3–4, Springer, Berlin, Heidelberg.

De Langen, P. W., 2004, Analysing the performance of seaport clusters, Shipping and Ports in the Twenty-first Century, Routledge, Abingdon.

De Langen, P. W., 2006, Stakeholders, conflicting interests and governance in port clusters, *Research in Transportation Economics*, 17(0), 457–477 [Chapter 20].

De Langen, P., 2015, Governance in seaport clusters, in H. Haralambides (Ed.), *Port Management*, pp. 138–154, Palgrave Macmillan, UK.

Ducruet, C., 2009, Port regions and globalization, in P. W. d. Langen, C. s. Ducruet, and T. Notteboom (Eds.), *Ports in Proximity: Competition and Coordination Among Adjacent Seaports*, pp. 41–53, Ashgate, Farnham.

Eisenhardt, K. M., 1989, Building theories from case study research, *The Academy of Management Review*, 14(4), 532–550.

Eisenhardt, K. M. and Graebner, M. E., 2007, Theory building from cases: Opportunities and challenges, *The Academy of Management Journal*, 50(1), 25–32.

Genrich, M., Kokkonen, A., Moormann, J., Muehlen, M., Tregear, R., Mendling, J. et al., 2008, Challenges for business process intelligence: Discussions at the BPI Workshop 2007, in A. ter Hofstede, B. Benatallah, and H.-Y. Paik (Eds.), *Business Process Management Workshops*, 4928, pp. 5–10, Springer, Berlin, Heidelberg.

Guy, E. and Lapointe, F., 2011, Building value into transport Chains: The challenges of multi-goal policies, in C. Comtois, B. Slack, P. V. Hall, and R. J. McCalla (Eds.), *Integrating Seaports and Trade Corridors*, pp. 154–164, Ashgate, Farnham.

Halabi-Echeverry, A., 2016, Computational intelligence to assist development of strategic decision making for the port integration, *Doctoral thesis*, Macquarie University, Sydney, Australia.

Hall, P., McCalla, R. J., Comtois, C., and Slack, B., 2011, *Integrating Seaports and Trade Corridors*, Ashgate, Farnham.

Han, J., Hayashi, Y., Cao, X., and Imura, H., 2009, Application of an integrated system dynamics and cellular automata model for urban growth assessment: A case study of Shanghai, China, *Landscape and Urban Planning*, 91(3), 133–141.

Haralambides, H., 2015, Competition, excess capacity and the pricing of port infrastructure, in H. Haralambides (Ed.), *Port Management*, pp. 221–252. Palgrave Macmillan, UK.

Henesey, L. E., 2006, *Multi-Agent Systems for Container Terminal Management*, Blekinge Institute of Technology, Sweden.

Hiranandani, V., 2014, Sustainable development in seaports: A multi-case study, *WMU Journal of Maritime Affairs*, 13(1), 127–172.

Kent, P. and Ashar, A., 2010, Indicators for port concession contracts and regulation: The Colombian case, http://asafashar.com/IAME_2010_Article_Performance_Indicators_for_Regulators_Final_Final.pdf accessed October 2016.

Lam, J. S. L. and Notteboom, T., 2014, The greening of ports: A comparison of port management tools used by leading ports in Asia and Europe, *Transport Reviews*, 34(2), 169–189.

Latin American and Caribbean Economic System (SELA), 2015, Digital ports in Latin America and the Caribbean: Situation and prospects, *XXVI Meeting of International Cooperation Directors for Latin America and the Caribbean*, Port Cooperation in Latin America and the Caribbean: Digital ports. Situation and Prospects Punta Cana, Dominican Republic, April 23 and 24. SP/XXVI-RDCIALC/DT N° 2-15.

LL 1966, Protocol of 1988 relating to the International Convention on Load Lines, 1966. (n.d.). Retrieved from http://www.admiraltylawguide.com/conven/protoload-lines1988.html.

Luan, W. X., Chen, H., and Wang, Y. W., 2010, Simulating mechanism of interaction between ports and cities based on system dynamics: A case of Dalian, China, *Chinese Geographical Science*, 20, 398–405.

Murty, K. G., Liu, J. Y., Wan, Y. W., and Linn, R., 2005, A decision support system for operations in a container terminal, *Decision Support Systems*, 39(3), 309–332.

Notteboom, T. E., 2011, *Economic Analysis of the Rijn, Schelde Delta Port Region*, ITMMA, Antwerp.

Organization for Economic Cooperation and Development (OECD). 2000, *Assessing the Environmental Effects of Trade Liberalisation Agreements*, OECD Publishing, Paris, France.

Rodrigue, J. P., 2008, Transport and spatial organization, in *The Geography of Transport Systems*, http://people.hofstra.edu/geotrans accessed July 2016.

Rodrigue, J. P., Comtois, C., and Slack, B., 2013, *The Geography of Transport Systems*, Taylor & Francis, retrieved from https://people.hofstra.edu/geotrans/about.html.

Rodrigue, J. P. and Notteboom, T., 2010, Comparative North American and European gateway logistics: The regionalism of freight distribution, *Journal of Transport Geography*, 18(4), 497–507.

SOLAS PROT 1978, Protocol of 1978 relating to the International Convention for Safety of Life at Sea (London 1978). (n.d.). Retrieved from http://webcache.googleusercontent.com/search?q=cache:0omtSAZakGMJ:www.admiraltylawguide.com/conven/protosolas1978.html+&cd=1&hl=en&ct=clnk&gl=co.

United Nations Conference on Trade and Development UNCTAD. 2015, Programme for the Creation of the Latin American and Caribbean Network of Digital and Collaborative Ports, in *Transport & Trade Facilitation Newsletter*, No. 65-Fifth Quarter 2014, UNCTAD Trade and Logistics Branch.

Vergara, H. A., Ghane-Ezabadi, M., Rahanjam, M., and Hall, M., 2015, Assessing the capacity of the Pacific Northwest as an intermodal freight transportation hub (No. 2013-S-OSU-0036), New York and Geneva.

Verhoeven, P., 2010, A review of port authority functions: Towards a renaissance? *Maritime Policy & Management*, 37(3), 247–270.

Wang, C., Ducruet, C., and Wang, W., 2015, Port integration in China: Temporal pathways, spatial patterns and dynamics, *Chinese Geographical Science*, 25(5), 612–628.

Woodside, A. G., 2010, *Building Theory from Case Study Research. Case Study Research: Theory, Methods and Practice*, Emerald, Bingley.

Yeo, G., Roe, M., and Dinwoodie, J., 2008, Evaluating the competitiveness of container ports in Korea and China, *Transportation Research Part A: Policy and Practice*, 42(6), 910–921.

Chapter 10

Data Analytics to Characterize University-Based Companies for Decision Making in Business Development Programs

León Darío Parra Bernal and
Milenka Linneth Argote Cusi

Contents

Summary..188
Introduction...189
Theoretical References 190
Definition of the Problem Analyzed 192
Research Questions or Hypotheses 192
What Was the Methodology of the Problem Resolution?...................................193
    What Was the Data Used? 193
    What Were the Models and Concepts Used in This Study? 194
What Was the Way to Test/Answer the Hypotheses/Research Questions? 195
    About Validity and Reliability in This Work 196

Why Is This Approach for the Solution Valuable? 196
What Are the Results and Their Interpretation? 197
How Are These Results Meaningful for Organizations and for Future Research? 199
Conclusions and Recommendations..199
Are the Objectives of the Research Achieved?...199
Operational and Tactical Implications...200
Strategic Implications 200
Statistical Appendix...203
References...203

Summary

Today, the topic of entrepreneurship has become of main importance in the structure of support that universities provide to their students. However, in Latin America the sources of statistical information and research to characterize the profile of the university entrepreneur are still embryonic, making it difficult to design and to make product development support adapted to the needs of university entrepreneurs. This situation demands the use of tools for the collection and analysis of data on the characteristics of the business of university students, in order to obtain data for decision making regarding the creation and promotion of support programs business in universities. In 2013, a census was conducted on business enterprises owned by undergraduate and graduate students, or their parents, as well as graduates in the EAN University in Colombia. The central purpose of this research was to characterize these companies into different dimensions of analysis, and thus to establish, among other things, business support needs, opportunities for growth, and improvement for these companies, and levels of differentiation among firms for academic programs, and other control variables (Parra and Argote 2015). The results of previous research aroused the interest in 2014 for this research project will be replicated in the Continental University in Peru, with the same methodology that was implemented in the EAN University. With data from the two Universities, it proceeded to elaborate an analysis with a logistic regression model, in order to discriminate the factors associated with the potential of business growth and product innovation, and traditional companies with a low level based on sales and no productive innovation. This is in order to design a portfolio of support services and business development differential for each group of companies. The analysis conducted in the two populations allowed discrimination against businesses owned by students and graduates according to their productive and economic characteristics, providing information about specific needs of each company business support, expressed in issues such as financing sources, marketing, and network management. The study allowed to identify that about 75% of the companies surveyed in both universities were associated with poor production characteristics, requiring more support in the commercial area, while another 25% showed production characteristics with potential growth, requiring greater support in areas such as networking and business innovation.

Introduction

Nowadays the access to several information systems is strategic for the investigation in different areas and to support decision making. Under the premise that the information is power, having the updated market information and the population characterization studies are really important not only for any edge research but also for business intelligence (Cañibano and Sanchez 2004).

While United States and Europe have extensive literature and experience about business and entrepreneurship, (Rothaermel et al. 2007) in Latin America the statistical information based in the characterization of the business network is in an embryonic stage, with some initiatives, such as the Global Entrepreneurship Monitor (GEM), that gather up information worldwide contemplate some variables for measuring the entrepreneurship rate. In particular cases, like the entrepreneurship inside the universities and its application in the processes of entrepreneurial incubation, the availability of primary information turns out to be more precarious (Kantis et al. 2002b).

In regard to previous situation, with the challenge to decrease the gap, in 2013 a survey was performed in EAN University located in Bogotá, Colombia. The main objective was to characterize the student's companies (or their parents), in order to have a basic information to classify companies according to its growth potential and therefore guide the entrepreneurial development and incubation programs created in that institution. According to the results obtained in 2013, the investigation was replicated in 2014 with the Continental University located in Huancayo City, Peru. The information gathered in both universities, in two Latin American countries, allows to identify the specific needs in terms of support and business development (Parra and Argote 2015).

This research has as its main contribution the characterization of the entrepreneurial profile in universities. The methodological field provides instruments to collect demographic, financial, technologic, and social features and the enterprise networks inside the universities; this knowledge allows us to design focused entrepreneurial support strategies. In the other way, the experiment design that was developed in the two different contexts (Colombia and Peru) allows one to make a contrast analysis of the case–control type. An analysis of such information enhances the decision making regarding the design and implementation of incubation programs and entrepreneurial development in both institutions.

This chapter develops in the following order. The first section contextualizes the study and the main theoretical references about university entrepreneurship topic; furthermore, it emphasizes the importance of the data analysis in the decision making in the incubation field and entrepreneurial development. In the second section, we present the methodology used to develop the entrepreneurial survey in both universities and the selected statistical model to determine the factors associated with the companies with productive growth potential in both universities. In the third section, the results of the entrepreneurial characterization in both universities are shown the same way as a statistical model regarding the explanation about the companies with growth potential. Finally, the fourth section closes with a discussion about the findings and its main applications for the decision making.

Theoretical References

There is a wide development in the theory regarding university entrepreneurship in general and in the four research streams that have emerged over the last decade: entrepreneurial research university, productivity of technology transfer offices, new firm creation, and environmental context including networks of innovation. Nevertheless, in Latin America there is a recent matter with investigations that strengthen the theoretical bases of the topic such as the creation through empiric studies. Among the most complete studies, we have the Rothaermel et al. (2007) theoretical review that systematizes the theoretical advances in the literature about university entrepreneurship in the United States and Europe, through the 173 articles published in academic journals. Among the empirical studies, the Global Entrepreneurship Monitor Project is noteworthy, which in the last decade has collected information from more than 11 countries worldwide characterizing the entrepreneurial activities of adult population and the empirical studies of Santarelli and Vivarelli (2006) with companies of the OECD and Italy. In Latin America, the first studies begin in 2000 with the research of Kantis et al. (2002a) on dynamic entrepreneurship, characterization of entrepreneurship in Latin America and East of Asia, and university entrepreneur characterization in Argentina, among other publications (Kantis et al. 2002b).

The investigations in university entrepreneurship is extensive. In the last decade, the research in university entrepreneurship rise in part due to the industry's growing demand for technological innovation and to reduce public funding for research (Thursby and Thursby 2002). There are investigations about the entrepreneurship intentions and motivations (Cowling and Taylor 2001, Liseras et al. 2003), about the new firm creation and development of spin-off* (Colombo and Delmastro 2002, Kantis et al. 2002b, Rothaermel et al. 2007, Pazos et al. 2008, Parra and Argote 2013, 2015), the impact of entrepreneurship training in the new firms' creation inside universities (Crissen 2013), and the influence of the·college training of the entrepreneur or businessman in the entrepreneurial growth (Kantis et al. 2002b).

Regarding the factors associated with entrepreneurship with the growth potential, some investigations indicate that there is more related to the specific features of the businessman or entrepreneur than to external factors (Parra 2016). Several studies delve into the competencies, knowledge, features, and motivations that lead

---

* Spin-off is an Anglo-Saxon term that refers to a project born as an extension of a previous one, or more of a company born from another by separating a subsidiary division or department of the company to become a business in itself.

to the entrepreneurs to create their own company and the way they manage to survive successfully in the market (Dubini 1989, Kantis et al. 2004, Van Gelderen and Jansen 2006).

One of the determinant variables of the potential growth is the age of the company. Through the years the company gains experience and knowledge useful to survive in the market. According to the research of Daepp et al. (2015) the age is a key variable to explain entrepreneurial mortality. Concomitantly, Mengistae (2006) explains the growth and survival of the companies from the entrepreneur's business expertise and the number of years of studies; this relation can be compared with the number of years of the company in the market. Furthermore, many authors have associated the concept of success with a temporary situation linked to the survival of organizations (Bosma et al. 2004). This perspective of the industrial organization indicates that companies with benefits and profits decide to remain in the market and those that generate losses end up giving up their entrepreneurial activity (Jovanovic 1982, Harada 2003).

Financing is an essential variable all along the entrepreneurial cycle. Financing of new firm creation can define the force of its start and its subsequent survival. For instance, Lasio et al. (2005) found that 75% of the Ecuatorians invest in family business, friends, or neighbors; this implies that a high percentage of new businesses are funded with own resources and closely 20% turned to the financial sector. Parra and Argote (2015) found in EAN (Colombia) and Continental (Peru) universities that companies financed their start stage with: family savings, previous jobs incomes, friends, or family loans and in the last instance with financial institutions or banks. Other studies have found that the type of financing in the early stages of the entrepreneurial creation process can lead to condition the stability and the continuity of them in the market on midterm (Echecopar et al. 2006; Fracica et al. 2011). Then, companies that have enough resources to finance their initial phase could have a better chance of survival in "the valley of death" than those who do not have.

On the other hand, Kelley et al. (2012) carried out an analysis about the development and success of companies in relation to the context where they operate and the economic field where they are created. It is found that the companies have differences between countries with different levels of development; hence, the GEM differentiates among factor-driven economies and efficiency-driven economies.* About that Mengistae (2006) states that the growth and development of companies are influenced by the sector where the business operates. Regarding this, Rothaermel et al. (2007) include in their conceptual model about university

---

* The GEM ranks countries according to their level of productive development into three categories: Economies driven by factors that have the basic requirement to institutional and infrastructure to generate new business, driven by efficiency. Economies whose level of institutional maturity has allowed the efficient use of resources such as labor market, higher education, and a sophisticated financial market to generate new business, and innovation-driven economies whose economic development has generated them all an institutional ecosystem and enabling knowledge transfer to generate a new business (Kelley et al. 2012).

entrepreneurship, the context where the companies are immerse and identify four factors that influence the university entrepreneurship: the innovation networks, science parks, incubation processes, and geographical location.

Another important variable according to the analyzed studies are the entrepreneurial networks. Hansen (1995) found that the founders with wide social and professional networks had more access to knowledge sources, capital resources, and more customers. Kantis et al. (2004) concluded that the networks play an important role for the dynamic companies; it allows them to gain access to non-monetary resources such as information, technology, raw materials, or equipment, among others. Tornikoski and Newbert (2007) in their conceptual model with nine dimensions also give importance to networking because once the entrepreneur establishes a network, the entrepreneur can gain access to its resources.

Definition of the Problem Analyzed

At present, the promotion of the entrepreneurship is an important area in the support structure that universities give to their students as part of the current educational and economic command that has been given to these institutions (Rothaermel et al. 2007). However, one of the problems in the entrepreneurial accompaniment and incubation process inside universities is the lack of primary information about the productive and economic profile of entrepreneurial students and their companies, making difficult to design and create entrepreneurial programs according to the needs of this population.

In that order, the investigation outlines the relevance of primary data that gives essential information about socio-productive features and the stage of the cycle where the companies are. This information bring us elements to design a portfolio for companies' traditional base characterized by low impact in the employment generation and with subsistence incomes, as for those which their entrepreneurial profile has the potential of productive growth.

Research Questions or Hypotheses

The present investigation was focused on solving the following research questions: (1) Which are the features of the companies owned by students or graduates in the universities of the study? (2) Which are the factors associated with the university entrepreneurship with growth potential? (3) Which are the differences in both universities of the study? The answer to these questions gives the essential elements to the decision making in the incubation programs and entrepreneurial development in both institutions.

One of the hypothesis considered at the beginning of the investigation was that the features of the university entrepreneurship in the Continental University in Peru are more precarious than the EAN University students companies in Colombia, because Colombia counts with an ecosystem of entrepreneurship more developed, which would boost the existence of a greater percentage of companies with the growth potential. Therefore, the entrepreneurial development strategies should be different in both universities in response of these differences.

What Was the Methodology of the Problem Resolution?

The interest in university entrepreneurship initiated in EAN University, Colombia, an educational institution since 1967 that includes the entrepreneurship topic in its curriculum and counts with a high percentage of students that own or want to create their own company or students whose parents have company. According to the last perception survey that was carried out with the National Consulting Center (CNC, for its acronym in Spanish) in 2012, 35% of the graduates and 15% of the students state having a company. The mission of the university in the training of the entrepreneurs was taken as an opportunity to do an entrepreneurial survey indoors in 2013, complying a study case in the field of university-based entrepreneurship.

The entrepreneurial survey was executed in phases. The preoperative phase included compilation and analysis about the state of the art of entrepreneurial surveys and the methodologies and collect instruments, important activities for the fieldwork planning. Parallelly, the team was trained in the application of the instrument. Afterwards, the phase two implied the development of the fieldwork, which was subdivided into two stages: the pilot test and the execution of the survey *in situ*. Finally, the phase three implied the elaboration of the survey database, information processing, data evaluation, and the result analysis (Table 10.1).

The instrument had eight sections: demographic characteristics of students, company information, technological level, financial system access, human resources, market access, entrepreneurial network, and entrepreneurial innovation. On the basis of the first section a basic record of the companies owned by students was built and the other sections allow to know the features of the companies related to the use of new technologies, investment and innovation, financial system access, exportation, if they are affiliated; the advantages and disadvantages, and all important topics in the entrepreneurial activity.

The survey in the EAN University was conducted on March 2013 and in the Continental University in June 2014, both surveys were made with the support of a team of tutors, who have been previously trained.

What Was the Data Used?

The number of companies surveyed in both universities exceeds the planning expectations considering the economic and logistic restrictions. For the EAN University case, 346 companies owned by students and graduates or their parents was surveyed,

Table 10.1   Description of the Phases and Activities that Form the Development of the College Entrepreneurial Survey

Phase I Preoperative (POP)		Phase II Field Work (FWP)		Phase III Data Analysis (DAP)	
	Information collection for the Conceptual Framework		Pilot Test		Data Physical Validation Test (Random)
	Information collection from other surveys and the Colombian context		Feedback		Survey database design
	Survey planning coordination		Survey logistic strategy		Typing, debug, and validation
	Survey design form				Data analysis of the EAN University students companies
	Communication and marketing strategy definition				Information consolidation generated from the phases POP and FWP and diagnosis
	Training of the survey tutors and supervisors		Survey execution		Results communication
	Coordination of the survey implementation				Official results publication

Source: Own creation.

while for the Continental University 298 companies were surveyed. A total of 644 companies were surveyed, considering the pilot test and the extended survey.

What Were the Models and Concepts Used in This Study?

According to the literature, the study of a dynamic company requires longitudinal information (Kantis et al. 2002a). Currently, this kind of information about university-based companies is not available in Colombia and Peru, which is not the case of developed countries like United States (Daepp et al. 2015) and others (Delmar et al. 2003, Rothaermel et al. 2007). In this sense, the concept of "companies with growth potential" like an approximation to the concept of "dynamic company" because the information was collected in one moment of time. Likewise, it is assumed a company with growth potential, as one that receives an annual sale of more than US 50 thousand dollars (more than 100 million Colombian pesos and more than 70.000 Soles for Peru) and more than 10 employees at the moment of the survey.

The sample of the companies surveyed, allowed to build the dependent variable "potential" that discriminates among those companies that have a growth potential from those that do not have it, considering for its construction the total amount of annual sales and number of employees.* On the other side, the independent selected variables were the age of the company, the economic sector where the company develops, the availability of having external financing at the moment of creation, and the membership of some kind of entrepreneurial network. The selection of the independent variables was based on the theoretical referents described previously and that are associated with the theories of entrepreneurial growth (Delmar et al. 2003), the factors associated with the dynamic companies (Kantis et al. 2002a), the entrepreneurship and the process of start, survival, and entrepreneurial growth (Penrose 1959, Siegel et al. 1993, Agarwal and Gort 1996, Brassiolo and Arreaza 2013).

A logistic model[†] is used to shape the relation between the variables because it is considered that the prevalence of the companies with growth potential in an economic system increases as the company's economic contextual conditions improve. In this sense, the model allows us to know which is the prevalence of companies with growth potential in the sample and which factors are associated to that prevalence.

What Was the Way to Test/Answer the Hypotheses/Research Questions?

The logistic model allows us to answer the research questions. The model represents a dependent variable and a group of independent variables related by the logistic function that allows to predict the result of the categorical variable Y with "0" non-potential growth company and "1" growth potential company, according to the

---

* For this study it is assumed that a company has potential productivity growth in the two universities of studies (EAN University in Colombia and University Continental in Peru) when employing more than 10 employees and their sales exceed one hundred thousand dollars a year.

† In the section "Statistical Appendix" models of the multicollinearity tests are explained.

independent or predictor variables. The model target is to find the prevalence rate based on the number of cases and the information that the predictor variables can offer in order to estimate a final occurrence rate:

$$\text{log}it(p_i) = ln\left(\frac{p_i}{1 - p_i}\right) = \beta_0 + \beta_1 x_{1,i} + \cdots + \beta_k x_{k,i}. \tag{10.1}$$

The odds ratio are modeled by the linear function of the predictor variables. The beta variables are the additive effects in the odds ratio logarithm corresponding to a change unit in the *j–esima* explicatory variable (as shown in Equation 10.1).

To evaluate the variable significance in the model the test Ji-squared or the distribution Ji-squared is used to accept or reject the null hypothesis. If the *p*-value is lower than the significance level, the null hypothesis is rejected, while the lower the *p*-value the more significant the result is. In this case, the null hypothesis is that the independent variable x_i has no incidence in the dependent variable y_i "growth potential companies." That is to say that the significant variables have an impact on the dependent variable.

About Validity and Reliability in This Work

The present investigation involves two parts: the design and implementation of an entrepreneurial university-based survey and a logistic model to evaluate the study hypothesis. They were developed following a methodology that allowed obtaining in a systematic way the information and the results that are used to evaluate the investigation hypothesis.

The systematization and the generated documentation of the entrepreneurial survey in the EAN University allowed to replicate the process in the Continental University in Peru. Note that in order to guarantee that the samples could be comparable, we considered as control variables the features of the entrepreneurship processes in each university, at the same time the survey was the same for both institutions. Finally, the logistic model allowed to evaluate the investigation hypothesis through the odds ratio interpretation, the regression coefficient, and the *p*-values.

Why Is This Approach for the Solution Valuable?

The statistical data analysis is a powerful tool that allows making affirmations based on the evidence. However, for the data analysis it is necessary to have primary information. Although, in the thematic of Business university, there have been studies from entrepreneurial databases in developed countries (Rothaermel et al. 2007), in Latin America these studies are scarce (Kantis et al. 2002a), even more when it refers to university entrepreneurship.

In this sense, this investigation provides the creation of databases information of entrepreneurship in two Latin American universities, two different countries and two different economic contexts, which allows a contrast analysis of the case–control type. The different stages of each entrepreneurship ecosystems in each country assess the impact of the entrepreneurial activities inside the two universities.

What Are the Results and Their Interpretation?

The logistic model explains 10% of the variability for the surveyed companies in the EAN University and 15% for the surveyed companies in the Continental University, the results were consistent with the sample type and the variability associated with this multivariate analysis type.

The factors with more impact in the growth potential of enterprises are the age of each company and the business networks in both universities. The chance of being a potential growth company is 3.5 times bigger in those companies that are more than five years old in EAN University and 4.6 times in the Continental University. If the company is affiliated to some kind of entrepreneurial university network, it has 2.3 times more chances of having growth potential in EAN University and 7.1 times in Continental University (Tables 10.2 and 10.3).

The age of the company is an important demographic variable. In an economic system, as the company prevails through time and generates experience in the market it has a bigger probability of maintaining itself successfully (Prostigo and Fracica 2002). Likewise, Kantis et al. (2002a) found that the companies in the East

Table 10.2 Logistic Binominal Model for the Surveyed Companies in the EAN University, Bogota, Colombia, 2013

Variables	Odds Ratio	Coef.	P > |z|	Sig.
Seniority (0 = less than five years)	3.5269	1.2604	0.0000	
	2.1045	0.7441	0.0520	**
Sector (0 = manufacturing)	1.7953	0.5852	0.0910	*
	2.3582	0.8579	0.0470	**
Financing (0 = own resources)		−2.8162	0.0000	***
Networks (0 = it is not affiliated)				
_cons				

Note: Reference category: Nongrowth Potential Companies (NGPC). Dichotomy- dependent variable: 0 = NGP companies, 1 = GP companies. Odds ratio and coefficient regarding the reference category. Pseudo R^2: 0.1015.

*Significant to 0.1; **Significant to 0.05; ***Significant to 0.001.

Table 10.3 Logistic Binominal Model for the Surveyed Companies in the Continental University, Huancayo, Peru, 2013

Variables	Odds Ratio	Coef.	P > |z|	Sig.
Seniority (0 = less than five years)	4.6280	2.3644	0.0030	***
	1.1396	0.9332	0.8730	NS
Sector (0 = manufacturing)	1.3312	0.6470	0.5560	NS
	7.1723	3.8036	0.0000	***
Financing (0 = own resources)		−3.8686	0.0000	***
Networks (0 = it is not affiliated)				
_cons				

Note: Reference category: Nongrowth Potential Companies (NGPC). Dichotomy-dependent variable: 0 = NGP companies, 1 = GP companies. Odds ratio and coefficient regarding the reference category. Pseudo R^2: 0.1013.
NS—Nonsignificant; ***Significant to 0.001.

Asia have an important support in entrepreneurial networks, something that does not occur in the Latin American countries. It is noteworthy that the network variable was significant to the 0.001 in the Continental University; this result indicates if a company is affiliated to some kind of business network in Peru (mining sector, extractive sector, or machinery production) has seven times more opportunity of having growth potential than those are not affiliated.

The sector and financing variables were not significant for the Peru case as for the Colombian case. An exploratory review of the Colombian context in relation to the incubation and entrepreneurship processes in Parra and Argote (2013) shows that this context offers a wide financing portfolio (DANE 2012) and an advanced ecosystem that pretends to strengthen the industry through a Productive Transformation Program (Parra and Argote, 2015). In this sense, it is found that the companies surveyed by the EAN University that unfold in the manufacturing sector (industry and transformation) have two times more of opportunity of becoming in companies with growth potential than those that are placed in the nonmanufacturing sector (services, trade, and agricultural). In contrast, in the Continental University the difference by sector is not significant (see Table 10.3), perhaps due to the weight of the trade and services sector in the total number of companies. When the distribution of the companies is observed by productive sectors the EAN University counts with a bigger participation in the manufacturing industry sector (18.2%), while in the Continental University it is 8.1%.

The financing topic is decisive in the companies for its start and survival in the market. From the surveyed companies, it is clear that even though they affirmed that they would access the bank system, only a smaller percentage has real access to this financing mechanism, this is an indicator of the problem that the Latin American companies are facing. In the EAN University model the companies that access to third party resources such as banks and financing entities have 1.7 times more of being companies with growth potential than those that only have own resources. In the case of Continental University, the variable was not significant because most of the surveyed companies affirmed to get started with own and/or family resources.

How Are These Results Meaningful for Organizations and for Future Research?

The findings of the investigations about the topic of entrepreneurship in general and business entrepreneurship in particular match the surveyed companies in EAN University in Colombia and Continental University in Peru. The independent variables: age of the company, sector, financing, and the networks are factors that influence the growth potential of the entrepreneurship (Galloway and Brown 2002, Kantis et al. 2004, Camacho 2007, Rothaermel et al. 2007).

The 17% of the surveyed companies in the EAN University and 7.4% in the Continental University are classified as companies with growth potential. Most of the surveyed companies counts with less than 10 employees (85.2% in Continental University and 74.35% in the EAN University) and more than 50% of them have more than five years of experience in the market (62.3% in the Continental University and 51.7% in the EAN University), which reflects the persistence of the entrepreneurs to keep up with the market.

The most important challenge for the two universities is to create companies that survive over time, and improve their incomes, generate jobs, and have a steady growth in an independent way or that are part of a conglomerate, which implies a bigger level of organization.

At the university level, in which the entrepreneurship-training topic is a major component to create a company, as in the case of the EAN University, it is observed that there exists other variables that promote the transit to companies with growth potential, and that are exogenous to the training process as well as have access to networks and financing sources. No doubt, the work University—private sector and state—is very important and decisive for the future public policy agenda on this topic (Parra and Argote 2013).

Conclusions and Recommendations

Are the Objectives of the Research Achieved?

The census data analysis in both institutions and the results of the model allowed us to arrive at the following conclusions:

About 17% of the surveyed companies in the EAN University and the 7.4% in the Continental University are classified as companies with growth potential, considering the total of the annual sales and the number of employees. Of the companies, 85.2% in the Continental University and 74.35% in the EAN University count with less than 10 employees.

The previous aspects imply that the incubation programs and the strengthening entrepreneurial that generates inside these two institutions must have in mind the base traditional structure companies of the students. In this sense, it is convenient to focus the efforts on the growth of companies with growth potential before focusing on other kinds of factors.

Operational and Tactical Implications

For the tactical and operational part, the results indicate that the incubation programs and strengthening entrepreneurial must focus on the accomplishment of the business owners in the first years of creation of their companies. The age variable, being significant in both study populations, indicates that if the companies survive in the first two years, the likelihood of becoming companies with growth potential increases significantly. Moreover, the entrepreneurial incubation programs must be emphasized on the participation and the articulation in entrepreneurial networks among their beneficiaries. In both universities, was found that the configuration of the networks increases radically the possibility that a company manifests productive growth potential.

Additionally, the financing support lines and the seed capital that the EAN University offers to its entrepreneurs, according to the results in which most companies have own resources, contribute to the creation of companies with growth potential. It is also desirable that the incubation program and entrepreneurial promotion in the EAN University consider focusing its efforts on the creation and support to companies in the diffuser sectors of knowledge related with the manufacturing industry.

Strategic Implications

Although, the experience of other countries that are working in the entrepreneurship field since previous years shows us the way forward, this must adjust to local realities. In Latin America, the productivity issue is characterized by its narrow base with minor differences between countries. To that, it is added the low information availability to measure these productive phenomena, which allows knowing the situation, identifying the challenges, and planning into the future in order to obtain the results wanted, as for the economic development (Peña-Vinces et al. 2010). Therefore, it is strategic the generation of contextual information for public policy design according the geographic location (Rothaermel et al. 2007).

Table 10.4 Correlation Matrix for the Independent Variables in the Logistic Model for the Case of EAN University

Variables	Anti-güedad	VIF_i	T_i	Sector1	VIF_i	T_i	Finan	VIF_i	T_i	Redes	VIF_i	T_i	Innova	VIF_i	T_i	Export
Antigüedad	1.0000															
Sector1	0.0590	1.0035	0.9965	1												
Finan	0.0293	1.0009	0.9991	−0.0509	1.0026	0.9974	1									
Redes	0.1533	1.0241	0.9765	−0.0047	1.0000	1.0000	−0.047	1.0022	0.9978	1						
Innova	0.0815	1.0067	0.9934	0.0153	1.0002	0.9998	0.084	1.0071	0.9929	0.1118	1.0127	0.9875	1			
Export	0.0570	1.0033	0.9968	0.0998	1.0101	0.9900	0.0391	1.0015	0.9985	0.129	1.0169	0.9834	0.0789	1.0063	0.9938	1

Source: Compiled from the business census of the EAN University.

Table 10.5 Correlation Matrix for the Independent Variables in the Logistic Model for the Case of the Continental University

Variables	Antigüedad	VIF_i	T_i	Sector1	VIF_i	T_i	Finan	VIF_i	T_i	Redes	VIF_i	T_i	Innova	VIF_i	T_i	Export
Antigüedad	1.0000															
Sector1	0.0497	1.0025	0.9975	1												
Finan	0.0371	1.0014	0.9986	−0.0099	1.0001	0.9999	1									
Redes	−0.0820	1.0068	0.9933	0.0121	1.0001	0.9999	0.0464	1.0022	0.9978	1						
Innova	−0.1983	1.0409	0.9607	−0.0066	1.0000	1.0000	−0.0137	1.0002	0.9998	0.0962	1.0093	0.9907	1			
Export	0.0322	1.0010	0.9990	−0.2023	1.0427	0.9591	−0.0842	1.0071	0.9929	0.1265	1.0163	0.9840	0.1656	1.0282	0.9726	1

Source: Compiled from the business census of the Continental University.

In this sense, the current investigation gives major lessons for the incubation processes and strengthening entrepreneurial in universities in two different contexts. Although, the same experiment was designed and implemented in two different countries and universities, the results were similar. It was expected that the Colombian context would have the bigger impact in the type of companies found and even though a bigger percentage of companies were identified with growth potential in relation to Peru, this difference was not of great magnitude.

In the college field, in which the training for the entrepreneurship topic is given great importance (Parra and Argote 2013), as in the EAN University case, it is observed that there are other intervene variables that benefit the transition of companies with growth potential and that are exogenous to the college field like the access to financing and network resources. This implies that the incubation strengthening entrepreneurial universities programs must be considered as part of their strategic planning the Articulation University—private sector and state—for the design of their entrepreneurial promotion programs.

Statistical Appendix

Multicollinearity between the explanatory variables in the model, for both universities, was conducted using both factor inflation variance (VIF_i) as the tolerance factor (T_i) measures were widely used in the analysis of multicollinearity (Belsley 1991). An empiric rule cited by Kleinbaum et al. (2013) is to consider that there are problems of collinearity if some VIF_i is greater than 10, which corresponds to an $R_i^2 > 0.9$ and $T_i < 0.1$. As can be seen from Tables 10.4 and 10.5, in either case, it appears that the rule is met: $VIF_i > 10$ and $R_i^2 > 0.9$ and $T_i < 0.1$ where no multicollinearity problems are observed.

References

Agarwal, R. and Gort, M., 1996, The evolution of markets and entry, exit and survival of firms. *The review of Economics and Statistics*, 489–498.

Belsley, D. A., 1991, *Conditioning Diagnostics: Collinearity and Weak Data in Regression*, John Wiley & Sons, New York.

Bosma, N., Van Praag, M., Thurik, R., and De Wit, G., 2004, The value of human and social capital investments for the business performance of startups, *Small Business Economics*, 23(3), 227–236.

Brassiolo, P. and Arreaza, A., 2013, Who are the entrepreneurs in Latin America? In the Report on Economy and Development, Latin American Development Bank (CAF), Entrepreneurship in Latin America, from subsistence to productive transformation, Bogotá, Colombia.

Camacho, D. Y., 2007, Towards a model of university entrepreneurship, Notes from CENES, Technical University of Tunja (UPTC), Tunja.

Cañibano, L. and Sánchez, P., 2004, Measurement, management and information of intangibles: The newest. *Accounting and Management Review*, 1, 99–139.

Colombo, M. G. and Delmastro, M., 2002, How effective are technology incubators?: Evidence from Italy. *Research Policy*, 31(7), 1103–1122.

Cowling, M. and Taylor, M., 2001, Entrepreneurial women and men: Two different species?. *Small Business Economics*, 16(3), 167–175.

Crissen, J. C. 2013, Entrepreneurship as a strategy of competitiveness and economic development. *EAN Review*, (57), 103–118.

Daepp, M., Hamilton, M. J., West, G. B., and Bettencourt, L., 2015, *The Mortality of Companies*, 12(106), doi: 10.1098/rsif.2015.0120.

Delmar, F., Davidsson, P., and Gartner, W., 2003, Arriving at the high growth firm, *Journal of Business Venturing*, 18(2), 189–216.

Dubini, P., 1989, The influence of motivations and environment on business start-ups: Some hints for public policies, *Journal of Business Venturing*, 4(1), 11–26.

Echecopar, G., Angelelli, P., Galleguillos, G., and Schorr, M., 2006, Seed capital for financing new businesses, Progress and Lessons Learned in Latin America, Washington, DC.

Fracica, G., Vaca Vaca, P., and Sepúlveda, M. D. P., 2011, El empresario en el Start Up, Memorias XXI Congreso Latinoamericano sobre Espíritu Empresarial, 216–231.

Galloway, L. and Brown, W., 2002, Entrepreneurship education at university: A driver in the creation of high growth firms?. Education+ Training, 44(8/9), 398–405.

Hansen, E. L., 1995, Entrepreneurial networks and new organization growth, *Entrepreneurship Theory Practice*, 19(4), 7–19.

Harada, N. 2003, Who succeeds as an entrepreneur? An analysis of the post-entry performance of new firms in Japan. *Japan and the World Economy*, 15(2), 211–222.

Jovanovic, B. 1982, Selection and the Evolution of Industry. *Econometrica: Journal of the Econometric Society*, 649–670.

Kantis, H., Angelelli, P., and Moori, V., 2004, Entrepreneurial development: Latin America and the international experience, BID-FUNDES International, Buenos Aires, Argentina.

Kantis, H., Ishida, M., and Komori, M., 2002a, Entrepreneurship in emerging economies: The creation and development of new businesses in Latin America and East Asia (No. 56558), Inter-American Development Bank.

Kantis, H., Postigo, S., Federico, J., and Tamborini, F., 2002b, The emergence of university-based entrepreneurs: How do they differ? In the case of empirical evidence Argentina. *RENT XVI Conference*, Barcelona, Spain.

Kelley, D. J., Singer, S., and Herrington, M., 2012, The global entrepreneurship monitor. 2011–2012 Global Report, GEM 2012, 7. Ed. Global Entrepreneurship Monitor, London UK.

Kleinbaum, D., Kupper, L., Nizam, A., and Rosenberg, E., 2013, *Applied Regression Analysis and other Multivariable Methods*, Cengage Learning, Independence, KY.

Lasio, V., Arteaga, M. E., and Caicedo, G., 2005, Global Entrepreneurship Monitor Ecuador 2008, Escuela Superior Politécnica del Litoral.

Liseras, N., de Rearte, G., María, A., and Graña, F. M., 2003, *Factors associated with the entrepreneurial vocation in university students*. Mar del Plata University, Argentina.

Mengistae, T., 2006, Competition and entrepreneurs' human capital in small business, longevity and growth, *Journal of Development Studies*, 42(5), 812–836.

Parra, L. D., 2016, Analisis de brechas tecnologicas en el sector metalmecanico desde el estudio de casos de contraste, EAN University, Bogotá, Colombia.

Parra, L. D. and Argote, M. L., 2013, Management in the process of business creation: The case of the EAN IN3 University of Colombia, *Entrepreneurship: Different Approaches, Research Notebook EAN University*, EAN University, Bogotá, Colombia.

Parra, L. D. and Argote, M. L., 2015, University entrepreneurship: Analysis of contrast between the EAN University in Colombia and the Continental University in Peru, Technical Report of the Research Project "Compared the Business Census EAN University (Colombia) and the Continental University (Peru) Study, EAN University.

Pazos, D., Fernández López, S., Otero González, L., and Rodríguez Sandiás, A. 2008, The creation of companies in the university field: An application of the theory of resources. *Management Notebooks Review*. (1), 2008.

Peña-Vinces, P. and del Carmen, J. 2010, Determinants of international competitiveness: Empirical application in developing countries. Doctoral Dissertation. Sevilla University, Spain.

Penrose, E., 1959, *The Theory of the Growth of The Firm*, Oxford University Press, Oxford.

Rothaermel, F. T., Agung, S. D., and Jiang, L. 2007, University entrepreneurship: A taxonomy of the literature. *Industrial and Corporate Change*, 16(4), 691–791.

Santarelli, E. and Vivarelli, M., 2006, Entrepreneurship and the process of firms' entry, survival and growth, IZA Discussion Papers, No. 2475, http://nbnresolving.de/urn:nbn:de:101:1-2008051649.

Siegel, R., Siegel, E., and MacMillan, I. C., 1993, Characteristics distinguishing high-growth ventures, *Journal of Business Venturing*, 8(2), 169–180.

Thursby, J. G. and Thursby, M. C., 2002, Who is selling the Ivory tower? Sources of growth in university licensing, *Contemporary Economic Policy*, 22(2), 162–178.

Tornikoski, E. T. and Newbert, S. L., 2007, Exploring the determinants of organizational emergence: A legitimacy perspective, *Journal of Business Venturing*, 22(2), 311–335.

Van Gelderen, M. and Jansen, P., 2006, Autonomy as a start-up motive, *Journal of Small Business and Enterprise Development*, 13(1), 23–32.

Chapter 11

Statistical Software Reliability Models

Francisco Iván Zuluaga Díaz and
José Daniel Gallego Posada

Contents

Summary.. 208
Introduction.. 208
   Purpose of the Study.. 208
About the Background of This Work.. 209
   Definition of the Key Concepts 209
Definition of the Problem That Is Analyzed... 211
What Was the Methodology? 211
   Research Question and Design 212
   What Were the Models and Concepts Used in This Study? 212
      Jelinski–Moranda with Imperfect Debugging.. 212
      Moranda Geometric.. 215
      Musa Basic 217
      The Musa–Okumoto Model.. 219
      Duane 220
      The Littlewood–Verrall Linear... 222
What Were the Results and Their Meaning/Context? 224
   What Are the Results and Their Interpretation? 224
   How Are These Results Meaningful for Organizations and for Future
   Research? 226
Conclusions 228
References 228

Summary

Software quality analysis has become a key factor of analysis in development due to the considerable increase in the use of such systems in the current world. Owing to this, several models for describing this quality in terms of reliability have been proposed, some of which are presented in this study. The purpose of this study is to evaluate the performance of several statistical software reliability models given the experimental times between failures obtained from Musa's software reliability data benchmark. For the analytics, an R-based platform was implemented with parameter estimation routines for a variety of statistical software reliability structures. This tool provided a visual representation of the behavior of the number of failures described by each model. The statistical models provided an effective tool along with a theoretical background to describe software reliability. Owing to the complexity of the functions, parameter estimation may pose fairly complicated challenges from the computational point of view. The sort of models described in this work could be used to characterize software quality from the perspective of its reliability given the collected information regarding times between failures. These tools could also be integrated to an online system which creates an information loop between failure detection, reliability measurement, and debugging processes. The application developed in Shiny by RStudio has been implemented for monitoring in the virtual branch of the largest financial institution in Colombia. This research provides a starting point for developing a software reliability analysis tool, which could be expanded to a greater number of models and to further techniques related to the study of software reliability. These tools not only include the parameter estimation for such models but also a visualization of the estimations and predictions made by each model, providing valuable insights on their behavior.

Introduction

Purpose of the Study

The use of software in everyday life has increased considerably and has become a major factor in transcendental applications. Owing to this increasing use and importance, the software quality becomes an issue of primary concern. Software quality can be expressed by requirements or attributes such as reliability, availability, security, and performance (Mahapatra and Roy 2012).

Among these attributes regarding software quality, reliability is generally seen as the most important factor. Reliability quantifies faults and failures in the software, which can lead to serious consequences in systems which may be critical for information safety and business normality. Therefore, evaluation, assessment, and prediction of software reliability has been increasingly requested within projects to achieve highly trustworthy software systems (Amin et al. 2013).

For these reasons, in this work we implement an R-based platform including parameter estimation routines for several statistical software reliability structures in order to evaluate their performance at modeling information about times between failures from benchmark data sets on software reliability.

About the Background of This Work

Since 1972, with the work of Jelinski and Moranda, a considerable amount of Software Reliability Growth Models or SRGMs have been proposed (Mahapatra and Roy 2012). These models specify the form of a stochastic process that describes the behavior of the system regarding software failures in order to use these failures for the estimation of reliability, measurement of the current state, and prediction of future states.

However, the applicability of SRGMs has been widely discussed because no particular model can be used in all situations. Additionally, new alternative methodologies based on neural networks and time series (Amin et al. 2013) have been proposed. Nevertheless, the latter have complications regarding the verification of the assumptions of the ARIMA model (autoregressive integrated moving average model) and the definition of the practical steps required to build a time series model for a given software reliability data set.

Definition of the Key Concepts

We define *reliability* as the probability of the system to perform its function under specific operating conditions for a period of time.

Mathematically, the reliability function $R(t)$ is the probability of the system to operate without failures in an interval $[0,t]$:

$$R(t) = P(T > t) \quad t \geq 0 \tag{11.1}$$

where T is a random variable that represents the failure time or time between failures.

The failure probability (cumulative distribution function of T) is given by

$$F(t) = 1 - R(t) = P(T \leq t) \tag{11.2}$$

Thus, if the time to failure T has a density function $f(t)$, which can be interpreted as the probability that failure occurs in the infinitesimal interval of time $[t, t + \Delta t]$, we have

$$R(t) = \int_t^\infty f(x)\,dx \tag{11.3}$$

The failure rate function $\lambda(t)$ describes the impact of age on the behavior of the system itself. This allows to differentiate designs that provide similar reliabilities in a specific instant according to the variation rate in the aging behavior during the use of its components:

$$\lambda(t) = \lim_{\Delta t \to 0} \frac{R(t) - R(t + \Delta t)}{\Delta t R(t)} = \frac{f(t)}{R(t)} \tag{11.4}$$

The expression $\lambda(t)dt$ represents the probability of a component (or system) aged to fail in an infinitesimal interval between t and $t + dt$.

Now consider a nonhomogeneous continuous time Poisson process $\{N(t): t \geq 0\}$ with state space $\{0, 1, \ldots\}$ and as parameter the positive and locally integrable function $\lambda(t)$, which satisfies the following properties:

1. $N(0) = 0$
2. Independent increments
3. For each $t \geq 0$ and $h \to 0$
   a. $P(N(t + h) - N(t) = 1) = \lambda(t) + o(h)$
   b. $P(N(t + h) - N(t) \geq 2) = o(h)$
   where $o(h)$ satisfies $\lim_{h \to 0}(o(h)/h) = 0$

If $N(t)$ denotes the number of observed failures until time t, the function

$$\mu(t) = \int_0^t \lambda(x) \, dx, \tag{11.5}$$

which is called the *mean value function,* describes the expected value of the cumulative number of failures in the interval $[0, t)$. Thereby, $\mu(t)$ provides a descriptive measure of the failure behavior in the system.

Under these conditions, it is possible to prove that

$$P(N(t) = n) = \frac{[\mu(t)]^n}{n!} \exp\{-\mu(t)\} \quad n = 0, 1, \ldots \tag{11.6}$$

Thus, given the mean value function it is possible to calculate the failure intensity rate function and the reliability function in time t_0:

$$\lambda(t) = \frac{d\mu(t)}{dt} \tag{11.7}$$

$$R(t \mid t_0) = \exp\{\mu(t_0) - \mu(t + t_0)\} \tag{11.8}$$

Thus, using the various forms of the mean value function, it is possible to obtain different nonhomogeneous Poisson processes that describe the behavior of faults within the system.

Definition of the Problem That Is Analyzed

Software reliability is defined as the probability of failure-free operation in a defined environment for a specific period of time (Grottke 2001). A *failure* is the divergence between the behavior of the software and the requirements of the user. This dynamic phenomenon must be distinguished from static concept of failure (or *bug*) in software coding, which causes the occurrence of the fault as soon as it is activated during program execution.

As the software does not deteriorate in the same way as that of the hardware, software reliability remains constant over time if changes to the coding or environmental conditions are undertaken, including the user behavior. However, if after each failure, the underlying error is detected and corrected perfectly, software reliability increases over time, as shown in Figure 11.1.

Typically, during the test phases, since the occurrence of each failure generates the removal of the causative error, the expected number of detected faults to time t, denoted by $\mu(t)$, can be interpreted as a reflection of reliability growth. Those models that can explain the behavior of $\mu(t)$ are called Reliability Growth Models. Each SRGM implicitly assumes a functional form for $\mu(t)$. Then, using failure times t_1, t_2, ... or times between failures, Δt_1, Δt_2,... collected over a testing period, SRGM parameters can be estimated.

What Was the Methodology?

John Musa's valuable sets of software reliability data are regarded as of high quality and a carefully performed collection process. This data has been extensively used by modelers in this area to illustrate and validate their models (Davies et al. 1987). For this reason, we have used Musa's benchmark data set number 1 (Musa 1980) for the numerical aspects of this work.

Figure 11.1 Fault detection and repair.

Research Question and Design

To assess the performance of statistical software reliability models for describing the behavior of experimental measurements of times between failures, we implemented a platform in *R* language with parameter estimation routines and error calculation for each of the selected models.

It is worth to state that (contrary to simply comparing the presented models) the aim of this work was to validate the use of this sort of models in the analysis of software reliability as part of a larger project in the same area which included additional techniques such as Fault Tree Analysis (FTA) and time series.

What Were the Models and Concepts Used in This Study?

Some of the software reliability models mostly used in the literature (Dai et al. 2004) are described; some of which are implemented in the *R* statistical software package *Reliability* developed by Andreas Wittman (Wittman 2009).

There is a set of assumptions regarding the applicability of such models to the processes of reliability analysis. They are often called *Standard Assumptions* in which we assume the following:

1. The software is operated under the same conditions in which it is desired to make predictions about its reliability.
2. All failures of equal severity have equal chances of being found.
3. The system errors are independent when the failures are detected.

The first assumption ensures that the estimates provided by the model using the data obtained in a particular environment are applicable to the scenario under which it is intended to make reliable projections. The second assumption ensures that the various failures have the same distributional properties. Finally, the third assumption simplifies the analysis carried out by the estimates using maximum likelihood methods.

Jelinski–Moranda with Imperfect Debugging

One of the basic software reliability models based on Markov stochastic processes was the one developed by Jelinski and Moranda in 1972 and much of the Markov-based models developed later represent variations or extensions of this model.

A generalization of this initial model, which relaxes the assumption of perfect failure debugging in the system was proposed by Mahapatra and Roy (2012). The Jelinski–Moranda model represents a particular case in which the probability of a perfect correction of faults is 1.

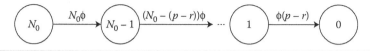

Figure 11.2   Markov process of the Jelinski–Moranda model.

Model Description

The time between failures is assumed to have an exponential distribution with the parameter being proportional to the number of remaining failures in the system, so the mean time between failures at time t is $[\phi(N_0 - (i-1)(p-r))]^{-1}$, where t is a time between the occurrence of the $(i-1)$th and ith failures. In this case, ϕ represents the proportionality constant; N_0 the total number of failures in the system from the initial moment at which the system can be observed; p the probability of an imperfect failure debugging; and r is the likelihood of introducing a new failure during debugging. The process is illustrated in Figure 11.2.

Input Data and Assumptions

1. The fault detection rate is proportional to the current remaining amount of failures in the software.
2. The fault detection rate remains constant over intervals between occurrences.
3. When an error occurs in the system, the detected fault is corrected with probability p, the failure is not completely removed with probability r, and a new fault is entered into the system with probability r, so that $p + q + r = 1$ and $q \geq r$.

The data required to implement this model are the times between failures $\{x_i\}_{i=1,\ldots,n}$, or the times at which failures occurred $\{t_i\}_{i=1,\ldots,n}$, where $x_i = t_i - t_{i-1}$ with $t_0 = 0$.

Model Structure and Reliability Prediction

Let T_i be the time in which ith failure occurs. By assumption, T_i is a random variable with exponential distribution and parameter

$$\lambda(i) = \phi[N_0 - p(i-1) + r(i-1)] = \phi(N_0 - (i-1)(p-r)) \quad i = 1, 2, \ldots, N_0 \qquad (11.9)$$

Then, the density and mean value functions associated with this model are given by

$$f(t_i) = \phi(N_0 - (i-1)(p-r)) \exp\{-\phi(N_0 - (i-1)(p-r))t_i\} \qquad (11.10)$$

$$\mu(t) = N_0(1 - \exp\{-\phi(p-r)t\}) \qquad (11.11)$$

Parameter Estimation

Given a set of failure times $\mathbf{t} = \{t_i\}_{i=1,\ldots,n}$ it is possible to estimate the parameters ϕ and N_0 in Jelinski–Moranda model by maximizing the likelihood function defined by

$$L(\mathbf{t}, N_0, \phi) = \prod_{i=1}^{n} \phi(N_0 - (i-1)(p-r)) \exp\{-\phi(N_0 - (i-1)(p-r))t_i\} \qquad (11.12)$$

$$= \phi^n \prod_{i=1}^{n} (N_0 - (i-1)(p-r)) \exp\left\{-\phi \sum_{i=1}^{n} (N_0 - (i-1)(p-r))t_i\right\} \qquad (11.13)$$

This function's natural logarithm is

$$L = \ln\left[\phi^n \prod_{i=1}^{n} (N_0 - (i-1)(p-r)) \exp\left\{-\phi \sum_{i=1}^{n} (N_0 - (i-1)(p-r))t_i\right\}\right] \qquad (11.14)$$

$$= n\log\phi + \sum_{i=1}^{n} \log(N_0 - (i-1)(p-r)) - \phi \sum_{i=1}^{n} (N_0 - (i-1)(p-r))t_i \qquad (11.15)$$

Taking partial derivatives with respect to N_0 and ϕ, respectively, we obtain the first-order conditions

$$\frac{\partial L}{\partial N_0} = \sum_{i=1}^{n} \frac{1}{N_0 - (i-1)(p-r)} - \sum_{i=1}^{n} \phi t_i = 0 \qquad (11.16)$$

$$\frac{\partial L}{\partial \phi} = \frac{n}{\phi} - \sum_{i=1}^{n} (N_0 - (i-1)(p-r))t_i = 0 \qquad (11.17)$$

Solving for ϕ in Equation 11.17, we have

$$\hat{\phi} = n\left[\sum_{i=1}^{n} (\hat{N}_0 - (i-1)(p-r))t_i\right]^{-1} \qquad (11.18)$$

Replacing this expression in Equation 11.16, we have an equation for N_0 which does not depend on ϕ:

$$\sum_{i=1}^{n} \frac{1}{\hat{N}_0 - (i-1)(p-r)} = \frac{n \sum_{i=1}^{n} t_i}{\sum_{i=1}^{n} (\hat{N}_0 - (i-1)(p-r)) t_i} \qquad (11.19)$$

This equation must be solved using numerical algorithms. Replacing this result in Equation 11.18 the maximum likelihood estimators for the Jelinksi–Moranda model are obtained.

Moranda Geometric

Model Description

The geometric model presents a variation from the initial model proposed by Jelinski and Moranda in section "Introduction". We assume that the time between failures has an exponential distribution with geometrically decreasing mean, so that the discovery of faults in the early stages has a greater impact in reducing the risk rate during later stages. The function is initially constant in D but decreases geometrically with parameter $0 < \phi < 1$ whenever a failure occurs. The change in the function is smaller as more failures occur, reflecting the lower impact of the discovery of flaws in the later stages of execution.

Input Data and Assumptions

Along with the *Standard Assumptions* presented earlier, we assume the following:

1. The fault detection rate forms a geometric progression and is constant over the intervals between failure occurrences, that is, $z(t) = D\phi^{i-1}$, where $0 < \phi < 1$ and $t_{i-1} \le t < t_i$; and t_{i-1} represents the time in which $(i-1)$th failure occurs.
2. There exists an infinite number of failures in the system.
3. Time between failure detection has an exponential distribution.

The data required to implement this model are the times between failures $\{x_i\}_{i=1,\dots,n}$, or the times at which failures occurred $\{t_i\}_{i=1,\dots,n}$, where $x_i = t_i - t_{i-1}$ with $t_0 = 0$.

Model Structure and Reliability Prediction

Let X_i be the time between $(i-1)$th and ith failures. By assumption, X_i is a random variable with exponential distribution and density function

$$f(x_i) = D\phi^{i-1} \exp\{-D\phi^{i-1} x_i\} \qquad (11.20)$$

In this case, the failure rate and mean value functions associated with this model are given by

$$\lambda(t) = \frac{D\exp\{\beta\}}{[D\beta\exp\{\beta\}]t + 1}$$

(11.21)

$$\mu(t) = \frac{1}{\beta}\log([D\beta\exp\{\beta\}]t + 1)$$

(11.22)

where $\beta = -\log(\phi)$. Note that $\lim_{t\to\infty}\mu(t) = \infty$.

Parameter Estimation

Given a set of times between failures $\mathbf{x} = \{x_i\}_{i=1,\ldots,n}$ it is possible to estimate parameters β and D in Jelinski–Moranda model by maximizing the likelihood function defined by

$$L(\mathbf{t}, N_0, \phi) = \prod_{i=1}^{n} D\phi^{i-1}\exp\{-D\phi^{i-1}x_i\}$$

(11.23)

$$= D^n \exp\left\{-D\sum_{i=1}^{n}\phi^{i-1}x_i\right\}\prod_{i=1}^{n}\phi^{i-1}$$

(11.24)

This function's natural logarithm is

$$L = \ln\left[D^n \exp\left\{-D\sum_{i=1}^{n}\phi^{i-1}x_i\right\}\prod_{i=1}^{n}\phi^{i-1}\right]$$

(11.25)

$$= n\log D - D\sum_{i=1}^{n}\phi^{i-1}x_i + \frac{n(n-1)\log\phi}{2}$$

(11.26)

Taking partial derivatives with respect to D and β, respectively, we obtain the first-order conditions

$$\frac{\partial L}{\partial D} = \frac{n}{D} - \sum_{i=1}^{n}\phi^{i-1}x_i = 0$$

(11.27)

$$\frac{\partial L}{\partial \phi} = -D\sum_{i=1}^{n}(i-1)\phi^{i-2}x_i + \frac{n(n+1)}{2\phi} = 0$$

(11.28)

Solving for D in Equation 11.27, we have

$$\hat{D} = \frac{n\hat{\phi}}{\sum_{i=1}^{n} \hat{\phi}^i x_i} \tag{11.29}$$

Replacing this expression in Equation 11.28, we have an equation for ϕ which does not depend on D:

$$\frac{\sum_{i=1}^{n} i\hat{\phi}^i x_i}{\sum_{i=1}^{n} \hat{\phi}^i x_i} = \frac{n+1}{2} \tag{11.30}$$

Solving this equation using numerical algorithms and replacing this result in Equation 11.29 we can obtain the maximum likelihood estimators for the Moranda geometric model.

Musa Basic

This model, developed by John Musa, one of the largest contributors to the study of the reliability of software systems using statistical models, has the widest distribution among the various proposed models of software reliability and has been applied in a variety of areas.

Specifically, Musa intends to use this model to make early predictions of reliability, for example, prior to the execution of the system or to assess the impact of new software engineering techniques in the development process (Lyu 1996).

Model Description

The time between failures is assumed to have a piecewise exponential distribution with a constant parameter for individual failures. The mean value function satisfies the property that the number of expected failures in each interval is proportional to the number of failures not detected in that time. Since $\lim_{t \to \infty} \mu(t) = \beta_0$, this is a finite-failure model and β_0 represents the total number of failures to be detected in the limit.

Input Data and Assumptions

Along with the *Standard Assumptions* presented earlier, we assume the following:

1. The cumulative number of failures until time t, $N(t)$, follows a Possion process with the mean value function $\mu(t) = \beta_0[1 - \exp\{-\beta_1 t\}]$, $\beta_0, \beta_1 > 0$.

2. Times between failures are piecewise exponential, that is, the risk rate is constant for each individual failure.

The data required to implement this model are the times between failures $\{x_i\}_{i=1,...,n}$, or the times at which failures occurred $\{t_i\}_{i=1,...,n}$, where $x_i = t_i - t_{i-1}$ with $t_0 = 0$.

Model Structure and Reliability Prediction

Since $\mu(t) = \beta_0[1 - \exp\{-\beta_1 t\}]$, the failure rate function is

$$\lambda(t) = \mu'(t) = \beta_0 \beta_1 \exp\{-\beta_1 t\} \tag{11.31}$$

Note that the speed of the decay is determined by the magnitude of β_1. In any case, however, the function diminishes exponentially starting at $\beta_0 \beta_1$ at time 0 until the limit.

Parameter Estimation

Having a set of failure times $\mathbf{t} = \{t_i\}_{i=1,...,n}$ and a time interval of length $x \geq 0$ since the last failure time t_n in which the system operated correctly, so that the total observation time is $t_n + x$, it is possible to estimate parameters β_0 and β_1 in Musa's model by maximizing the likelihood function given by

$$L(\mathbf{t}, \beta_0, \beta_1) = \beta_0^n \beta_1^n \left[\prod_{i=1}^{n} \exp\{-\beta_1 t_i\} \right] \exp\{-\beta_0[1 - \exp\{-\beta_1(t_n + x)\}]\} \tag{11.32}$$

The natural logarithm of this function is

$$L = \ln \left[\beta_0^n \beta_1^n \left[\prod_{i=1}^{n} \exp\{-\beta_1 t_i\} \right] \exp\{-\beta_0[1 - \exp\{-\beta_1(t_n + x)\}]\} \right] \tag{11.33}$$

$$= n \log \beta_0 + n \log \beta_1 - \beta_1 \sum_{i=1}^{n} t_i - \beta_0 (1 - \exp\{-\beta_1(t_n + x)\}) \tag{11.34}$$

Taking partial derivatives on this function with respect to β_0 and β_1, respectively, the following first-order conditions are obtained:

$$\frac{\partial L}{\partial \beta_0} = \frac{n}{\beta_0} - 1 + \exp\{-\beta_1(t_n + x)\} = 0 \tag{11.35}$$

$$\frac{\partial L}{\partial \beta_1} = \frac{n}{\beta_1} - \sum_{i=1}^{n} t_i - \beta_0 (t_n + x) \exp\{-\beta_1 (t_n + x)\} = 0 \qquad (11.36)$$

Solving for β_0 in Equation 11.35, we have

$$\hat{\beta}_0 = \frac{n}{1 - \exp\{-\hat{\beta}_1 (t_n + x)\}} \qquad (11.37)$$

Replacing this result in Equation 11.36 we have an equation for β_1 that does not depend on β_0:

$$\frac{n}{\hat{\beta}_1} = \sum_{i=1}^{n} t_i + \frac{n(t_n + x)}{\exp\{\hat{\beta}_1 (t_n + x)\} - 1} \qquad (11.38)$$

This equation must be solved using numerical algorithms. Replacing this result in Equation 11.37 both parameters' maximum likelihood estimators for the Musa model are established.

The Musa–Okumoto Model

Model Description

The logarithmic Poisson process proposed by John Musa and Kazu Okumoto has been widely used. It represents a nonhomogeneous Poisson process in which the failure intensity decreases exponentially as failures occur. As in the Moranda geometric model, failures detected at early stages are attributed greater relevance.

Input Data and Assumptions

1. The failure intensity rate decays exponentially according to the expected number of failures, that is, $\lambda(t) = \lambda_0 \exp\{-\theta \mu(t)\}$, where $\mu(t)$ represents the mean value function; θ is the decreasing parameter; and $\lambda_0 > 0$ is the initial failure rate.
2. The cumulative number of failures until time t, $N(t)$, follows a Possion process.

The data required to implement this model are the times between failures $\{x_i\}_{i=1,\dots,n}$, or the times at which failures occurred $\{t_i\}_{i=1,\dots,n}$, where $x_i = t_i - t_{i-1}$ with $t_0 = 0$.

Model Structure and Reliability Prediction

Let $\beta_0 = \theta^{-1}$ and $\beta_1 = \lambda_0\theta$. Then, the failure rate and mean value functions are given by

$$\lambda(t) = \frac{\beta_0\beta_1}{\beta_1 t + 1} \tag{11.39}$$

$$\mu(t) = \beta_0 \log(\beta_1 t + 1) \tag{11.40}$$

Parameter Estimation

Using a set of failure times $\mathbf{t} = \{t_i\}_{i=1,\dots,n}$, Musa derived the maximum likelihood estimators for the parameters given by

$$\hat{\beta}_0 = \frac{n}{\log(1 + \hat{\beta}_1 t_n)} \tag{11.41}$$

$$\frac{1}{\hat{\beta}_1} \sum_{i=1}^{n} \frac{1}{1 + \hat{\beta}_1 t_i} = \frac{n t_n}{(1 + \hat{\beta}_1 t_n)\log(1 + \hat{\beta}_1 t_n)} \tag{11.42}$$

This equation must be solved using numerical algorithms. Replacing this result in Equation 11.41 both parameters' maximum likelihood estimators for the Musa–Okumoto model are established.

Duane

Model Description

This model is a generalization of the homogeneous Poisson process and was originally proposed in the hardware reliability analysis taking into account the quasi-linear log–log relationship existing between the cumulative failure rate and the cumulative test time. This behavior can be represented by a Weibull-type process which is a nonhomogeneous Poisson process where the failure intensity function has the same shape of the hazard rate of the Weibull distribution. Since similar behaviors have been identified in software systems, this model has been used to describe these phenomena. Note that this is an infinite failure model since

$$\lim_{t\to\infty} \mu(t) = \lim_{t\to\infty} \alpha t^\beta = \infty \quad \text{with } \alpha, \beta > 0$$

Input Data and Assumptions

Along with the *Standard Assumptions*, the key assumption in this model is

1. The cumulative number of failures until time t, $N(t)$, follows a Possion process with the mean value function $\mu(t) = \alpha t^\beta$ with $\alpha, \beta > 0$.

The data required to implement this model are the times between failures $\{x_i\}_{i=1,\ldots,n}$, or the times at which failures occurred $\{t_i\}_{i=1,\ldots,n}$, where $x_i = t_i - t_{i-1}$ with $t_0 = 0$.

Model Structure and Reliability Prediction

Let T be the total observation time of the system, according to Assumption 1, we have

$$\frac{\mu(T)}{T} = \frac{\alpha T^\beta}{T} = \frac{\text{Expected number of failures at time } T}{\text{Total observation time}} \qquad (11.43)$$

Applying the natural logarithm on both sides of this equation we have a log–log linear relationship between both variables given by

$$Y = \log\frac{\mu(T)}{T} = \log\frac{\alpha T^\beta}{T} = \log\alpha + (\beta - 1)\log T \qquad (11.44)$$

In this case, the failure rate function is defined by

$$\lambda(t) = \alpha\beta t^{\beta-1} \qquad (11.45)$$

Note that this function is strictly increasing for $\beta > 1$, constant under a homogeneous Poisson process ($\beta = 1$) and strictly decreasing for $1 > \beta > 0$. Then, it is not possible to have a growth in reliability for values of β greater than 1.

Parameter Estimation

In Crow (1974) the deduction of the maximum likelihood estimators of α and β in the Duane model are performed, having as input a set of failure times $\mathbf{t} = \{t_i\}_{i=1,\ldots,n}$:

$$\hat{\alpha} = \frac{n}{t_n^{\hat{\beta}}} \qquad (11.46)$$

$$\hat{\beta} = \frac{n}{\displaystyle\sum_{i=1}^{n-1}\log(t_n) - \log(t_i)} \qquad (11.47)$$

The Littlewood–Verrall Linear

The models presented above restrict variations in system reliability to the moments at which failures occur. A Bayesian model, like the Littlewood–Verrall model, assumes a subjective point of view from which, if no failures occur while the system is being observed, reliability should grow, reflecting an increase in confidence toward the software used. Thus, reliability is a mixture between the number of faults that have been detected and the amount of time the system remains free of faults.

Model Description

This model tries to account for the generation of failures during the debugging process allowing the possibility that the system becomes less reliable in later times. With the correction of each of the faults a sequence of software programs, each with the aim of solving the failure by its predecessor, is generated. Owing to the uncertainties, the new version may have different performances (of varying quality); thus a new source of variation is introduced to the model, a fact which is reflected in the random choice of the parameters.

The distribution of failure times is, as in other models, exponential with a randomly chosen rate using a gamma distribution, replacing the constant choice made previously.

Input Data and Assumptions

Along with the *Standard Assumptions* presented earlier, we assume the following:

1. Successive times between failures, x_i, are random variables with parameters ξ_i $i = 1,...,n$.
2. The set ξ_i forms a sequence of random variables with gamma distribution determined by paramaters α and $\psi(i)$. It is assumed that the function $\psi(i)$ is an increasing function in i, which represents the quality of the programmer and the difficulty of the debugging process, so a good-quality programmer would have a function with greater growth.

The data required to implement this model are the times between failures $\{x_i\}_{i=1,...,n}$, or the times at which failures occurred $\{t_i\}_{i=1,...,n}$, where $x_i = t_i - t_{i-1}$ with $t_0 = 0$.

Model Structure and Reliability Prediction

First, it is necessary to have a marginal distribution of the x_i variables. The initial distribution has the form

$$g(\xi_i, \psi(i), \alpha) = \frac{[\psi(i)]^\alpha \xi_i^{\alpha-1} \exp\{-\psi(i)\xi_i\}}{\Gamma(\alpha)} \quad \xi_i > 0 \tag{11.48}$$

Using a conditional distribution for the x_i given by $f_{x_i}(x_i | \xi_i) = \xi_i \exp\{-\xi_i x_i\}$ for $x_i > 0$, the marginal distribution of x_i has a Pareto distribution form, described by

$$f(x_i | \alpha, \psi(i)) = \frac{\alpha[\psi(i)]^\alpha}{[x_i + \psi(i)]^{\alpha+1}} \tag{11.49}$$

Therefore, the joint density function of the failure times is

$$f(x_1, \ldots, x_n) = \frac{\alpha^n \prod_{i=1}^{n} [\psi(i)]^\alpha}{\prod_{i=1}^{n} [x_i + \psi(i)]^{\alpha+1}} \tag{11.50}$$

So, the distribution for the ξ_i can be found by

$$h(\xi_1, \ldots, \xi_n) = \frac{\prod_{i=1}^{n} \xi_i^\alpha \exp\left\{-\sum_{i=1}^{n} \xi_i(x_i + \psi(i))\right\}}{[\Gamma(\alpha+1)]^n \prod_{i=1}^{n} (x_i + \psi(i))^{\alpha+1}} \tag{11.51}$$

Each ξ_i is a random variable with gamma distribution with parameters $\alpha + 1$ and $1/(x_i + \psi(i))$. In the linear case, Littlewood and Verrall propose failure rate and mean value functions, given by

$$\lambda(t) = \frac{\alpha - 1}{\sqrt{\beta_0^2 + 2\beta_1(\alpha - 1)t}} \tag{11.52}$$

$$\mu(t) = \frac{1}{\beta_1} \sqrt{\beta_0^2 + 2\beta_1(\alpha - 1)t} \tag{11.53}$$

Parameter Estimation

Using the marginal distribution functions for x_i, the maximum likelihood estimators for parameters α, β_0, and β_1 can be obtained by solving the following system of nonlinear equations:

$$\frac{n}{\hat{\alpha}} + \sum_{i=1}^{n} \log(\hat{\psi}(i)) - \sum_{i=1}^{n} \log(x_i + \hat{\psi}(i)) = 0 \tag{11.54}$$

$$\hat{\alpha} \sum_{i=1}^{n} \frac{1}{\hat{\psi}(i)} - (\hat{\alpha}+1) \sum_{i=1}^{n} \frac{1}{x_i + \hat{\psi}(i)} = 0 \qquad (11.55)$$

$$\hat{\alpha} \sum_{i=1}^{n} \frac{i}{\hat{\psi}(i)} - (\hat{\alpha}+1) \sum_{i=1}^{n} \frac{i}{x_i + \hat{\psi}(i)} = 0 \qquad (11.56)$$

What Were the Results and Their Meaning/Context?

What Are the Results and Their Interpretation?

Now, we present a study case which illustrates the use of the computational tool developed in the statistical software *R*, using the set number 1 from Musa's software reliability data compilations (Musa 1980).

After accessing the platform, it is possible to view the main screen of the application, which includes a panel for model selection and parameter settings and several tabs for exploring the different features of the models, which is presented in Figure 11.3.

The data required for the tool is a comma separated values (*.csv) file with the observed times between failures. This information can be imported using the corresponding option in the graphic interface, as shown in Figure 11.4.

Figure 11.3 Welcome screen of the application.

Figure 11.4   Data upload process.

After uploading the data from Musa's data sets to the *R* platform—which is available upon request to the authors—and performing the parameter estimation for every model, the following mean absolute relative errors were obtained. The displayed results were rounded off to four decimal places.

Figure 11.5 shows the behavior of each mean value functions for the models described above. It can be seen that the fitted curves differ among them, the Moranda geometric model being the one that resembles the most to the original data, which is consistent with the residual analysis presented in Table 11.1, as this model has approximately 8% mean absolute relative error. Naturally, since this exercise has only considered one data set, it may be possible to obtain different performance indicators on the models while using a different input.

In Figure 11.6, the dynamics of the relative error from each model compared with the experimental data are plotted. In this case we can see that, in spite of having large discrepancies at the beginning, most of the models tend to reach a low level error in advanced stages of the analysis.

An interesting feature of these models is that, since they estimate the parameters of the mean value function, based on information up to a certain instant, it is possible to calculate the predictions of the model regarding future failure occurrences. This is presented in Figure 11.7. Clearly, models with better performance at the in-sample prediction stage exhibit more reasonable estimates on the failure times and, consequently, on the reliability of the system.

As an additional remark, it is important to mention the role that well-implemented parameter estimation routines play in this analysis. Owing to the complex structures

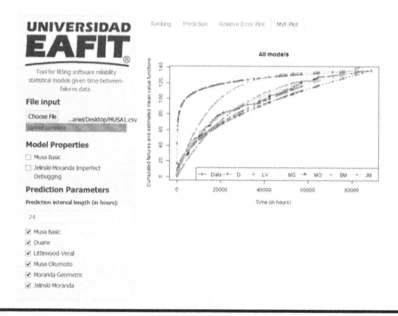

Figure 11.5 Plot of the experimental data and the fitted mean value functions.

Table 11.1 Mean Absolute Relative Errors for the Fitted Models versus Experimental Data

Method	Mean Absolute Relative Error
Duane	0.1226
Littlewood–Verrall	0.1015
Moranda Geometric	0.0849
Musa–Okumoto	1.9519
Musa Basic	0.2393
Jelinski–Moranda	0.2214

that likelihood functions may have, the (systems of) equations obtained from the first-order conditions might be badly conditioned and even non-convex, which could be reflected in the slow or possibly no convergence of the numerical methods used.

How Are These Results Meaningful for Organizations and for Future Research?

Given that the original data used to carry out this research came from real-world computational processes, there is a natural application field for this sort of tools and

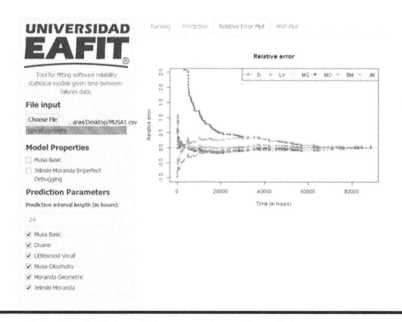

Figure 11.6   Graph of the relative errors for each model.

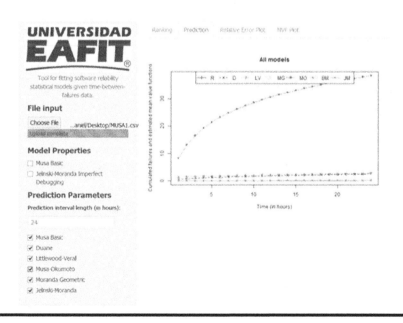

Figure 11.7   Plot of the predicted failures in the system.

analysis in the industry, especially in organizations that depend strongly on their computational structure like, for example, banking.

Conclusions

Statistical models provide an effective tool along with a theoretical background to describe software reliability. Owing to the complexity of the functions, parameter estimation may pose fairly complicated challenges from a computational point of view.

As stated earlier, one of the aims of this project is to extend it to additional statistical models of similar natures as the one presented, but also to include different theoretical backgrounds to approach the problem like the time series analysis or FTA.

As another possible subject for a future development on this topic, it may be interesting to establish confidence intervals for the estimations and projections provided by each model. This information could provide a broader perspective on the state of the system at a specific instant, and may be a valuable tool to analyze the reliability of the system or its components.

References

Amin, A., Grunske, L., and Colman, A., 2013, An approach to software reliability prediction based on time series modeling, *Journal of Systems and Software*, 86, 1923–1932.

Crow, L. H., 1974, Reliability analysis for complex repairable systems, in F. Proschan, and R. J. Serfling (Eds.), *Reliability and Biometry*, pp. 379–410, SIAM, Philadelphia.

Dai, Y. S., Xie, M., and Poh, K. L., 2004, *Computing System Reliability: Models and Analysis*, Springer, New York.

Davies, N., Marriot, J. M., Wightman, D. W., and Bendell, A., 1987, The Musa data revisited: Alternative methods and structure, in B. K. Daniels (Ed.), *Software Reliability Modelling and Analysis, de Achieving Safety and Reliability with Computer Systems*, pp. 118–130, Springer, Netherlands.

Grottke, M., 2001, *Software reliability model study*, Research Report A.2, University of Erlangen-Nuremberg, Nürnberg.

Lyu, M., 1996, *Handbook of Software Reliability Engineering*, vol. 1, Computing McGraw-Hill, New York.

Mahapatra, G. and Roy, P., 2012, Modified Jelinski–Moranda software reliability model with imperfect debugging phenomenon, *International Journal of Computer Applications*, 48(18), 38–46.

Musa, J. D., 1980, Software life cycle empirical/experience data, data & analysis center for software, available at http://www.dacs.org. accessed September 17, 2010.

Wittman, A., 2009, The Reliability Package: Functions for estimating parameters in software reliability models, *R-Cran Repository*. Version: 0.0-2, pp. 1–27.

Chapter 12

What Latin America Says about Entrepreneurship? An Approach Based on Data Analytics Applications and Social Media Contents

Laura Rojas de Francisco, Izaias Martins, Eduardo Gómez-Araujo, and Laura Fernanda Morales de la Vega

Contents

Summary...230
Introduction...230
Background...231
    The Concept of Entrepreneurship..231
    Entrepreneurship in the Online Context..232
Methodology..233
    Analytics Process... 234
Findings 235

Main Insights..235
   An Interpretation of Entrepreneurship Social Uses in the Internet
   Context...236
Content Analysis 238
   Education and Entrepreneurship Learning..238
   Funding and Support...242
   Entrepreneurship Development...243
Discussion and Implications..245
   Education and Entrepreneurship Learning..245
   Funding and Support...246
   Entrepreneurship Development 247
Limitations and Future Research 248
References...249

Summary

This chapter provides a first attempt to analyze and understand the social media use of the concept "entrepreneurship" in Latin America. In this chapter, we use the analytics methods to study the data available and provided by individuals in the social media. The data available online has been used to study the online exchange of resources between individuals, groups, or organizations, to locate patterns revealing actors, nodes, relationships, and their connections. Latin America is a region that has a very active conversation around entrepreneurship; at first glance the conversation has a clearly neutral and positive sentiment around it. This study found a relationship between entrepreneurship and the category of social entrepreneurship in Latin America. Social entrepreneurship, in countries such as Chile, Venezuela, and Colombia, does not refer to a philanthropic activity, but indicates how people can be an agent of change from this type of entrepreneurial activity, helping to solve global problems, to inspire optimism, and to collaborate, especially in countries with serious problems of poverty.

Introduction

Despite all the attention to definition of entrepreneurship by scholars and experts over the past years, we lack understanding about what are the social use and what society thinks about this subject.

This chapter provides a first attempt to analyze and understand the social media use of the concept "entrepreneurship" in Latin America. Our study analyzes the use of the entrepreneurship word and hashtag in its Spanish version *#Emprendimiento* and Portuguese version *#Empreendedorismo* by tracking microblogging messages shared on social media, in order to describe its social uses in the online exchange of contents between users, clustering those messages according to patterns, identifying topics, thematic and main contributors and interpret them in order to find and describe the common features about entrepreneurship in Latin America. Furthermore, this study contributes to the discussion on the many definitions of entrepreneurship in the literature and in the practice describing the business processes from a new approach based on analytics and social listening by using the data publicly available in social media networks.

The following is a description of the theoretical framework, the methodology used in the study, the main findings, and, finally, its implications, limitations, and future lines of research.

Background

The Concept of Entrepreneurship

Throughout the years, the concept of entrepreneurship has been inevitably associated with the activities of business creation and self-employment, which is not the most accurate definition of the term (Chow 2006). The term entrepreneurship often is associated with different and varied names such as: entrepreneurial factor, business function, entrepreneurial initiatives, business behavior, and even entrepreneurial spirit (Cuervo et al. 2007). Each of these are covering some concepts and ideas that aim to submit terminological precision and simultaneously, the historical evolution and theoretical location, which explains the different approaches to the definition of entrepreneurship.

However, there seems to be a consensus that the essence of entrepreneurship is the willingness to pursue and exploit an opportunity (Stevenson and Jarillo 1990). Opportunity is defined as a future situation according to desires and goals of individuals or organizations.

Entrepreneurship can be seen as "entrepreneurial function," which involves more than the creation of a new business. Entrepreneurship implies the pursuit of opportunity, evaluation, and exploitation of opportunities and the set of individuals who discover, evaluate, and exploit them (Shane and Venkataraman 2000). In brief, in a firm-level perspective, these opportunities are not specifically related to business creation but rather through new products, services and process, new strategic behaviors, and new market opportunities. Thus, entrepreneurial opportunities come in a variety of forms: opportunities in product markets, opportunities in factor markets, as in the case of the discovery of new things—innovation. As noted above, we can identify that the two streams of research have denominated the entrepreneurship literature. The first has largely focused on the individual entrepreneur as the unit of analysis, especially on identifying the traits which distinguished successful entrepreneurs from less successful ones. At the same time, in this stream is also included the relationship between education and entrepreneurship (Acs and Szerb 2007, Naudé et al. 2008, O'Connor 2013). Education has become one of the strategies that worldwide governments use to increase entrepreneurial activity (Von Graevenitz et al. 2010, Sánchez 2013). Entrepreneurship education refers to instructing individuals on the attitudes and aptitudes that they need to experience and know to be an entrepreneur, run-manage a business and make it successful (OECD 1998, Duval-Couetil 2013).

In contrast, the second stream of research tends to view entrepreneurial activities as a firm-level phenomenon, labeled intrapreneurship or corporate entrepreneurship. This second stream is also linked with entrepreneurial development; it is understood as every action related to encouraging and supporting individuals, in a territory, for creating new business. Encouraging and supporting entrepreneurship requires that a territory generates actions related to awareness, education and training, business incubation, business growth, R&D transfer, networking, financial support, business infrastructure, regulation of business procedures and taxes, the structure of the labor force, and any other aspect required to improve the business climate and entrepreneurial ecosystem (Ribeiro-Soriano and Galindo-Martín 2012, Mason and Brown 2014).

On the other hand, studies have demonstrated that financial support or funding is crucial for entrepreneurial development (World Bank 2013, Mason and Brown 2014). Funding is defined as the study of the resource allocation applied to new ventures; it is related to the mechanisms that entrepreneurs use to access the capital that they need to invest in startups or business growth such as, for instance, bootstrapping, business angels, investors, venture capital fund, risk capital fund, crowdfunding, loans, public stock offering, among others (Colombo and Grilli 2007, World Bank 2013, World Economic Forum 2013).

But, what about the social use of this concept? Where is it located?

Having in mind that Internet and information and communications technologies (ICTs) offer a space to perform multiple actions and is a context in which a lot of information is generated by many sources and nowadays the social monitoring tools available are heavily used by major brands all over the world in order to get to know their consumers better, we decided to explore this context to find what people is saying about entrepreneurship in Latin America using social media sites as a channel to share, participate, and generate conversations.

Entrepreneurship in the Online Context

It is widely acknowledged that communication has definitely changed and the influence of Internet and social media on people and on the organizations' ability to interact and communicate are visible in all areas of society. Nowadays the social media and Web 2.0 technologies provide dynamism, interaction, collaboration, participation, and opportunities to create places where people learn together and share their experiences (Bonsón and Flores 2011). Equally important, the digital environment offers advantages for entrepreneurs (López 2012), not only for digital ventures, it is also about the opportunities that ICTs offer to entrepreneurs to publish, produce content, and follow the market (Guthrie 2014), or to attract consumers, reduce uncertainty or redirected toward innovation in products, services, distribution, marketing, or processes (Franklin et al. 2013); or use environments that can track consumers in order to give value to the business (Culnan et al. 2010) and all this with global reach.

Over the last decade, social media also emerged as one of the most important tools for conducting business and marketing activities (Alarcón et al. 2015). Scholars also highlight the influence of the Internet and firms' social media usage on entrepreneurial activities. Along with the Internet "Revolution" in the 1990s new opportunities to access to new audiences have arrived, as well as new ideas and resources with lower costs making it more attractive to start a business. In particular, social media was recognized as an important strategic mechanism for international business achievement because it provides firms with faster access to market, consumer and competitor information (Mathews and Healy 2007), and also facilitates the internationalization of small- and medium-sized companies (Gabrielsson and Gabrielsson 2011).

That means there is data available on websites, social networks, and social media that leaves a trail that can be identified and interpreted from the actions made by those who use the online context. So, it has been studied in order to find regular patterns, actors, and actions, relationships and exchanges of information and resources to obtain knowledge on how the exchanges work, who are information providers, how it is exploited to guide information and find opportunities and changes; all this by analyzing the behavior of those who use ICTs (Kaushik 2007).

For this reason, the use of web analytics has been implemented in many areas of research. It is a resource for research in marketing (Jackson 2009), strategic decisions (Seufert and Schiefer 2005), business intelligence (Chen et al. 2012), and information management as a strategy in organizations (Vom Brocke and Rosemann 2015). A variety of methods are used, including data mining (Hema and Malik 2010), mining of opinion (Pang and Lee 2008), text mining (He et al. 2013), digital social network analysis (Bonchi et al. 2011), or classification in tiers, polarity of words and phrases, and sentiment analysis (Speriosu et al. 2011) that can be used to analyze what users produce and share on the web.

Methodology

This chapter provides an attempt to analyze entrepreneurship in Latin America by the use of analytics and social listening on the data available provided by individuals in the social media. The data available online has been used to study the online exchange of resources between individuals, groups, or organizations, to locate patterns revealing actors, nodes, relationships, and their connections. It is possible to obtain knowledge about how these trade routes work, with a variety of techniques and methods to convert them into primary sources by processing and reducing through refining data and identifying and grouping similar items, leverage content by categorization on textual data, monitoring the tweet stream by its relations to the study objectives, and utilizing contextual intelligence to discern meaning by matching (Mohanty et al. 2013).

In this chapter, we used the web analytics on the data available on the web to obtain the general trends and then identify by analytics on Twitter, the social media uses of entrepreneurship as the keyword and hashtag in order to identify topics of interest, contributors, trends, and how they are used (Kumar et al. 2014, Batrinca and Treleaven 2015).

Analytics Process

The process started by using digital analytics tools of IBM Social Media Analytics for business social insight, which allowed us to do an initial exploratory round of data mining performed with the keywords and hashtags *emprendimiento* (entrepreneurship in Spanish), *empreendedorismo* (entrepreneurship in Portuguese) in the Latin American context, setting a period of six months (May–October 2015), within the historical archive, using the content analytics and the language processing tool to measure: volume by the number of snippets (units of content); share of voice (percentage of a keyword relative to the total conversation); reach: volume of snippets by source; sentiment: natural language processing that tells us if the content is mainly positive, negative, neutral, or ambivalent; relationships: the relationships between analyzed keywords; top Influencers: authors with the most volume of generated content and evolving topics: other topics related to the keywords that lead us to a first insight on the entrepreneurship uses. Then to refine data we used the search queries to obtain smaller quantities, limiting the search to a maximum amount of 25,000 snippets and filtering out data from Spain.

For text mining and interpretation we made a historical tracking monitoring keywords and hashtags in Twitter contents, sampling and bubbling up data by reach, users, words and popularity, and having in account their impact by the total number of impressions presented as most relevant tweets, (tweets received by many users) considering just original tweets and filtering tweets in Spanish from the United States. At this point, the sample was reduced to 867,000 tweets.

From this, we made a random sample of tweets using word clouds to find the most used words to bring together a set of tweets by tags and by topic, finding common features which allowed us to find categories that were classified by querying tools in a CADQAS software and organizing them into clusters: Education and Entrepreneurship Learning, Funding and Support, and Entrepreneurship Development. The final sample of tweets to interpret by content analysis was 2824 tweets. The corpus collected was systematically analyzed in each category in order understand the information that people post in social media messages publicly available, analyze what is revealed within the contents of a message, and find common topics and thematic (Krippendorff 2004). To do this, we used as a guide the entrepreneurship theory first as a codebook and then interpret and describe in a qualitative way, the social uses of entrepreneurship in Latin America.

Findings

Main Insights

Latin America is a region that has a very active conversation around entrepreneurship; at first glance the conversation has a clearly neutral and positive sentiment around it. The analysis shows conversation is coming from or is related to the news (70%), blogs (24%), video channels (3%), and social media sites (3%).

Regarding the share of voice and volume in all the conversation on the web, when we look at the countries that are generating the most conversation around the subject, the country with the majority of snippets is Brazil, followed by Chile, Argentina, Mexico, Colombia, Venezuela, Bolivia, and Peru. The conversation in Spanish speaking countries of Latin America presented a steady growth from June, reaching its maximum in September. This growth is driven by the keyword *emprendimiento*. It is interesting that when we split the three analyzed terms, the conversation about *empreendedorismo* (Brazil) presented the highest number in October, while the word *emprendimiento* started to decline in that month. Topic *empreendedorismo*, monitored in Brazil accounts for the 28.45% of the total conversation in LATAM. The behavior of the volume over time in the whole conversation—with all the keywords—presents a steady growth from July 1, reaching its top on September 30 and a slight drop during the months of June and October.

Overall, the sentiment of the conversation in *emprendimiento* is mostly neutral with a tendency to be positive and that implies that the conversation is more informational than opinionated, for the word *empreendedorismo* the positive trend is higher (+50%) and between the sources the positive trend of the conversation remains and gets portrayed in the news. Brazil talks the most about the subject entrepreneurship in the region. Chile has a very active conversation promoting the entrepreneurship culture as well as communicating about the opportunities for entrepreneurs.

In Chile and Colombia the word Social was highly associated. Argentina has also presented several content around the entrepreneurship subject and government.

Influencers of the conversation by volume of content top 10 are *Pulsosocial* (Colombian blog), José Martin (Pulso Social blogger), *El Mercurio* (Chilean digital newspaper), Copesa (Chilean Media Group—*La Tercera* digital newspaper), *Portal Minero* (Information and business online community of the mining industry of Chile), *Emprendo Verde* (Sustainable entrepreneurship network Chile), Fernanda Santos (Brazilian collaborator for *Camacari Fatos e Fotos*, Startupi com.br and portalexame.abril.com.br), *El Comercio* (digital newspaper from Peru), and *Extra Noticias* (Chilean newspaper).

The main sources for entrepreneurship conversations were YouTube, followed by *Organización Editorial Mexicana* (Mexican media group), *Pulso social* (Colombian online publication covering entrepreneurship and technology), segs. com.br (Brazilian insurance industry specialized portal), economiaynegocios.cl (Chilean business and economy centered portal), latercera.com (Chilean newspaper), diario.elmercurio.com (Chilean digital newspaper), portafolio.co (a finance oriented digital magazine from Colombia), startupi.com.br (Brazilian knowledge based on innovation market, business, entrepreneurship, and technology), and df.cl (Chilean blog).

The evolving topics in news are about startups, entrepreneurs, platform, and technology, followed by development and financing and blogs seem to replicate what's talked in the news.

When search is about entrepreneurship topics related in Peru and Mexico are startups, entrepreneurs, platform, technology, development and financing; Bolivia is talking more about province and work; Venezuela and Argentina are portraying a highly important discourse on government and themselves and Brazil's main topics are business, people, entrepreneurs, lectures, and innovation Figure 12.1.

An Interpretation of Entrepreneurship Social Uses in the Internet Context

The contents using this hashtag have been shared in Twitter since 2009. An average of 18,500 tweets can be shared in a day as original texts, retweets, and replies and is mostly used along with hashtags innovation, enterprise, entrepreneur, entrepreneurs, startups, marketing, and companies (Figure 12.2). Venezuela is the country from where most social media is used to share content about entrepreneurship, followed by Mexico and Brazil, with a significant difference by Colombia, Chile, Peru, then by Ecuador, Guatemala, Panama, and Argentina. The top users of the *#Emprendimiento* in their tweets are from Venezuela (4), México (2), Ecuador, Chile, and Colombia (Figure 12.3).

However, there are other versions of *#Emprendimiento* in LATAM. We can find the hashtag *#Emprendedorismo* related with the Portuguese word without the ee-, which is commonly used in Argentina, Uruguay, from Brazilian users writing in Spanish, and sometimes in Venezuela and Colombia. There is also *#Empresarismo*, used in Puerto Rico and sometimes in Colombia and Venezuela. The hashtag #Entrepreneurship is also used in tweets written in Spanish or Portuguese, mostly in Chile, Brazil, and México. *Emprendimiento* as a keyword is mostly used in Venezuela, followed by Chile and Colombia; it is also used in nonspeaking Spanish countries and United States showing significant use (Figure 12.4). The most used keywords are startup, marketing, enterprise, success, companies, brands, and management. Brazil is not in the graphic due to the use of a different word; however, if we compare the *empreendedorismo* uses to other LATAM countries it is similar to Venezuela.

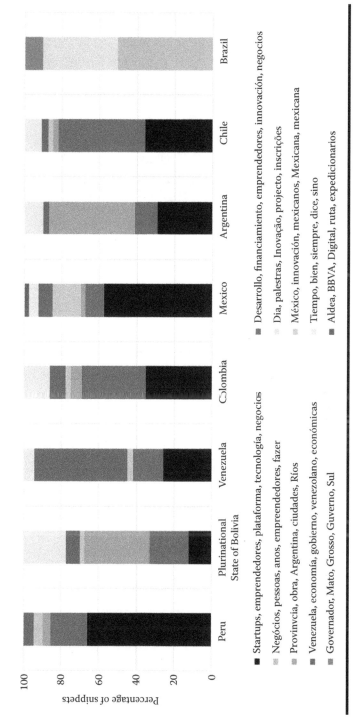

Figure 12.1 Keywords sentiment analysis. (Courtesy of I3M Social Analytics Tools.)

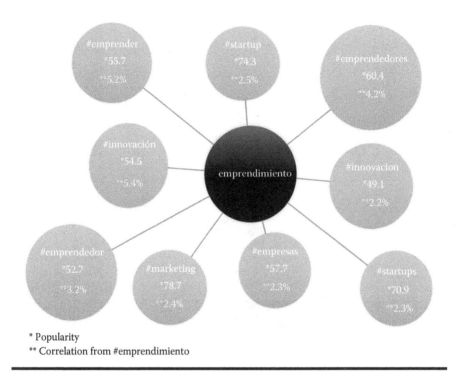

* Popularity
** Correlation from #emprendimiento

Figure 12.2 Related hashtags. (From IBM Social Analytics Tools.)

Content Analysis

The common features identified as categories of entrepreneurship were classified into clusters and after analyzing the sets, these were subdivided for descriptions. Education is presented as entrepreneurship learning, informal learning (events), and coaching for entrepreneurs; funding and support have additional sections with bootstrapping, crowdfunding, marketing and promotion; and entrepreneurship development has two more sections: digital entrepreneurship and social entrepreneurship.

Education and Entrepreneurship Learning

According to universities entrepreneurship spirit is something that can be taught by #mentoring the process. Entrepreneurship learning in formal education is carried out with workshops for middle school, by meetings with entrepreneurs, and events such as entrepreneurship weeks or Startup Weekends and formal training in the educational curricula.

Tweets exposes themes like: Youth business in Peru; assessment with young college students; entrepreneurship in the stock market in Ecuador; entrepreneurship

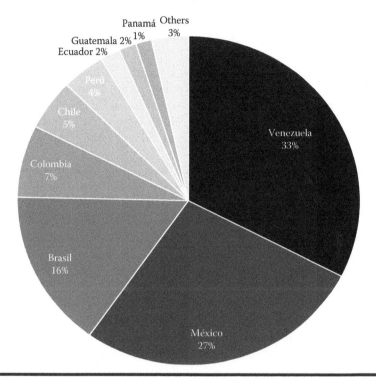

Figure 12.3 **Entrepreneurship hashtags used in Twitter LATAM. (From IBM Social Analytics Tools.)**

Figure 12.4 **Keyword *emprendimiento*. (From IBM Social Analytics Tools.)**

experiences, sustainable entrepreneurship, forums in Venezuela; or workshops for entrepreneurs in Chile and Ecuador.

The public University of Santiago, Chile, says entrepreneurship learning is within the "Triple Helix": State–Company–University. According to that, the academic events have sponsorship from organizations such as bioincuba.com, Peruvian incubator, Corfo, production development corporation of Chile; MeetLatam.com, a channel meeting between entrepreneurs of Silicon Valley and LATAM; or Polisofia. com that helps organizations develop skills to innovate, allow Crowdsourcing, or Co-Create Innovation.

Informal learning events for entrepreneurship training are organized by government agencies such as @SenaSoft and @FórmulaSena or the Chamber of Commerce of Bogotá from Colombia and the municipality of Coacalco, Mexico; community-based associations and Accelerators Communities as http://aliadasencadena. org/ organized by the female entrepreneurs association in Baruta, Venezuela, and Groups of investors such as HubBOG of Colombia.

To promote events, key topics are inserted as hashtags as innovation, financial solutions, training indicators, rotation, portfolio, digital marketing, and social networks such as ELIGE Congress in México for #leadership and #Management, the online congress #SMLatam on entrepreneurship and business with high #Technology, or #socialmedia and #DigitalMarketing for #digitalentrepreneurship for the congress #OlhóCON 2015 in Brazil. Twitter becomes a billboard to advertise events as Symposium of #leadership and #management and Entrepreneurship in Venezuela. Or Media is used by the Global Entrepreneurship Week of GEM with accounts that share information in sites such as @empreendeweb, degerencia.com, or EmpreendedorOnline.Net.Br; also blogs like @blogdoecommerce from Rio de Janeiro, offering articles, tutorials, courses and news and a directory of articles is also available at directory of articles at @ArtigosEcommerc and @empreendemia focused on accelerating business between companies with practical tips for entrepreneurs in Brazil.

It is also possible to find the linked key words in a hashtag like training for #youngentrepreneurs and #successfulleaders; or #DigitalMarketingGames with videos in #E-Commerce at cursodeecommerc YouTube channel.

Coaching hashtags in tweets are used to disseminate items for inspiration: Meet the "Mark Zuckerberg" of Latin America, 10 tips on entrepreneurship given by the founder of Digg and the entrepreneur without dying in the attempt. Also to get followers: "Join the culture of entrepreneurship, success awaits you! to know it and apply it, follow me!"; or advertise books "*Skudmart, Chemistry Death,*" book designed to encourage innovation, creation, and the birth of new companies based on the mix between the academic and the entrepreneurial spirit of students and graduates and Guy Kawasaki presents its manual for a successful entrepreneur. Additionally advantages and disadvantages of entrepreneurship are exposed as: you are your own boss, you manage your schedule, and you know how far you want to go, attractive isn't it?

Motivating phrases calls to: "Make a change, don't let continue a world short on vision!"; "Even if you do not know what can happen, do not hesitate to do it, the limit is up to you, do not hesitate!"; "A complaint about a product or service always emerges, this is an opportunity to undertake a solution and succeed"; "Unreachable goals does not exist, only people who get tired halfway"; "Overcome fear and learn to take the plunge; If someone says that entrepreneurship is easy, do not believe is hard, but it's worth it."

Messages about business plans are common: "in the first 5 years of a company; there are obstacles and course corrections, so make a plan"; "Implement an idea without a good business plan is like going on a trip route"; "Develop a plan taking into account possible setbacks on the road, even if that sound crazy"; "Having an idea is not enough to start a business, you must develop a plan and evaluate the market"; "Define mission and vision is the best exercise to define the north of the business and scope." Those messages make people ask: "I would like opinions, links, and information about business plan and how to create a good business plan for a startup?" And they can find: "Test and validate your business model; download the master Startup Guide"; the most common mistakes in preparing a business plan.

Information for entrepreneur's actions is shared for those who have already started: "Keys for innovative entrepreneurship"; "What does a Marketing Professional, Cool Hunting—Trend Hunters secrets to develop a good sales forecast services, business"; "Tips to strengthen corporate governance, such as preserving a family business or turning your child into an entrepreneur"; "How to make the most of a conference or networking event." "To avoid stumbling: Major mistakes in entrepreneurship"; "How to prevent someone from stealing your idea about a new startup"; "why the venture fails?"; "Make mistakes Marketing entrepreneurs?"; "The money from my business is really mine?" Or about the attitude: "Transforming the passion in entrepreneurship"; "Decalogue to be a good leader; Anyone who is successful is because knew how to manage its own mind and think unimaginable things and make them entrepreneurship"; "Try to improve those skills that will make more effective and productive in what you undertake."

Someone shares: "thinking about next project…suggestions???" Answers could be: "low investment franchises to undertake with success or motivation"; "lessons to learn from Israel, birthplace of successful startups"; "How to turn a hobby into a business." On digital entrepreneurship: "Dive into the world of entrepreneurship 3.0"; "improve the usability of your online store"; "The easy creation of web pages boosts the business entrepreneurs to make your venture a global business, selling abroad and seek new markets."

Entrepreneurs are seeking support to become known and get customers asking users to re-tweet: "Hey, you help me spread my venture with RT? Pompoms Paper, Thanks"; "Can you help me please disclose this? Looking for partners to boost CRM entrepreneurship in Bogotá"; "Look is my venture for birth gifts I hope you likeBabyFlowersGift—Argentina"; "I still programming, structuring, webmastering my future web entrepreneurship check it out"; "In Loja we already have a company of inks, made with quality inks."

Funding and Support

The figure of angel investors is found when angels offer financing entrepreneurs in Colombia or Mexico saying: "Do you know why I will finance your company?" Or "Undertake startup venture funding." Mentors announce: "Inclusive Business Program develops with IDB Masisa"; "We want to help and support the successful development of your enterprise account with us!"; "We continue supporting your entrepreneurial ideas—Wayra; Fundación Impulsar from Argentina trains young entrepreneurs through mentoring and economic orientation"; "HubBOG offers acceleration Startups and Campus program in academia and investment" or "co working for new digital companies and invite entrepreneurs to let them know their venture registering it and then receive information on opportunities for Colombian State support." The funding by the government is reflected indirectly in messages like the one about the Law for the Promotion of Corporate Finance "crowdfunding startup undertake Mexico." On the other hand, organizations such as *Banca Comunitaria* process microcredit for venture, entrepreneurship, and encourages organization and citizen participation.

There are also contests and prizes as *Concurso Ideas* in Venezuela or Fintech-Challenge, an incubator which promises seed capital and the possibility of implementing digital entrepreneurship in Colombia.

Tweets are also sharing contents about "What is Bootstrapping?" and users answer: "A way to get funding"; "The business philosophy of the twenty-first century, Economic Freedom, with little do much and ideal for starting;" Everything can be with bootstrapping. A user explains that it is like starting a venture "to pure lung" or, as Uruguayans say row in it, or start a venture with "what you're wearing," "with what is at hand; but start!." So it is possible to find announces about how to start a business without a penny with Bootstrapping hashtag or The 10 Commandments of Bootstrapping.

The growing entrepreneurial projects are led by several investors through crowdfunding platforms where entrepreneurs ask for help to raise funds, to find sponsorship and partnership or a network of cooperation for entrepreneurs sharing to users that will come funding investors: Kickstarter coupled with a platform that drives or accompanies entrepreneurs promoting creative projects led by artists and other entrepreneurs, or a portal called crowdfunding micochinito.com shares: "Together we can afford what we need. If you have a project, you can ask for help from your community to support you. If you want to support, you can find the projects that are in your community. Go ahead!" This tweets are shared with links and ID users saying: "Looking for a digital venture funders to support crowdfunding campaign"; "Looking Visionary contributors or Taxpayers who are visionaries in platforms like

Indiegogo"; or directly like an initiative: "seeking funds to be in a global competition with their product in Peru."

The hashtag is also used to call for venture crowdfunding in platforms and give notice of opportunities in events like the Startup Nations Summit capstone of Global Entrepreneurship Week or joining initiatives such as the Chilean Red Digital. There are also those who think that crowdfunding is a resource that goes beyond raising funds and can be used as a platform for helping local development in Colombia.

Entrepreneurship Development

The information shares: "what really makes an entrepreneur"; "What is the ideal training for an entrepreneur"; "The right age to be an entrepreneur"; "How to register the mark of your business and secure your identity or the lessons learned and difficulties faced by a startup." Then it is possible to find entrepreneurship advice in messages about: "Advantages and challenges for the small entrepreneur business at home"; "Image consultant, a good choice for a company in your own home," or "difficulties and solutions for administration of interests in family businesses."

And share posts about entrepreneurship ideas: "Steps to take a business idea of the paper and turn it into reality"; "What is the profile of the food truck entrepreneurs"; "Tips to build a snack bar for those who are already in the industry"; "Is there still room for new entrepreneurs in collective purchases or tips on how to assemble a buffet parties."

In Brazil, the media says digital entrepreneurship is undertaking all economic sectors by allowing optimization, opening of markets, and internationalization at low cost. This kind of messages can also be seen in a Chilean company that says that they live on technology, a seed venture @Vive Digital @ParqueSoft that facilitates online purchases or the launch of apps in Colombia, in events like the digital entrepreneurship forums organized by the association of young entrepreneurs Vzlaemprende from Venezuela or the user experience in Chile or contests like Fintech Challenge in Colombia.

Digital entrepreneurship is present in the social media thanks to bloggers that answer tweets saying: I want ideas to start a business at home with online entrepreneurship by tweets sharing: profitable business #ideas on the Internet with high growth potential. Users say:

> "digital entrepreneurship is mainstream and opens the door to new markets; Online entrepreneurship is the best way for young and creative companies"; "With online entrepreneurship you have your slice of #virtualcake"; "Web entrepreneurship is the new business model and is necessary to facilitate access to the new entrepreneur the online business."

It is possible to find information about how to become a digital entrepreneur in: "what kind of business works on the web"; "Tips to Make Your digital enterprise"; "Take off sites that offer discounts are the newest form of online entrepreneurship"; "tips for the entrepreneur who want to choose a good domain for a website shop"; "Advantages and difficulties of new online entrepreneurs"; "The profile and online entrepreneurship paths"; "What are the advantages of having an online business"; "See how to reduce risks in an e-commerce project"; "Tips for those wishing to start a business on the Internet."

Social entrepreneurship is highly mentioned, we found that in Costa Rica a university announced a social entrepreneurship workshop with the theme expectations of the social investors; in Mexico, organizations identify opportunities for joint work to promote it; Venezuela announced the social change maker day-#SChMD2015, a space of cocreation driven by Ashoka a global association of social entrepreneurs and Impact Hub Caracas; Mexico launches the Ruta BBVA in its XXXI Edition associated to the education in values and social entrepreneurship; in Chile the #FIIES2015 is an organization that seeks to create massive social impact through identifying and supporting social entrepreneurs in early stage, or in Valparaiso, Chile a master class is given in social entrepreneurship in #TallerVIVA supported by investors and achievements related to the innovation theme are announced in igLatino an initiative of the center for democracy and development in the Americas.

Social entrepreneurs become influencers: @JuanDelCerro has a column focused on entrepreneurs and SMEs (small- and medium-sized enterprises) (OECD 2005) and gives lectures on social entrepreneurship in organizations in Guadalajara, Mexico, on social and technological innovation; @felixxi is a social entrepreneur committed to @OpcionVenezuela teaching social entrepreneurship to young people and @EnriqueJacobR identify opportunities in Mexico to work together and to promote it with @fominbid.

There are also meetings like #senseCamp an alternative conference or #emprecamp from the global initiative MakeSense.org that focuses on talents, skills, and social entrepreneurs to solve social challenges, make connections in the international organization Fellows Ashoka for citizens, leading the way for #Changemakers.

Social entrepreneurship can be seen in initiatives like the center for entrepreneurship and cultural recovery in Chile; @Ruta_N for building peace through Social Entrepreneurship and Social Innovation in Colombia; The Laboratoria.la a tech social enterprise empowering Latin American women, or in events such as the indigenous craft fair in Venezuela, and in invitations to join the team or @conquitodmq at socialtocrowd.org.

To understand what social entrepreneurship is, it is stated that it is not philanthropy and rather is how you can be an agent of change doing this kind of enterprise, which is usually classified as disruptive, something to solve global problems, for inspiring optimism, collaboration, diversity, and also as a model that can help entrepreneurs.

The relationship between innovation and entrepreneurship is constant and that is why an accelerator in Mexico says: "Education, entrepreneurship and innovation are linked actions that promote development."

We found that the @DesignThinking is an invitation to the development of creativity in Chile promoting a dream sustained by an innovative plan; entrepreneurship, business, and innovation meet in a Chilean community; there is a national congress of agricultural innovation and entrepreneurship in Chile and the INE (National Institute of Entrepreneurship) from Mexico say the country has an environment of entrepreneurship and innovation to grow steadily.

There are also awards and competitions like Avonni of Chile, the national university entrepreneurship competition organized by the innovation center UC Anacleto Angelini and Sura in Colombia, or the #PremiosEi2015awards in Ecuador. Meetings are also organized: Heroesfest.co and #MakeenSummit in Colombia or a fair of social entrepreneurship and Scientific Research Talents in Ecuador.

Discussion and Implications

The study, on which this chapter is based, provides an approach to understand the entrepreneurship concept in LATAM following it as keyword or hashtag in the web and specifically on a corpus of contents shared in Twitter obtained randomly from historical data. That allowed us to analyze its social uses and practice by describing and interpreting the online exchange and common features to find thematic and topics set out below.

Education and Entrepreneurship Learning

Recently, interest on entrepreneurship education has risen due to the recognition of its contribution toward fomenting the creation of new companies and jobs, as well as the generation of innovation within already established organizations (Lima et al. 2014), which generates social progress, economic strength, and regional development (Fayolle et al. 2006). Given the above, the relation found between the use of *#emprendimiento* and higher education in entrepreneurship is not surprising. Our findings point that especially from the universities standpoint, there is a constant use of *#emprendimiento* to promote their courses of formal education in entrepreneurship, and also to divulge academic events in this field of knowledge. These results confirm what Lima et al. (2014) highlighted, sustaining that higher education has been driven toward creating surroundings, activities, and courses in the entrepreneurship field, thus opening an important space in academia for this subject.

Simultaneously, there is evidence of the frequent use of *#emprendimiento* associated with other category of entrepreneurship education that can be associated with informal formation. Governmental entities especially use this term to divulge courses oriented toward bringing people into entrepreneurship. The relevance of the subject is in the public political agendas in Latin America and the Caribbean. Countries such as Chile, Colombia, and Mexico lead the publications from public institutions such as agencies for socioeconomic development oriented to improve competitiveness and the productive diversification of the country. This is required through the promotion of the formation of human capital. In this sense, the need to strengthen the generation of high-impact technology-based enterprises in the region (Léderman et al. 2014, Martins et al. 2015) explains that the main purposes established in the publications relate with the formation in innovation and technological capabilities, such as digital marketing and social media, besides the formation in leadership and management oriented toward generating productive and highly competitive ecosystems.

Finally, even under the concept of entrepreneurship education, our findings aim toward the frequent usage of motivational messages about entrepreneurship, considering coaching as a tool toward the creation and good management of businesses. This is understood, given the need to foster a change in the mindset to overcome certain cultural paradigms which are especially evident in Latin America and that prevent more cases of business success, such as fear to failure.

Overall, it is observed that the association or use of *#emprendimiento* in the context of education is present and is subject to paramount relevance for the universities and the government. The universities foster the integral formation throughout entrepreneurship courses in their undergraduate and graduate programs, such as informal formation through academic events and spaces for discussion about successful practices that drive the entrepreneurial spirit. Simultaneously, the governments participate in programs of informal formation, with the objective of strengthening the actors in the entrepreneurial ecosystem in the key regions for each country to foster high-impact entrepreneurship within their territories.

Funding and Support

Our findings have shown that *#emprendimiento* is often used in publications related with the search for funding sources that may well be the formal and informal options of risk capital, the public calls of seed capital or certain emergent funding alternatives, such as crowdfunding and bootstrapping. Other frequent use is related to the formation in investment subjects, this being of investors looking for tools to mitigate risk, or entrepreneurs looking for capital to start their business or leverage the activity of a company in an early stage.

These findings confirm that funding is a transcendental topic of the entrepreneurial activity, especially for startups and companies in an early stage facing difficulties to fund their business due to the risk of a possible failure and lacking the history to make up for this risk, which leads to an even greater difficulty to access bank funding. For this reason, the frequent use of *#emprendimiento* associated with publications related to the search for early stage partners such as venture capital funds, angel investors, crowdfunding platforms, and information about bootstrapping, is justified. In this case, many of the publications come from entrepreneurs who seek funding, advice, and access to value-added networks.

In Latin America, the social use of the word entrepreneurship is directly associated with different alternative sources of funding, showing a new trend which aims toward the growth of the venture capital culture and is justified with the identification of different venture capital funds, as well as business angel networks that have started to operate in recent years in the region. This type of investment is important not only in developed countries, but also in developing ones. Thus, if we consider that the market for potential investors is much larger than the market for active investors (San José et al. 2005), the generation of knowledge, as presented in our findings, can help overcome a major obstacle: the lack of private investment culture in the region.

Entrepreneurship Development

Developing a suitable business climate is a key factor in countries to stimulate their entrepreneurial activity (World Bank 2013, World Economic Forum 2013, Mason and Brown 2014). Achieving entrepreneurial development not only depends on the involvement of the government and the private sector, but also depends on molding cultural norms and the education system, eliminating regulatory barriers, providing financial support for new business initiatives, creating effective market strategies and network access and encouraging the creation of clusters, among others (Isenberg 2011, Sánchez 2013).

Latin American countries are one of the world's regions with the highest rate of entrepreneurial activity (Amoros and Bosma 2014); however, it is also one of the regions showing undeveloped entrepreneurial ecosystems (World Economic Forum 2013). A recent study has indicated that Latin America is a region with many entrepreneurs but with very few innovations (Léderman et al. 2014). One of the main reasons for this is the low investment in R&D from companies and governments. As a consequence of the above, nowadays the use of ICTs in Latin America is being consolidated like a key tool to develop entrepreneurial innovative projects with low budget, while reducing the technological gap in the business of this region (Karol and Vélez 2013). According to Karol and Vélez (2013), there is a strong tendency to relate entrepreneurial activity, digital entrepreneurship, and ICT in Latin America.

The present study confirms this relationship, by finding a strong connection between the use of *#emprendimiento* and entrepreneurship development and digital entrepreneurship. Regarding the first, this result indicates that the Internet is increasingly being consolidated as a key channel for providing support to entrepreneurial activity in Latin America, especially in countries such as Chile and Argentina, through consulting and courses online, crowdfunding and networking. Concerning the digital entrepreneurship, this study shows that this category is a trend that permeates all economic sectors that transcends the actual economic situation by allowing optimization, opening of markets, and internationalization at low cost for startups.

These findings, regarding the relationship between *#emprendimiento* and the category of digital entrepreneurship, are consistent with the results of other studies. Researches have shown that ICTs have reduced transaction costs and have expanded the efficient scale industries, which has opened doors for many small businesses to start productive investment plans in various areas of the economy (Jensen 1993). At the same time, studies have shown that ICTs have reduced the importance of economies of scale in many sectors, which has encouraged the creation of small and new businesses (Audretsch and Thurik 2001a, Stiroh 2002, Vélez 2011).

In consequence, it is reasonable that we found a relationship as well between entrepreneurship and innovation. Karol and Vélez (2013) and Léderman et al. (2014) indicate that the use of ICTs in Latin America is being consolidated like a strategy to develop entrepreneurial innovative projects. In countries such as Colombia, Chile, and Mexico this relationship refers to the generation of innovative ideas to start up through various methodologies, especially design thinking, as well as the promotion of events and the support for entrepreneurs that encourage innovation and entrepreneurial culture. The results found are also in line with the studies mentioned above, which support the connection between entrepreneurship and innovation (Audretsch and Thurik 2001b, Thurik and Wennekers 2001, Carree and Thurik 2003, Acs and Amorós 2008).

Finally, this study found a relationship between entrepreneurship and the category of social entrepreneurship in Latin America. Social entrepreneurship, in countries such as Chile, Venezuela, and Colombia, does not refer to a philanthropy activity, but indicates how people can be an agent of change from this type of entrepreneurial activity, helping to solve global problems, to inspire optimism and to collaborate, especially in countries with serious problems of poverty. Precisely, the "agents of change" is the key concept used by scientific literature to define social entrepreneurs (Leadbeater 1997, Dees 1998, Drayton 2002, Bornstein 2004, Austin et al. 2006, Sen 2007, Short et al. 2009, Zahra et al. 2009, Yunus and Weber 2011). It is not a secret that many Latin American countries have several problems that affect the social and economic development; social entrepreneurship can be used as an initiative to solve these pressing social problems, creating social ventures or partaking in the social responsibility of profit companies.

Limitations and Future Research

Given the amount of data collected, the analysis was made on the highlights without going into detail by country, although the data obtained allows one to raise it, this requires an additional step or a different study. In that sense, the cases of Argentina and Venezuela and Brazil would be interesting to deepen, due to the political role in the case of the former two countries and the impact of the last in the region.

On the other hand, in the social media different words that are synonymous with entrepreneurship are used; those words were not analyzed in terms of generating an interpretation; however, there is a body of data that can be analyzed in further stages.

The work does not focus on studying the production of news content, content of blogs, boards, or audiovisual channels, which can be studied particularly taking into account the characteristics of each medium. Also tweets collected contain images shared by users, but these have not been analyzed in this study.

In the filtration process data from Spain and the United States was removed, but the role from both countries must be considered for further studies to shed light on the process of entrepreneurship in Latin America.

References

Acs, Z. J. and Amorós, J. E., 2008, Entrepreneurship and competitiveness dynamics in Latin America, *Small Business Economics*, 31(3), 305–322.

Acs, Z. J. and Szerb, L., 2007, Entrepreneurship, economic growth and public policy, *Small Business Economics*, 28(2–3), 109–122.

Alarcón, M. C., Rialp, A., and Rialp, J., 2015, *The Effect of Social Media Adoption on Exporting Firms' Performance, Entrepreneurship in International Marketing (Advances in International Marketing*, vol. 25, Emerald Group Publishing Limited, London UK, pp. 161–186.

Amoros, J. E. and Bosma, N., 2014, *GEM Global Entrepreneurship Monitor, 2013 Global Report*, Global Entrepreneurship Research Association (GERA).

Audretsch, D. B. and Thurik, A. R., 2001a, What's new about the new economy? Sources of growth in the managed and entrepreneurial economies, *Industrial and Corporate Change*, 10(1), 267–315.

Audretsch, D. B. and Thurik, A. R., 2001b, *Linking Entrepreneurship to Growth*, OECD Science, Technology and Industry Working Papers, 2001/2, OECD Publishing. doi:10.1787/736170038056.

Austin, J., Stevenson, H., and Wei-Skillern, J., 2006, Social and commercial entrepreneurship: Same, *Different, or Both? Entrepreneurship Theory and Practice*, 30(1), 1–22.

Batrinca, B. and Treleaven, P. C., 2015, Social media analytics: A survey of techniques, tools and platforms, *AI & SOCIETY*, 30(1), 89–116.

Bonchi, F., Castillo, C., Gionis, A., and Jaimes, A., 2011, Social network analysis and mining for business applications, ACM Transactions on Intelligent Systems and Technology (TIST), ACM, 2(3), 22.

Bonsón, E. and Flores, F., 2011, Social media and corporate dialogue: The response of global financial institutions, *Online Information Review*, 35(1), 34–49.

Bornstein, D., 2004, *How to Change the World: Social Entrepreneurship and the Power of Ideas*, University Press Oxford, Oxford.

Carree, M. A. and Thurik, A. R., 2003, The impact of entrepreneurship on economic growth, in Z. J. Acs and D. B. Audretsch (Eds.), *Handbook of Entrepreneurship Research*, pp. 437–471, Springer, Rotterdam.

Chen, H., Chiang, R., and Storey, V. C., 2012, Business intelligence and analytics: From big data to big impact, *MIS Quarterly*, 36(4), 1165–1188.

Chow, I. H., 2006, The relationship between entrepreneurial orientation and firm performance in China, *SAM Advanced Management Journal*, 71(3), 11–20.

Colombo, M. G. and Grilli, l., 2007, Funding gaps? Access to bank loans by high-tech start-ups, *Small Business Economics*, 29(1–2), 25–46.

Cuervo, A., Ribeiro, D., and Roig, S., 2007, *Entrepreneurship: Conceptos, Teoría Y Perspectiva*, Fundacion Bancaja, Madrid.

Culnan, M. J., McHugh, P. J., and Zubillaga, J. I., 2010, How large US companies can use twitter and other social media to gain business value, *MIS Quarterly Executive*, 9(4), 243–259.

Dees, G., 1998, Enterprising non-profits, *Harvard Business Review*, 76(1), 55–66.

Drayton, B., 2002, The citizen sector: Becoming as entrepreneurial and competitive as business, *California Management Review*, 44(3), 120–132.

Duval-Couetil, N., 2013, Assessing the impact of entrepreneurship education programs: Challenges and approaches, *Journal of Small Business Management*, 51(3), 394–409.

Fayolle, A., Gailly, B., and Lassas-Clerc, N., 2006, Effect and counter-effect of entrepreneurship education and social context on student's intentions, *Estudios de Economía Aplicada*, 24(2), 509–524.

Franklin, M., Searle, N., Stoyanova, D., and Townley, B., 2013, Innovation in the application of digital tools for managing uncertainty: The case of UK independent film, *Creativity and Innovation Management*, 22(3), 320–333.

Gabrielsson, M. and Gabrielsson, P., 2011, Internet-based sales channel strategies of born global firms, *International Business Review*, 20(1), 88–99.

Guthrie, C., 2014, The digital factory: A hands-on learning project in digital entrepreneurship, *Journal of Entrepreneurship Education*, 17(1), 115–133.

He, W., Zha, S., and Li, L., 2013, Social media competitive analysis and text mining: A case study in the pizza industry, *International Journal of Information Management*, 33(3), 464–472.

Hema, R. and Malik, N., 2010, Data mining and business intelligence, *Proceedings of the 4th National Conference*, Bharati Vidyapeeth's Institute of Computer Applications and Management, New Delhi.

Isenberg, D., 2011, The entrepreneurship ecosystem strategy as a new paradigm for economic policy: Principles for cultivating entrepreneurship, *Presentation at the Institute of International and European Affairs*, Institute of International and European Affairs, May 12, 2011, Dublin, Ireland.

Jackson, S., 2009, *Cult of Analytics: Driving Online Marketing Strategies Using Web Analytics*, Routledge, London.

Jensen, M. C., 1993, The modern industrial revolution, exit, and the failure of internal control systems, *Journal of Finance*, 48(3), 831–880.

Karol, R. and Vélez, J., 2013, Impact of ICT on the level of innovation in Latin America and the Caribbean: Econometric estimates at a panel, *Documentos de Trabajo*, 19(4), 1–18.

Kaushik, A., 2007, *Web Analytics: An Hour a Day (W/Cd)*, John Wiley & Sons, New York.

Krippendorff, K., 2004, *Content Analysis: An Introduction to its Methodology*, Sage, Los Angeles.

Kumar, S., Morstatter, F., and Liu, H., 2014, *Twitter Data Analytics*, Springer, New York.

Leadbeater, C., 1997, *The Rise of the Social Entrepreneur*, Demos, London.

Léderman, D., Messina, J., Pienknagura, S., and Rigolini, J., 2014, *El Emprendimiento En América Latina: Muchas Empresas Y Poca Innovación*, Banco Mundial, Washington, DC.

Lima, E., Lopes, R. M., Nassif, V., and da Silva, D., 2014, Opportunities to improve entrepreneurship education: Contributions considering Brazilian challenges, *Journal of Small Business Management*, 53(4), 1033–1051.

López, A., 2012, Internet entrepreneurs use digital strategies to enter the global marketplace, *Caribbean Business*, 40(23), 14.

Martins, I., Goméz-Araujo, E., and Vaillant, Y., 2015, Mutual effects between innovation commitment and exports: Evidence from the owner-manager in Colombia, *Journal of Technology Management & Innovation*, 10(1), 103–116.

Mason, C. and Brown, R., 2014, *Entrepreneurial ecosystems and growth oriented entrepreneurship*, Final Report to OECD, OECD Publishing, Paris. Available at https://www.oecd.org/cfe/leed/Entrepreneurial-ecosystems.pdf.

Mathews, S. W. and Healy, M. J., 2007, The internet and information capability reduces perceived risk of internationalisation: An Australian SME perspective, *International Journal of Organisational Behaviour*, 12(1), 71–87.

Mohanty, S., Jagadeesh, M., and Srivatsa, H., 2013, Big data imperatives: Enterprise "big data" warehouse," *BI"Implementations and Analytics*, Apress, doi: 10.1007/978-1-4302-4873-6.

Naudé, W., Gries, T., Wood, E., and Meintjies, A., 2008, Regional determinants of entrepreneurial start-ups in a developing country, *Entrepreneurship and Regional Development*, 20(2), 111–124.

O'Connor, A., 2013, A conceptual framework for entrepreneurship education policy: Meeting government and economic purposes, *Journal of Business Venturing*, 28(4), 546–563.

OECD, 1998, *The OECD Jobs Strategy Fostering Entrepreneurship*, OECD Publishing, Paris. Available at http://www.oecd.org/cfe/leed/fosteringentrepreneurship.htm.

OECD, 2005, *OECD Glossary of Statistical Terms —Small and medium-sized enterprises (SMEs) Definition*, Retrieved April 19, 2017, from Available at https://stats.oecd.org/glossary/detail.asp?ID=3123.

Pang, B. and Lee, L., 2008, Opinion mining and sentiment analysis, *Foundations and Trends in Information Retrieval*, 2(1–2), 1–135.

Ribeiro-Soriano, D. and Galindo-Martín, M. A., 2012, Government policies to support entrepreneurship, *Entrepreneurship & Regional Development*, 24(9–10), 861–864.

Sánchez, J. C., 2013, The impact of an entrepreneurship education program on entrepreneurial competencies and intention, *Journal of Small Business Management*, 51(3), 447–465.

San José, A., Roure, J., and Aernoudt, R., 2005, Business Angel academies: Unleashing the potential for business Angel investment, *Venture Capital*, 7(2), 149–165.

Sen, P., 2007, Ashoka's big idea: Transforming the world through social entrepreneurship, *Futures*, 39(5), 534–553.

Seufert, A. and Schiefer, J., 2005, Enhanced business intelligence-supporting business processes with real-time business analytics, in *16th International Workshop on Database and Expert Systems Applications (DEXA 2005)*, August 22–26, 2005, pp. 919–925, IEEE, Copenhagen, Denmark.

Shane, S. and Venkataraman, S., 2000, The promise of entrepreneurship as a field of research, *Academy of Management Review*, 25(1), 217–226.

Short, J. C., Moss, T. W., and Lumpkin, G. T., 2009, Research in social entrepreneurship: Past contributions and future opportunities, *Strategic Entrepreneurship Journal*, 3(2), 161–194.

Speriosu, M., Sudan, N., Upadhyay, S., and Baldridge, J., 2011, Twitter polarity classification with label propagation over lexical links and the follower graph, in *Proceedings of the First Workshop on Unsupervised Learning in NLP*, pp. 53–63, Association for Computational Linguistics, Edinburgh, Scotland.

Stevenson, H. H. and Jarillo, J. C., 1990, A paradigm of entrepreneurship: Entrepreneurial management, *Strategic Management Journal*, 11(5), 17–27.

Stiroh, K. J., 2002, Are ICT spillovers driving the new economy?, *Review of Income and Wealth*, 48(1), 33–57.

Thurik, R. and Wennekers, S., 2001, *A note on entrepreneurship, small business and economic growth, small business and economic growth (January 11, 2001)*, ERIM Report Series Reference No. ERS-2001-60-STR.

Vélez, J. A., 2011, Impacto de Las TIC En El Emprendimiento Empresarial: Estimaciones Econométricas a Nivel de Un Panel de Países, in *Actas de La V Conferencia ACORN-REDECOM*, Lima.

Vom Brocke, J. and Rosemann, M. (Eds.), 2015, *Handbook on Business Process Management 2: Strategic Alignment, Governance, People and Culture*, Springer, Berlin.

Von Graevenitz, G., Harhoff, D., and Weber, R., 2010, The effects of entrepreneurship education, *Journal of Economic Behavior & Organization*, 76(1), 90–112.

World Bank, 2013, *Doing Business 2014: Understanding Regulations for Small and Medium-Size Enterprises*, World Bank Publications, Washington, DC.

World Economic Forum, 2013, The Global Competitiveness Report 2013–2014, in K. Schwab (Ed.), World Economic Forum, Geneva.

Yunus, M. and Weber, K., 2011, *Building Social Business: The New Kind of Capitalism That Serves Humanity's Most Pressing Needs*, PublicAffairs, New York.

Zahra, S. A., Gedajlovic, E., Neubaum, D. O., and Shulman, J. M., 2009, A typology of social entrepreneurs: Motives, search processes and ethical challenges, *Journal of Business Venturing*, 24(5), 519–532.

Chapter 13

Healthcare Topics with Data Science: Exploratory Research with Social Network Analysis

Cinthya Leonor Vergara Silva

Contents

Summary...253
Introduction...254
Social Network Analysis 255
    Methodology and Data Collection..256
Experiments and Results 257
Conclusion and Discussion 261
References...263

Summary

Data management and analysis is advancing to enable organizations to convert their data sources into information and knowledge in order to understand the several kinds of social issues and achieve their objectives. Social transformations and competitive environments have forced all kinds of organizations to evolve and adapt to the social demands. Chile, during the last decade, faces more social pressure and increasing citizen participation in pursuit of quality improvements and effective coverage within the public health system. With this, an important place where citizens and institutions can dialog directly has been twitter, which is a social networking service (SNS), where people and organizations generate a great data source with millions of commentaries each day. Its dynamics allows analysis of a wide spectrum of human behavior and is an important source for data scientists' investigations. This brief study examines the opinion on health issues from Chilean twitter's commentaries linked with government campaigns. The results show that virtual conversations give rich information on what is important for public opinion, if some campaign is appropriate or not, and if there exists relations between topics. Thereby, Twitter has shown, in the Chilean case, to be a good source of information to analyze public opinion and the effectiveness of government campaigns.

Introduction

The management of both public and private organizations has been one of the great challenges of the last decades. Since the Industrial Revolution until today we were facing increasingly complex social situations and competitive environments, which have forced to all kinds of organizations to evolve and adapt to social needs.

Nowadays the analysis of large volumes of data has changed the technological landscape expecting a rapid growth of several analyses based on the data toward integration of the business processes, orchestration flow processes, and social partnership in the management and development of activities in different types of organizations. During the last decade, more social pressure and increasing citizen participation in pursuit of quality improvements and effective coverage within the public system have been a key issue for policy decision makers.

The interaction between people and institutions has been moving into the digital world, where an increasing number of people give their opinion thorough web platforms, generating multiple sources of data for analysis with multiple data types and formats. One of them are the social networking sites (SNS), where different people voluntarily generates content and leave it publicly available to share all kinds of experiences. The large number of people interacting through the Internet in such platforms has generated a large amount of data, due to which its analysis becomes a part of Data Science and Big Data applications.

In particular, Twitter is an important SNS which is growing in its importance. It is noted for its simplicity and speed in generating the social content. With 288 million active users per month in June 2015 and with around 347,000 tweets per minute allowing various analyzes as: Summaries, like daily measurement, monthly, and annual volumes; category trends and analysis of data volumes (e.g., campaigns and key influencers); identification of the correlations between categories, in order to understand whether the issues are related or not; hashtags, to explore and perform effective filters in the search for a relevant data; predictive analysis, where we can identify the patterns of behavior, among others.

In this context, it is interesting to explore what is the relationship between citizens and certain topics related to public policies in Chile. In particular, health topics are one of the most relevant for political public relations, where public opinion and people health status and coverture is a key issue in developing a better society and improving the quality of life (UN Global Pulse 2014).

Thus, an exploratory analysis with published content in Twitter was carried out according to the keywords related to health in the Chilean context. To find the most important tweets, it was used concepts with hashtag related with the Chilean health context. Retrieving those keywords, health-related tweets were collected using the Twitter API and they were processed using the analytical tools and databases.

As a result, after performing an exploratory analysis, the content of the tweets were mainly linked to the quality, contingency, and criticism of the political class and governance. The analysis also showed that it is possible to identify distinctive patterns guided primarily by the contingency period, such as the issue of legalization of marijuana medical use in Chile. The present study provided a baseline that could be used to monitor the effectiveness of public policies, evaluating communication campaigns or estimate needs in population and public opinion using social network analysis techniques.

Social Network Analysis

Data Science is a concept used to describe the techniques for exploration and analysis of large volumes of data that reveal meaningful patterns and rules that could not be discovered by simple observation. A typical process enables one to carry out the stages of selection, preprocessing and integration, transformation of data, application of algorithms, interpretation of results, and for obtaining knowledge (Fayyad et al. 1996, Cleveland 2001, Pei et al. 2005, Dhar 2013).

Social network analysis (SNA) has its origins in both social science and in the broader fields of network analysis and graph theory. Social network analysis is related to mathematical or computer science theory and it consists in visualizing and modeling the entities of a network, identifying the relationships between these entities through algorithms, statistics, and computational tools (Scott 2012).

SNS is a web platform where people can connect with different users where people or organizations voluntarily generated content and leave it publicly available to share experiences. The large number of people interacting through the Internet in such platforms has generated a large amount of data with social content. To analyze social networks over an SNS, globally speaking, applications such as the following can be found:

▪ *General trends:* This is the measurement of volumes of data during some period.

- *Categories and correlations:* Analysis of data volumes over-infers causes of higher frequencies (e.g., events, campaigns, and key influencers) and analyzes correlations between the categories in order to understand if the issues are related.
- *Hashtag analysis:* Exploring hashtags that are used frequently in tweets to perform effective filters in the search for relevant data.
- *Predictive analysis:* Identify and predict behavior patterns through the publication of the publications of individuals.
- *Network dynamics and structure:* How a network is structured and its changes over the time.

In particular, Twitter is a very popular SNS, which provides access to its data and is one of the most open social media site (Kwak et al. 2010). Thanks to its structure, it allows communication between many people without account friendship restriction connections which gives to its users the possibility of interacting more freely (Jansen et al. 2009, Bifet and Frank 2010, O'Connor et al. 2010). Also, Twitter offers an application programming interface (API) for collecting tweets, which allows to search older tweets, with some restriction, and gets streaming tweets to follow a continuing live stream of new tweets based on a user-defined criterion.

Methodology and Data Collection

This exploratory research follows to explore the relationship between citizens' opinion and certain topics related to public policies and identify if it is possible to obtain relevant information in Chilean comments, in particular from information of health topics. Thus it is necessary to capture relevant relations between public opinion and health issues in Chile according to the opinions expressed in text format.

In this study, the microblogging site Twitter was used as the source of data. Also to find a good starting point Google Insights was used as a validator of keywords. It is important to notice that Twitter API has restrictions, in this case. The *"search/tweets"* method from *Twitter API* was used with *"oauth"* authentication from *"Twitter"* library providing the R-cran tool (Gentry 2015), and the restrictions consists in obtaining, as limit, 180 tweets requests in 15-min window if you sign in as a user and 450 tweets requests/15-min window if you sign in as an app. Also, if you search past comments there is a time window limit of seven days, then no tweets will be found for a date older, and if the search query has few comments it returns an empty data set. Owing to that when planned to explore comments in this SNS, it is necessary to do a research plan, use the relevant keywords, and to organize data recollection.

Accordingly, an analysis was carried out with published content in Twitter according to the keywords related to health. Where to find the most important words Google Insights was used, which capture frequently searches in Google and retrieving those keywords, health-related tweets were collected. Data were collected during 10 days between 2015-10-04 and 2015-10-24, 104965 tweets were recollected from the following keywords: (1) "salud chile," (2) "MINSAL,"; (3) "#VacunacionContraSarampion," (4) "FONASA," (5) "#PresupuestoSalud2016," (6) "#LeyRicarteSoto," and (7) "#MasMedicosyEspecialistas."

To store tweets, a transactional Data Base Management System (DBMS) was used; in this case, MYSQL DBMS was used as a database and "MySQL" Driver from R packages (Ooms et al. 2016) as user interface. Therefore, to obtain the necessary structure the Text Mining package was used (Feinerer et al. 2015), where clean tweets was a key step removing the following: (1) accounts cited in the tweets, (2) punctuation symbols, (3) numbers and blank spaces, (4) links, and (5) illative and stop words. After that, the vector space model was used with the Document Term Matrix structure with the resulting data set:

<<Vcorpus>>	<<DocumentTermMatrix>>
Metadata: corpus specific: 0, document level (indexed): 0 Content: documents: 89532	(documents: 89532, terms: 20448) Non-/sparse entries: 82216/1830168120 Sparsity: 100% Maximal term length: 91 Weighting: term frequency (tf)

Finally, to present the results "*wordcloud*" (Fellows 2015) and "*igraph*" (Csardi 2015) packages where used.

Experiments and Results

According to data recollection and methodology, data analysis was made based on the classical statistical methods and clustering techniques. As a first stage, keywords were found stating from an *insight* (Figure 13.1) analysis of relevance based on historical search in *google* which allows to validate the topic. Therefore, using the Twitter API, 3500 tweets were retrieved, captured on July 19 using "*Salud,*" "*Centro de Salud,*" "*Ministerio de Salud*" as keywords for the search.

With it, it was possible understand the conversations in this context and some knowledge about people behavior around this topic. After a cleaning process it was found that people who used these words are primarily looking for information related with coverture, public health enclosures, and some public and private health institutions. To show results a *wordcloud* was (Figure 13.2) made resuming in a visually friendly manner the most frequent words.

After that, a deeper analysis using a vector space model with the most frequent words was made, filtering them with more than 50 appearances and using a dendrogram aproximation to define the number of clusters. Results show that the topics can be separated into three or four subtopics (Figure 13.3) under the time windows used.

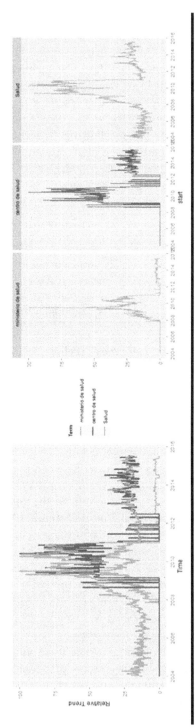

Figure 13.1 Search starting keywords in Google Insight.

Figure 13.2   Wordcloud from a tweet search based on keywords.

As clusters analysis shows, the subtopics can resume as follows:

1. *Cluster* 1: food-related commentaries and daily alimentation.
2. *Cluster* 2: politics and public issues.
3. *Cluster* 3: commentaries linked to health centers and attentions.
4. *Cluster* 4: contingent issues related with health (as in this case the approbation of marijuana law which was being discussed at the time the information was retrieved).

Therefore, once the topic was validated and the keywords selected based on this first approach, the final keywords were selected and during 10 days at 20:00 between 2015-10-04 and 2015-10-24 the tweets were retrieved and stored in a database. The most frequent tweets found are shown in Table 13.1. Tweets that were found went through.

A cleaning process called *wordcloud* (Figure 13.4) to understand the conversation in a simple and fast way.

Results have shown, for Twitter Chilean users, that there is a vast quantity of people talking and interested in health issues, giving their opinion on several topics mostly grouped under four segments or clusters. The most frequent opinion threads have relation with the current issues or contingency factors without being detriment to spontaneous opinions. Commentaries over tweets seem to be serious and give a good approach about what people are talking around this topic and show some campaigns such as, for example, "#LeyRicarteSoto" or "#JuntosContraelCáncer"

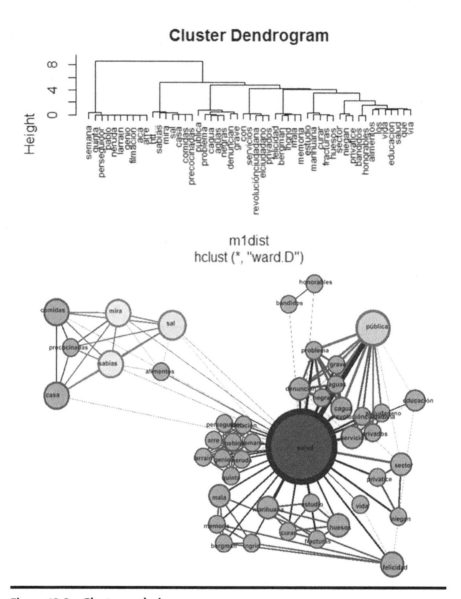

Figure 13.3   Cluster analysis.

were a success, given a good scenario to promote and inform. Nevertheless, other campaigns such as "#PresupuestoSalud2016" do not have important reactions. Another issue that can be seen is mostly of the opinion abeing negative in front of the political administration with adjectives such as "corruption," "problem," "denies," "bad administration," which can be explained because of the political scenario in Chile, where it has been faced with a decline in trust in institutions and political figures (Hola Chamy 2015).

Table 13.1 Most Frequent Tweets

Tweets	Fr.
RT @Clau_AlvaradoR: MINSAL withdraws $1.6 billion financing to Fundación las Rosas	2470
RT @joseantoniokast: Terrorism in La Araucanía, insecurity throughout Chile, illegal strikes, waiting lists in health and Pdta. MB talking about probity	2049
RT @LMayolB: Former Health Minister had three advisers, currently has 74 and most of them are relatives of politicians and leaders from NM. And MINSAL debt reach to $250 mm	1638
RT @ministeriosalud: Vaccination campaign	1070
RT @vanrysselberghe: Thanks to "popular government" medical examinations in Chile will cost 19% more. And the right to health?	1040
RT @ministeriosalud: #TogetherAgainstCancer	836
Ecuador and Chile sign 11 cooperation agreements on safety, education and health	774
RT @GobiernodeChile: #MoreMedicalDoctorsforChile	597
RT @hermesgamonal: #insulinebombAUGE Today until 24 hrs	554
Check the pharmacies schedules of each the region	511
RT @hermesgamonal: Thank you all for your support, more than 42 thousand signatures delivered to MINSAL # insulinebombAUGE	494
RT @ministeriosalud: #Vaccination Influenza vaccination	444
RT @miguelhuerta32: Bachelet government removes financial support from Fundación Las Rosas	438
RT @ministeriosalud: Participate in the Public Consultations	409
RT @GobiernodeChile: About 3000 women die each year from breast cancer. Prevent, self-test!	382

Finally, as an exploratory analysis, data collected and relationships found show that it is possible with simple techniques to understand the general opinion around a topic and evaluate if some campaigns or media influence are reaching people in the right direction or not.

Conclusion and Discussion

Organizations are facing an increased need to improve their operations, transparency and connection with its stakeholders where a new manner to deliver services

Figure 13.4 Wordcloud.

and products has appeared. An increasing number of companies and institutions give part of its services using social network tools, and its face-to-face contact has been changed to an online interchange of commentaries or messages. In this scenario, the rate of data collection is growing exponentially and translating this data into actionable knowledge is challenging in front of the social scenario and people behavior. Moreover, social demands and need are increasingly sophisticated requesting transparency, participation and quality services, and products especially in public institutions.

The data obtained give us a very good approach about public opinion and relevant topics, but it is of interest to see how virtual reality affects what eventually happens. Also we can see that people conversations are influenced by public figure, media and campaigns; therefore it is important to keep in mind the context and contingency while an analysis is made with special attention to get wrong conclusions. Causality in this data is not always in just one direction and causal analytics is challenging for data analysts.

Process text data is not an easy task and to choose tools and data structure is not a trivial decision. Data collection methods vary in relation to the data type and source and the method of collection, the design of the recording form and later analyses have to be well planned with a clear objective in mind. Techniques and algorithms also have limits depending of the data structure and type.

In the particular case of twitter data and search, "keywords" are another key issue to be considered. The quality of keywords and its relation with the target of the study can be the success factor to finish an investigation as is necessary to obtain the correct data. Moreover, given the large amount of data available and their possibility to convert to separate words, as the widely used "*vector space model*," it is very important to work with the necessary data, no more, facing the scenario where "less is more."

In terms of quality of data Twitter interactions give the relevant information and with a correct process of cleaning a wide range of analysis can be performed with reliable inputs. This makes it possible to conclude that people get involved in government campaigns and public issues with clear and classifiable views. Finally, the questions that remain are Is this a valid conclusion? Who interacts in Twitter-like platforms? Can we extend this result to the general citizens? Social networking sites seem to be a great source of data and the results are consistent, but how data can be loaded, clean, processed, analyzed, and, above all, explained still remain a challenge.

References

Bifet, A. and Frank, E., 2010, *Sentiment Knowledge Discovery in Twitter Streaming Data, Discovery Science*, Springer, Berlin.

Cleveland, W. S., 2001, Data science: An action plan for expanding the technical areas of the field of statistics, *International Statistical Review*, 69(1), 21–26.

Csardi, M. G., 2015, Network Analysis and Visualization, accessed June 26, 2015, https://cran.r-project.org/web/packages/igraph/igraph.pdf.

Dhar, V., 2013, Data science and prediction, *Communications of the ACM*, 56(12), 64–73.

Fayyad, U., Piatetsky-Shapiro, G., and Smyth, P., 1996, From data mining to knowledge discovery in databases, *American Association for Artificial Intelligence*, 17(3), 37–54.

Feinerer, I., Hornik, K., and Artifex Software Inc., 2015, Text Mining Package, accessed July 3, 2015, https://cran.r-project.org/web/packages/tm/tm.pdf.

Fellows, I., 2015, Word Clouds, accessed February 20, 2015, https://cran.r-project.org/web/packages/wordcloud/wordcloud.pdf.

Gentry, J., 2015, R Based Twitter Client, The R Foundation (Ed.), accessed July 29, 2015, http://lists.hexdump.org/listinfo.cgi/twitter-users-hexdump.org.

Hola Chamy, C., 2015, Cómo llegó Chile a la crisis política que terminó con la salida de todos sus ministros, BBC Mundo, accessed May 7, 2015, http://www.bbc.com/mundo/noticias/2015/05/150507_chile_bachelet_como_llego_crisis_politica_ch.

Jansen, B. J., Zhang, M., Sobel, K. and Chowdury, A., 2009, Twitter power: Tweets as electronic word of mouth, *Journal of the American Society for Information Science and Technology*, 60(11), 2169–2188.

Kwak, H., Lee, C., Park, H., and Moon, S., 2010, What is Twitter, a social network or a news media?, In *Proceedings of the 19th international conference on World wide web (WWW '10)*, ACM, New York, NY, USA, pp. 591–600. DOI=http://dx.doi.org/10.1145/1772690.1772751.

O'Connor, B., Balasubramanyan, R., Routledge, B. R., and Smith, N. A., 2010, From tweets to polls: Linking text sentiment to public opinion time series, *ICWSM*, 11(122–129), 1–2.

Ooms, J., James, D., DebRoy, S., Wickham, H., Horner, J., and RStudio, 2016, Database Interface and "MySQL" Driver for R, accessed January 29, 2016, https://cran.r-project.org/web/packages/RMySQL/RMySQL.pdf.

Pei, J., Kamber, M., and Han, J., 2005, *Data Mining: Concepts and Techniques*, 2nd ed., Morgan Kaufmann, Amsterdam.

Scott, J., 2012, *Social Network Analysis*, SAGE Publications, London.

UN Global Pulse, 2014, Analysing social media conversations to understand public perceptions of sanitation, Global Pulse Project Series, no. 5, accessed January 29, 2016, http://www.unglobalpulse.org/projects/sanitation-social-media.

Index

A

ACF, *see* Autocorrelation function
Adoption data, 77
Advanced planning systems (APS), 105
Analytics, 3, 6; *see also* Analytics knowledge
       management
  adoption of, 7, 28–29, 35–36
  and capabilities for operations, 40–42
  computational capacity, 11–12
  data mining methods, 10
  decision-making and problem-solving, 4
  Goldratt's theory of constraints, 14
  information systems, 11
  intelligent organization development, 15–18
  knowledge, 30
  machine/algorithm based solutions, 10
  management idea adoption, 9–11
  management theory principles, 13–15
  planning, 4–5
  scientific method in organizational
      studies, 9
  skillset and development, 12–13
  as technology, 24–25
  thinking, 7–8
  waste, 13
Analytics knowledge into healthcare, 53; *see also*
      Data; Healthcare data analytics;
      Healthcare data management
  fraud detection, 66, 69
  fraud identification, 68–70
  healthcare fraud, 66–68
  players in health systems, 66
  to prevent frauds, 70
Analytics knowledge management, 4, 12, 22;
      see also Analytics knowledge transfer
  analytics adoption, 23, 28–29, 35–36
  analytics and capabilities for operations,
      40–42

analytics as technology, 24–25
building on measurement results and
      benefits, 43–44
cloud computing, 31
creating capabilities, 35
CRM implementations, 39
developing, 29–30
Digital Technologies Maturity Index, 38
DVB-T2 technology, 26
e-business, 27
governance for technology adoption,
      44–47
innovation, 28–29
keeping organizational memories, 31
knowledge adoption, 23–24
knowledge application, 35
knowledge creation, 30–31
knowledge storage and retrieving, 31–32
measurement process, 43
mind and behavior influence, 38–40
problem understanding, 36–38
regression model, 25
stakeholder's needs, 42–43
technology use, 25–28, 35–36
Telco case, 41
USAA, 42–43
variation control, 37
VisiCalc, 26
Analytics knowledge transfer, 32; *see also*
      Analytics knowledge management
  barriers for good communication, 32
  human communication, 32
  needs in organizations, 33–34
API, *see* Application programming interface
Application programming interface (API), 256
APS, *see* Advanced planning systems
ARIMA model (autoregressive integrated
      moving average model), 209; *see also*
      Statistical software reliability models

Artificial neural networks, 142, 146–149,
152–154; *see also* Credit scoring
problems
Autocorrelation function (ACF), 175
Automated credit rating, 143
Average probability distribution function, 81

B

BI, *see* Business intelligence
Binary programming model, 94; *see also*
Prescriptive analytics
Biomedical imaging, 61
BPI, *see* Business process intelligence
Brownian motion, 10
Business intelligence (BI), 164
Business process intelligence (BPI), 160; *see also*
Informational port decision making
BPI-COLSETAM, 169
BPI-COSEDAM, 168
BPI-POFEDAM, 170
BPI-SELTIDAM, 170

C

Canadian Institute for Health Information
(CIHI), 59
Case studies, 116–127, 165
Catalogue of products, 94; *see also* Prescriptive
analytics
CCF, *see* Cross correlation function
Central tendency of data, 66
CIHI, *see* Canadian Institute for Health
Information
Classification techniques, 143
Client table attributes, 149
Cloud computing, 31
Cluster analysis, 260
Clustering ports, patterns of, 173
CNC, *see* National Consulting Center
Computational capacity, 11–12; *see also*
Analytics
Computed tomography scans (CT scans), 61
Consumer price index (CPI), 132; *see also*
Consumer price index estimation
Consumer price index estimation, 131
air transportation vs. CPI variation, 136
chicken vs. CPI variation, 137
data sources, 133
debugging process, 134
ground transportation vs. CPI variation, 135
methodology, 133–135

pork meat vs. CPI variation, 137
recommendations, 137–139
rent price variation, 138
results, 135–137
scanner data, 132–133
scraped data method, 132, 134
time series algorithms, 135
using Big Data, 132
Corporate social responsibility (CSR), 171
CPI, *see* Consumer price index
Creating capabilities, 35
Credit risk, 142–143; *see also* Credit scoring
problems
Credit scoring problems, 142, 145
application, 149
artificial neural networks, 146–149,
152–154
attributes of client table, 149
automated credit rating, 143
classification techniques, 143
comparison of results, 154–155
credit risk, 142–143
data, 149
logit model, 145–146, 150–152
multilevel neural network, 147
recommendations, 155
samples, 150
Cross correlation function (CCF), 175
Cross-regional spatial proximity, 182
CSR, *see* Corporate social responsibility
CT scans, *see* Computed tomography scans
Customer relationship management (CRM),
11, 31; *see also* Analytics knowledge
management
implementations, 39

D

Data, 62; *see also* Analytics; Analytics
knowledge into healthcare
adoption, 77
analyzing, 63
central tendency, 66
-driven methodologies, 75
frequency distribution, 65
histogram, 65
management and analysis, 253
network, 76–77
quality work cycle, 59
raw, 77
scanner, 132–133
Science, 255

scraped, 134
summaries, 64
types of, 62–63
use, 11–12
Data Base Management System (DBMS), 257;
    see also Social network analysis
Data mining (DM), 166
    methods, 10
Datasets, 76; *see also* Data; Dynamic social
    networks
DBMS, *see* Data Base Management System
Debugging process, 134; *see also* Consumer
    price index estimation
Decision; *see also* Prescriptive analytics
    making, 92–93
    -making and problem-solving, 4
    trees, 69
Decision support systems (DSSs), 164
Degree
    distribution function, 80
    probability function, 81
Design for Failure Mode Effect Analysis
    (DFMEA), 44
Deterministic equivalent model, 108; *see also*
    Stochastic hierarchical approach
Deterministic optimization models, 105
DFMEA, *see* Design for Failure Mode Effect
    Analysis
Digital Technologies Maturity Index, 38
Digital television terrestrial broadcasting
    (DTTB), 26
Digital video broadcasting-terrestrial second
    generation (DVB-T2), 26
Disaggregation levels, 109, 113–116, 126
Disaggregation structure, 109; *see also*
    Stochastic hierarchical approach
    for analyzed problem, 110
DM, *see* Data mining
DSSs, *see* Decision support systems
DTTB, *see* Digital television terrestrial
    broadcasting
Duane, 220–221; *see also* Statistical software
    reliability models
DVB-T2, *see* Digital video broadcasting-
    terrestrial second generation
Dynamic social networks, 74, 84; *see also*
    Support Vector Machine; Susceptible
    Infected Susceptible model
    adoption by fixed individual attributes, 81
    closeness centrality, 80
    data-driven methodologies, 75
    datasets, 76–77

degree distribution function, 80
degree probability function, 81
exploratory data analysis, 77
limitation and future work, 85
marketing instruments, 74
mean degree, 80
network heterogeneities, 80–82
practical implications, 84–85
probability distribution function, 81
social contagion, 74
transitions per month, 81
vertex-based centrality, 78–80

E

e-business, 27
EHR, *see* Electronic health records
Electronic health records (EHR), 60, 61
EMS, *see* Environmental management systems
Enterprise resource planning (ERP), 31
Enterprises, 105
Entrepreneurial survey, 193
Entrepreneurship, 230, 231–232
    analytics, 234–235
    content analysis, 238
    development, 243–245, 247–248
    funding and support, 235, 242–243,
        246–247
    future research, 248–249
    hashtags in Twitter LATAM, 239
    implications, 245
    insights, 235–236
    keyword *emprendimiento*, 239
    keywords sentiment analysis, 237
    in Latin America, 230, 235
    learning, 238–242, 245–246
    methodology, 233–234
    in online context, 232–233
    opportunity, 231
    related hashtags, 238
    social entrepreneurship, 244
    social uses in internet context, 236
    web analytics, 233
Environmental management systems (EMS), 168
ERP, *see* Enterprise resource planning
EVPI, *see* Expected value of perfect
    information
Expected value of perfect information (EVPI),
    127; *see also* Stochastic hierarchical
    approach
Explicit, 30
Exploratory data analysis, 77

F

Failure, 211
    probability, 209
    rate function, 210
FAO, *see* Food and Agriculture Organization the United Nations
Fault detection and repair, 211
Fault Tree Analysis (FTA), 212
Financing, 191; *see also* University-based companies
Food and Agriculture Organization the United Nations (FAO), 58
Fraud, 66
Frequency distribution, 65
FTA, *see* Fault Tree Analysis

G

Gaussian kernel, 87
GEM, *see* Global Entrepreneurship Monitor
Global Entrepreneurship Monitor (GEM), 189; *see also* University-based companies
    ranking, 191
Goldratt's theory of constraints, 14
Governance, 45; *see also* Analytics knowledge management

H

Health care, 67
Healthcare data analytics, 54–55; *see also* Analytics knowledge into healthcare
    components, 55–56
    in decision making, 55
    examples, 56
    fraud prevention, 56
    support for clinical decisions, 57
    workflow, 57
Healthcare data management, 57; *see also* Analytics knowledge into healthcare
    biomedical imaging, 61
    components of EHR, 61
    data quality, 58–60
    data quality work cycle, 59
    data sources, 60
    electronic records, 60
    healthcare data, 57–58
    sensor data, 61–62
Healthcare fraud, 66–68
    identification, 68–70
    prevention, 56, 70

Heuristic method, 70
Hierarchical production planning (HPP), 104; *see also* Stochastic hierarchical approach
HPP, *see* Hierarchical production planning

I

IAAS, *see* Infrastructure as a Service
ICT, *see* Information and communication technologies
IHS, *see* International Health Regulations
IMO, *see* International Maritime Organization
Inflation, 132; *see also* Consumer price index estimation
Informational integration, 160
Informational port decision making, 160, 183
    antecedents, 161–162
    BPI-COLSETAM, 169
    BPI-COSEDAM, 168
    BPI-POFEDAM, 170
    BPI-SELTIDAM, 170
    case study, 165
    complete multi-case chaining schema, 167
    cross-regional spatial proximity, 182
    data analytics, 160
    empirical evidence, 176–178
    finding evidence for each proposition, 175–179
    fostering proposition for each multiple case, 167
    linking propositions with BPIs, 167–171
    local spatial proximity in U.S., 181
    mapping spatial or institutional proximities, 179–182
    methodology to guide selected cases, 165
    multiple-case institutional proximity, 180
    multiple case studies, 165
    patterns of classification, 171
    patterns of clustering ports, 173
    port integration, 161–162, 163–164
    port jurisdictional case, 179
    prediction patterns, 174
    rationale of, 162–165
    regional learning systems, 166
    searching for patterns using outputs of DM workflows, 171–175
    theory building from cases, 165–167
Information and communication technologies (ICT), 47, 180
    internet and, 232
Information systems, 11
    access to, 189

Infrastructure as a Service (IAAS), 31
Innovation, 28–29
Integer programming model, 94; *see also*
Prescriptive analytics
Intelligent organization development, 15–18;
see also Analytics
International Health Regulations (IHS), 170
International Maritime Organization (IMO), 172
International Organization for Standardization
(ISO), 171
ISO, *see* International Organization for
Standardization

J

Jelinski–Moranda model, 212; *see also* Statistical
software reliability models
input data and assumptions, 213
Markov process of, 213
model description, 213
model structure and reliability
prediction, 213
parameter estimation, 214–215

K

Knowledge; *see also* Analytics knowledge
management
adoption, 23–24
application, 35
creation, 30–31
management, 12
storage and retrieving, 31–32
transfer, 32–34

L

Law enforcement (LE), 180
LE, *see* Law enforcement
Link rewiring, 75
Littlewood–Verrall linear, 222–224; *see also*
Statistical software reliability
models
Logit model, 142, 145–146, 150–152; *see also*
Credit scoring problems

M

Magnetic resonance imaging (MRI), 61
Make-to-order, 94; *see also* Prescriptive analytics
Management theory principles, 13–15

Manufacturing batch, 94; *see also* Prescriptive
analytics
Manufacturing order, 94
Mapping spatial or institutional proximities,
179–182
Marginal contribution, 94; *see also* Prescriptive
analytics
Marketing instruments, 74
Markov process, 213
Master production schedule (MPS), 105
behavior, 2, 127
Mathematical Programming, 95; *see also*
Prescriptive analytics
Mean value function, 210
Mind and behavior influence, 38–40
Mixed integer programming model, 94, 98;
see also Prescriptive analytics
Modeling, 95
Moranda geometric, 215; *see also* Statistical
software reliability models
input data and assumptions, 215
model description, 215
model structure and reliability prediction,
215–216
parameter estimation, 216–217
MPS, *see* Master production schedule
MRI, *see* Magnetic resonance imaging
Multi-case chaining schema, 167
Multilevel neural network, 147
Multiple-case institutional proximity, 180
Multistage stochastic programming models,
107; *see also* Stochastic hierarchical
approach
Musa basic, 217; *see also* Statistical software
reliability models
input data and assumptions, 217–218
model description, 217
model structure and reliability prediction, 218
parameter estimation, 218–219
Musa–Okumoto model, 219–220; *see also*
Statistical software reliability models

N

NAFTA, *see* North American Free Trade
Agreement
National Consulting Center (CNC), 193
National marine sanctuaries (NMS), 172
NDCP, *see* Network of Digital and
Collaborative Ports
Network data, 76–77
Network heterogeneities, 80–82

Network of Digital and Collaborative Ports (NDCP), 180
Neural networks, 69, 146
NMS, *see* National marine sanctuaries
Nonparametric techniques, 144
North American Free Trade Agreement (NAFTA), 175

O

Operational research (OR), 11
Opportunity, 231; *see also* Entrepreneurship
Optimization, 106
  models for HPP strategy, 110
OR, *see* Operational research
Order Acceptance, 93; *see also* Prescriptive analytics
Organizational memories, 31
Organizational studies, scientific method in, 9

P

Parametric techniques, 144
Partial correlation function (PCF), 175
Parts per billion (ppb), 172
PASS, *see* Platform as a Service
PCF, *see* Partial correlation function
PET, *see* Positron emission tomography
Planning, 4–5; *see also* Analytics
  horizon and disaggregation, 117
  production, 108–110
Platform as a Service (PASS), 31
PMMLs, *see* Predictive Model Markup Language models
Population, 63
Port integration, 161–164; *see also* Informational port decision making
  initiatives for port integration, 163–164
Port jurisdictional case, 179
Positron emission tomography (PET), 61
ppb, *see* Parts per billion
Predictive Model Markup Language models (PMMLs), 31
Prescriptive analytics, 92, 93, 99–101
  concepts in, 94, 97
  decision making, 92–93, 98
  extending problem, 98–99
  future research, 101
  mathematical programming, 95
  mixed integer programming model, 98
  model description, 95–96
  order acceptance, 93

problem solving, 96–97
project objectives, 96
research objectives, 101
scope, 93–94
strategy, 102
theoretical foundation, 94, 95
work performed in, 94
Problem understanding, 36–38
Product catalogue, 94; *see also* Prescriptive analytics
Production, 104
  planning, 108–110
Profit, 94; *see also* Prescriptive analytics

Q

QPP, *see* Quadratic programming problem
Quadratic programming problem (QPP), 87

R

Raw data, 77
Recourse problem (RP), 127
Regional learning systems, 166
Regression model, 25
Reliability, 209; *see also* Statistical software reliability models
Reliability Growth Models, 211
Re-setup, 94; *see also* Prescriptive analytics
RP, *see* Recourse problem

S

SAAS, *see* Software as a Service
Sales and operations planning (SOP), 108
Scanner data, 132–133
Scientific method in organizational studies, 9
SCM, *see* Supply chain management
Scraped data, 134; *see also* Consumer price index estimation
  method, 132, 133
SECI model (socialization, externalization, combination, internalization model), 30
Setup, 94; *see also* Prescriptive analytics
SIS model, *see* Susceptible Infected Susceptible model
SMEs (small-and medium-sized enterprises), 244; *see also* Entrepreneurship
SNA, *see* Social network analysis
SNS, *see* Social networking service
Social contagion, 74

Social network analysis (SNA), 253, 261–263;
    see also Social networking service
  cluster analysis, 260
  Data Science, 255
  keywords in Google Insight, 258
  methodology and data collection, 256–257
  MYSQL DBMS, 257
  results, 257–261
  subtopics, 259
  tweets, 261
  Twitter API, 256
  wordcloud, 259, 262
Social networking service (SNS), 254; *see also*
    Social network analysis; Twitter
Software as a Service (SAAS), 31
Software quality analysis, 208; *see also* Statistical
    software reliability models
Software Reliability Growth Models
    (SRGMs), 209
SOP, *see* Sales and operations planning
Spatial proximity in U.S., local, 181
Spin-off, 190
SRGMs, *see* Software Reliability Growth
    Models
SRM, *see* Supplier relationship management
Standard assumptions, 212
Statistical software reliability models, 208,
    209, 228
  data upload process, 225
  Duane, 220–221
  failure, 211
  failure probability, 209
  failure rate function, 210
  fault detection and repair, 211
  Jelinski–Moranda with imperfect
    debugging, 212–215
  key concepts, 209–211
  Littlewood–Verrall linear, 222–224
  mean absolute relative errors, 226
  mean value function, 210
  methodology, 211
  models and concepts used, 212
  Moranda geometric, 215–217
  Musa basic, 217–219
  Musa–Okumoto model, 219–220
  plot of data and fitted mean value, 226
  predicted failures, 227
  relative errors for each model, 227
  reliability, 209
  Reliability Growth Models, 211
  research question and design, 212
  results and interpretation, 224–228

software reliability, 211
Standard Assumptions, 212
Welcome screen of application, 224
Stochastic hierarchical approach, 104
  aggregate production plan, 110–113
  case study, 116–127
  demand, 4–3, 119–125
  deterministic equivalent model, 108
  deterministic optimization models, 105
  disaggregation levels, 109, 113–116, 126
  disaggregation model items, 116
  disaggregation structure, 110
  extensions, 127–128
  methodology flowchart, 117
  MPS behavior, 2, 127
  multistage stochastic programming
    models, 107
  objective of, 105
  optimal values models, 128
  optimization models for HPP strategy, 110
  planning horizon and disaggregation
    structure, 117
  production, 104, 108–110
  scenario tree in, 118
  stochastic optimization, 106–108
  two-stage stochastic program, 106
Stochastic programming model, 105; *see also*
    Stochastic hierarchical approach
Strategic planning, 5; *see also* Analytics
Supplier relationship management (SRM), 11
Supply chain management (SCM), 31
Support Vector Machine (SVM), 76; *see also*
    Dynamic social networks
  classification, 77, 86–88
  confusion matrix for Gaussian kernel, 87
  model characteristics after feature
    selection, 79
Susceptible Infected Susceptible model (SIS
    model), 75; *see also* Dynamic social
    networks
  adoptions, 82
  link rewiring, 75
  long-term prediction for adoption, 83
  parameters and variables, 86
  with rewiring, 82–84, 85–86
SVM, *see* Support Vector Machine

T

Tacit, 30
Technology adoption, 35–36
  governance, 44–47

Technology use, 25–28
Telco case, 41
Theory building from cases, 165–166; *see also* Informational port decision making
Time series algorithms, 135
Twitter, 254, 256; *see also* Social network analysis; Social networking service
Two-stage stochastic program, 106

U

UN, *see* United Nations
UNESCO, *see* United Nations Educational, Scientific and Cultural Organization
United Nations (UN), 58
United Nations Educational, Scientific and Cultural Organization (UNESCO), 58
United Services Automobile Association (USAA), 42–43
University-based companies, 188
    analyzed problem, 192
    correlation matrix, 201, 202
    data used, 193–194
    entrepreneurial survey, 193
    financing, 191
    GEM ranking, 191
    hypothesis testing, 195–196
    logistic binominal model, 197, 198
    models and concepts, 194–195
    operational and tactical implications, 200
    problem resolution, 193
    recommendations, 199
    research objectives, 199–200
    research questions or hypotheses, 192–193
    results and interpretation, 197–199

statistical analysis, 196
statistical appendix, 203
strategic implications, 200, 203
theoretical references, 190–192
validity and reliability in work, 196
USAA, *see* United Services Automobile Association
U.S. Geological survey (USGS), 172
USGS, *see* U.S. Geological survey

V

Value of the stochastic solution (VSS), 127; *see also* Stochastic hierarchical approach
Variation control, 37
Vertex-based centrality, 78–80
Vertex degree, 78
VisiCalc, 26
VSS, *see* Value of the stochastic solution

W

Wait-and-See solution (WS), 127
Waste, 13
Web 2.0 tools, 39
Web analytics, 233
Weibull-type process, 220; *see also* Statistical software reliability models
Welcome screen of application, 224
WOM, *see* Word of mouth
Wordcloud, 259, 262; *see also* Social network analysis
Word of mouth (WOM), 74
WS, *see* Wait-and-See solution